BUSINESS EXPECTATIONS

Are You Using Technology to its Fullest?

Bryan Bergeron
Jeffrey Blander

John Wiley & Sons, Inc.

Copyright© 2002 by John Wiley and Sons, Inc., New York. All rights reserved.

Published simultaneously in Canada.

Library of Congress Cataloging-in-Publication Data:

ISBN 0-471-20834-5

Printed in the United States of America.

10 9 8 7 6 5 4 3 2 1

To Miriam Goodman

Contents

Preface

The entire process of business and entrepreneurship is a form of alchemy. A visionary leader takes a handful of silicon, and zap! A handful of silicon chips appear. To the layperson, there's something alchemical about taking an idea and transforming it into something real, something from nothing. But for the seasoned and successful entrepreneur, the alchemical is best described as a well-defined set of beliefs and values that translate an initial vision into a discrete set of processes and products with salient benefits for the customer.

Alchemy involves magic, the power to create tangible benefits inexplicably in the mind of the customer. In this regard, even when customers know what they want, the product itself may continue to be a black box. To the modern farmer, magic might take the form of a genetically modified strain of corn that resists worms and other infestations without the expense and time of applying pesticides. For businesspeople always on the go, a Palm or RIM Blackberry PDA (personal digital assistant) is a magical device that transforms their professional activities into an understandable set of ever-present to-do lists and contact information. Similarly, for the exercise enthusiast, a watch that monitors energy expenditure, heart rate, and oxygen consumption is magic that allows her to achieve a level of fitness as quickly as possible.

Of course, from the perspective of the alchemist—the manufacturer or developer—the product is necessarily very real. While a product might appear magical to the uninitiated, the alchemist—like Intel, creating INTELigent silicon chips from sand, or Microsoft, creating the programs that bring the chips to life—employs management skills and product technologies that provide consistent, measurable, and controllable results.

Although the alchemists of the middle ages ostensibly concerned themselves with developing processes that could convert lead and other base metals to gold, the real alchemy has been in the conversion of gold to silicon. That is, over 8,000 years ago, the human race was characterized by tools made of alluvial gold.

Through the development of processes achieved through the social evolution of collective intellect, we progressed from gold to copper, bronze, iron, steel, and finally silicon and other solid-state substrates. Thus, alchemy has been achieved through the development of increasingly complex processes—technologies—that consistently and economically provide results.

The alchemists of the 21st century—the entrepreneurs, CEOs, and other leaders of the technologic age—are similarly creating magic every day through the application of technology. Modern alchemists are concerned with creating consistent results, as measured in terms of quality, time, money, and other resources. A hit-and-miss approach and sleight of hand do not survive in the modern marketplace, where the pace of innovation in fields from computing to drug discovery is increasing at an exponential rate. In this regard, every product development involves the magical transformation of a loosely defined idea by the developer into a completely known and knowable product from the end user's perspective. In other words, whereas magic is typically pervasive during the inception and development stage of a product's lifecycle, technology in the form of a defined set of benefits to the consumer is necessarily prevalent during the later stages.

This book explores how every product lies somewhere in the continuum between magic and technology during the alchemical transformation from idea to mature product. By determining where a product or service falls in this continuum and how to shift its position along the continuum, decision makers can create a value proposition that is internally transparent to their organization and externally transparent to investors as well as customers.

Business entrepreneurship, like any other endeavor, is fraught with risk. However, while risk is great, so are the rewards for succeeding. The proposition of this book is that by viewing business practices as an alchemical process that moves a product along the continuum between magic (a product idea) toward a tangible product technology, business leaders can make better decisions and increase their odds of a successful market introduction.

This book will be of interest to

- CEOs who orchestrate the developments within their company and direct the positioning of their products and services in the minds of their customers
- Product developers charged with transforming ideas generated by research and development (R&D) into tenable products in the marketplace
- Marketing executives involved in promoting technologic solutions for a variety of consumer wants and needs
- Sales professionals involved in selling technologic solutions to businesses and individuals
- Consumers who are interested in understanding the business processes within the corporate black box associated with the introduction of technologically innovative products to the marketplace

After reading this book, the reader will

- Understand the significance of the dynamic tension between magic and technology during the transformation of an initial idea into a viable product offering
- Appreciate the significance of defining the appropriate contributing amount of resource requirements, capital investment, time to market, and the ultimate commercial success for a product along the development continuum
- Understand how to best harness the dynamic tension that exists among product development, marketing, sales, and the consumer from a new, empowering perspective
- Review a set of tools that can help to identify the appropriate mix of magic and technology associated with a product, for internal uses and to accurately assess competitive offerings
- Have a roadmap detailing the alchemical process of transforming an idea into a market-driven product offering so that the internal product development effort remains credible internally, as well as in the eyes of customers and potential investors

In order to make this book accessible to the busy reader, it is divided into three parts: Proposition, Value, and Vision Maintenance.

Part One, Proposition, presents the alchemy–technology continuum model using common metaphors to refine the concept of magic and technology from product development, marketing, sales, and consumer perspectives. Part Two, Value, explores the practical monetary, predictive, and managerial value of viewing product development as a form of alchemy. Part Three, Vision Maintenance, illustrates how readers can apply business alchemy with respect to their particular organization's needs.

The New Economy is characterized by accelerating innovation, streamlining complexity, and managing customer-driven expectations. Given these pressures, information-based products and services are often offered for sale long before the alchemical transformation has been completed. One common pitfall of the New Economy is the discontinuity between the proposed marketing effort and the technology under development. A symptomatic by-product of the chasm that develops between internal R&D efforts and marketing managers is the inaccurate translation of available technologies' features and benefits to the customer. This miscommunication may create unrealistic initial expectations and a disgruntled consumer. As such, customers and investors who have been burned by immature technologies are more skeptical than ever before of the status of a purported technology.

The challenge for the business that wants to excel in the New Economy is to continually design and create products that transform the initial technology vision with a mercurial set of functionalities into a salient and tangible range of features and functions that are desired by the customer. The completion of this process from magic to the product in the hands of a satisfied customer signifies that the alchemical transformation has been completed successfully. To this end, this book provides business executives and marketing and sales professionals with a new perspective that they can use to not only satisfy but excite their customers.

Bryan Bergeron
Jeffrey Blander

Acknowledgments

To our literary assistant and mentor Miriam Goodman—poet, author, and photographer—for her technical expertise, wisdom, and mastery as a wordsmith. Special thanks to Daniel Sands and Steven Locke for their contributions to the conceptual framework of this book. To our readers, reviewers, students, and researchers, Bill Bauer, John Ryan, Joann Ryan, Rosalind Bergeron, Ron Rouse, Scott Tolle, Warner Slack, Howard Bleich, Michael and Laurie Gordon, Marguerite Lombardo, and Rose and Fred Blander, for their time, inspiration, insight, and constructive criticism.

PART ONE

PROPOSITION

1

Alchemy–Technology Continuum

The most successful businessman is the man who holds onto the old just as long as it is good and grabs the new just as soon as it is better.

Robert P. Vanderpoel

Despite all of our recent technologic achievements, from mapping the human genome to exploring the outer planets, humanity is still grounded in beliefs that span the centuries. While few of us could recite the process for converting iron ore into steel—one of the pillars of our modern technologic existence—most could recite parts of a belief system, such as that outlined by the Old Testament, that dates back to before the first smelters were conceived. Paradoxically, many of these belief systems are viable today because they provide a framework for dealing with the complexity of the man-made environment created by civilization.

Consider, for example, the applicability of classic Chinese cosmology in a modern, technologic society. In this belief system, the principles of *yin* and *yang* represent opposite and complementary forces in nature that combine to produce all that comes to be. Yin is the feminine, passive, dark, and wet; and yang, the masculine, active, bright, and dry. There is always an element of yang and an element of yin within any object, and yin and yang combine in various proportions to produce all the different objects in the universe.

In addition, the characteristics of yin cannot exist without those of yang, nor can the characteristics of yang exist without yin. As such, Chinese philosophers stress the importance of balance between the yin and yang to avoid rebellion, floods, and disease and assure social and political harmony.

In our modern, technologic society, the concepts of magic and technology represent opposite and complementary principles, especially as they relate to characterizing business products and activities. Magic is artistic, qualitative, unknown, and variable, while technology is rational, rooted in science, quantitative, known, and fixed. As such, business relies on technology for continued survival in the marketplace, but managers often consider technology to be as fleeting as magic. That is, the transformation of technology from the magical state to one of tangibility is the definition of customer wants and needs. Furthermore, commercial success is limited by the degree to which the consumer drives research and development.

From an entrepreneur's perspective, developing a product involves the alchemical transformation of a concept to a solid technology—a product offering. Modern high-tech products, from software to cell phones, are the result of this business alchemy. Moreover, during the alchemical transformation, the relative proportion of technology to magic—the unknown and variable—is different at each point in the transformation, both absolutely and in the perceptions of customers and the developers, engineers, marketing, sales, and corporate management involved in product creation. That is, depending on the experience of the customer, desktop copiers, communications satellites, genetic engineering, PCs, wristwatches, and operating systems all fall somewhere between known technological quantities and pure magic. However, regardless of the consumer's understanding of the inner workings of these devices, the benefits to the consumer of the proposed product offering must be readily apparent.

This chapter introduces the reciprocal relationship of magic and technology, thereby providing a framework for the discussions in the subsequent chapters. Specifically, the proposition advanced in this chapter provides decision makers with a set of predictive tools for knowing where a technology lies in the alchemical transformation from a qualitative, unmeasurable, magical state to a known, quantitative, measurable product. Decision makers can use these tools to

- Understand the process and risks involved in bringing a product to market, for example, how to move a software product out of an entrepreneur champion's head and out of the door in a "shrink-wrapped" concept box
- Clearly communicate the development status of an in-house project to those in R&D, sales, marketing, and investors
- Assess the status of the competition or any technology-oriented company, whether it is a supplier, competitor, substitute product, or a potential acquisition
- Appreciate the importance of timing in progressing from magic to product and the effect of delays at various stages of development and production on achieving a product
- Develop the appropriate hiring strategy along the continuum to maintain an on-target set of revenue and R&D goals

MAGIC VERSUS TECHNOLOGY

According to the *Encarta World English Dictionary* ([New York: St. Martin's Press, 1999], p. 1084), magic is defined as a special, mysterious, or inexplicable quality, talent, or skill. Technology, in contrast, is defined as the study, development, and application of devices, machines, and techniques for manufacturing and productive processes (p. 1831). Although these definitions are a good starting point for the discussion that follows, it may help to review the range of characteristics normally ascribed to magic and technology, shown in Figure 1.1. For example, the first item, Ancillary Uses, indicates that products with magical or undefined customer qualities tend to have limited application outside of a very specific domain or application. In contrast, products that are solid technologies can generally be successfully applied to a variety of application areas. For example, a sheet of Gore-Tex® can be used to make a rain-resistant hat, pair of boots, or coat; repair the lining of the aorta; or repair an inguinal hernia. In other words, there are economies of scale and scope because Gore-Tex can be used across multiple functional areas.

To illustrate the predictive value of knowing where a product or process lies in the alchemy–technology continuum, consider how the products and processes are characterized in the following discussion.

Figure 1.1   Magic versus Technology

Characteristic	Magic	Technology
Ancillary Uses	Few	Many
Compatibility	Low	High
Competition	Low	High
Complexity	High	Low
Configuration Time	High	Low
Consumer Acceptance	Low	High
Cost	Variable/High	Fixed/Low
Deliverable	Prototype	Commodity
Driving Force	Market	Requirements Specification
Economies of Scale	Low	High
Environment	Controlled	Variable
Expectation	Variable	Known
Goal	Capability	Profitability
Installed Base	Small	Large
Instances	Single	Multiple
Management Makeup	Technologists	Professional Managers
Marginal Cost	High	Low
Mechanism of Action	Unknown	Known
Perception	Emotive	Logical
Paradigm	Art	Science
Price	High	Low
Repeatability	Low	High
Resource Requirements	High/Variable	Low/Fixed
Results	Qualitative	Quantitative
Risk	High	Low
ROI	Unknown/Variable	Known/Fixed
Scalability	Low	High
Success Factors	Team Motivation	Sales
Supporters	Evangelists	Customers
Training Requirements	High	Moderate/Low
Usability	Single Event	Continuous

Products

For the purposes of illustration, consider two products, an ordinary countertop color TV and a prototype of a full-motion holographic video display. The TV is a sample of thousands of virtually identical units produced weekly at a plant in Singapore and sold in the United States under a variety of inexpensive brands. Compare the holographic display, one of a kind, tucked away in the high-security area of a research lab at a major electronics manufacturer. The holographic display shows animated images of objects from a three-dimensional (3-D) perspective. Now, compare and contrast the characteristics of each device from the perspective of magic and technology, using Figure 1.1 as a guide.

Countertop TV.   Consider a couple walking into one of the hundreds of electronic superstores across the United States in search of a color countertop TV for their kitchen. For most consumers, this sort of task represents an impulse buy, something conjured up over breakfast while reading through the sales in the Sunday paper. And that is as it should be, given that the color TV, commercially available in the United States since the early 1950s, represents a mature, stable technology, with a variety of related or ancillary uses. The couple can use the TV to view cable programs, a video on DVD or videotape, a movie from their roof-mounted satellite decoder, the baby on their remote baby monitor, home movies on their digital camcorder, the security camera at the front door, or the output of their computer game console.

Because the basic patents covering color TV expired long ago, there is considerable competition in the countertop color TV market from manufacturers in Mexico and Southeast Asia. This competition is a boon to the couple that can choose among a broad selection of models that offer a range of features and prices. Like most consumers, the couple's perspective toward their TV purchase is based on the traditional marketing concepts of product, price, place, and promotion for the company offering the TV. That is, they attend to the salient features, such as the number of channels, size of the screen, perhaps the number and type of input and output jacks, and the brand of the TV, for example. The price of a TV, a commodity item, tends to be stable, even with the occasional sale, in part because of competition among TV manufacturers.

Because variability in the production process and in the electronic components used by a manufacturer means that even though two TV units of the same make and model have the same specifications, there will be aesthetic and perceptual differences in side-by-side comparisons of the video images on their screens. Many of these differences may be difficult for customers to articulate, but customers can usually perceive differences in picture quality. For example, the couple visiting the superstore quickly spots a TV picture they like out of a floor-to-ceiling wall display of TVs playing the same DVD signal.

As a result, the couple believes that they are buying a known quantity, and part with their cash with a reasonable expectation of satisfaction. For the couple, the risk of buying a TV is relatively low, given the extended warranties most electronic superstores offer. In addition, there are numerous TV repair services in most cities that are capable of repairing a TV that is out of warranty. Similarly, the return on investment tends to be known, especially when a national brand is involved. Several brands of TVs stand for quality and value, either as a result of marketing or through consumers' personal experience.

From the manufacturer's perspective, customer expectations are generally known and quantifiable due to the large, existing body of market research for the home entertainment industry. Customers do not expect to have to know anything about the inner workings of the TV—the amount of RAM and ROM on board, for example—but expect to simply push the on–off button, select a channel, and begin enjoying their favorite programs. They understand what the TV is supposed to do from an operational perspective, and that certain conditions must be satisfied in order for the product to perform normally. For example, it is now common sense that a TV has to be plugged into a power source and connected to a cable or other signal source for normal operation.

As the couple expects, once they have the TV in their home, setup is trivial. The configuration time is very low and typically automatic. Assuming the TV is plugged in and is connected to an appropriate video source, it will automatically determine which channels are available and remove the others from the previous/next channel list that is accessed through the remote control.

Most customers do not consciously consider all of the issues listed in Figure 1.1 in purchasing a TV, in part because a TV for sale in a mall or an electronics outlet is assumed to fulfill the basic requirements for what constitutes a TV. Although it may be difficult to appreciate today, 30 years ago, before the color TV was really a commodity item, technical details were much more relevant. The front panels of TVs from different manufacturers would boast, for example, "solid-state tuner," to differentiate a TV from an older model based on vacuum tube technology, or "built-in pattern generator" to at least suggest that adjusting the color balance and the red, green, and blue guns could be performed without the assistance of a pattern-generator-toting repair technician.

This shift in sales focus from minutiae of technical details to an overall product-benefit gestalt can be appreciated by reviewing the history of the changing customer perception of personal computers (PCs) in the marketplace. The change moved PCs from technologic puzzles to commodities. In the 1980s PC purchases were rooted in discussions with technically savvy salespeople regarding the amount of RAM, ROM, disk space, nature of the input/output bus, CPU clock speed, and other technologic parameters. However, just as the number of transistors or ICs used in the tuner of a modern TV receiver has little if anything to do with picture quality, for most PC users, this level of technical detail is irrelevant. As long as a TV produces a clear picture and vibrant sound, it has fulfilled customer expectations. Similarly, as long as a PC runs the standard software suites without inordinate delays for saving data or spell-checking a document, it is normally considered good enough to satisfy most consumers' needs and wants. There are two factors important to the consumer in reaching a decision to buy a product: its functional durability and its cachet as a status symbol.

3-D Display. Now, consider a 3-D holographic video display intended to be the centerpiece for the home entertainment system of the future, which represents the magical product in Figure 1.1, somewhere between the leading edge and bleeding edge. The display is usable only as a demonstration prototype in a highly controlled laboratory setting. As far as the R&D staff knows, there isn't any significant competition, except perhaps for similar prototypes in one or two laboratories around the world. In any event, since the prototype is not for sale, there is no competition yet for customers.

Because of the custom circuitry, the complexity of the display is high and operation is finicky. Configuration time is high, in that modifying the display for different types of experimental video signals takes considerable time and effort, and the environmental conditions must be carefully controlled. Since the configuration is in constant flux, the cost of ownership is high and variable. The R&D department's deliverable is a stable prototype that demonstrates the *potential* of the device as product, whether for a specific customer, such as the military, or the general consumer market.

In either case, in a pure R&D shop there may be little concern at this point for issues such as scalability of the prototype for mass production. However, for a company with its sights set on eventually bringing the display to market, marketing should be involved at this point.

The marginal cost of creating additional 3-D displays is very high, and to those outside of the intimate circle of R&D, the mechanism of action of the 3-D display is generally unknown—hence magic. As such, the perception of the display from the point of view of observers not intimately involved with the technology is primarily emotional as opposed to technical. To the uninitiated, the display may seem like something out of a science fiction movie. Because there are so many unknowns, the risk of failure is high for the manufacturer; there is a chance that the investment in R&D may result in a dead end.

For example, even if the 3-D display is a technologic success, it may be a failure in the market because of compatibility or cost issues, for example. Thus, what we see here is the self-evident need to drive technological innovation via the consumer's need rather than the black-box approach to technology development. The primary success factor for the development group, which is motivated by pushing technology to the limit, is largely a function of its internal motivation and innate technical ability—that is, in the basic alchemical transformation of their idea into prototype. This is the crux of the tension between R&D and product marketing. Marketing is driven by the need to satisfy the customer, not the insatiable appetite of the developer, to build the latest and greatest gadget. Without an infusion of marketplace *realism,* as generated through market research, the prototype may be completely different from what research says consumers want.

The differences between the mature TV market and the new 3-D display market show that the Alchemy–Technology Continuum should be understood by comparing and contrasting a product's market and technology maturity as two distinct yet interrelated facets. Looking at these two facets will lead to information about the types of people that are required to lead the organization (see Figure 1.2).

Processes

The two products discussed in the preceding section, the "magical" 3-D display and the technologically stable countertop TV, illustrate the Alchemy–Technology Continuum from a product perspective. However, a technology can be expressed as a process as well as a product. Process development, like product development, undergoes a transformation from an idea to a specific prescription linked to a certain outcome. The alchemical transformation of ideas into processes is often difficult to appreciate because the transformation occurs in the context of the complexity of everyday life.

The degree of alchemical transformation of an idea to a practical process is evident when we encounter something new or experience

Figure 1.2 The Transformation

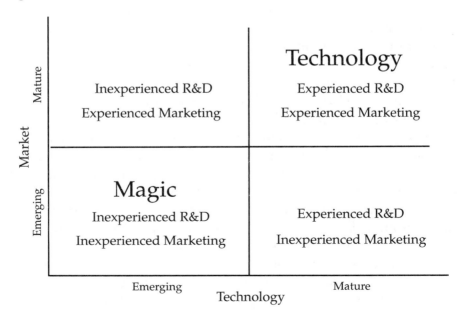

something familiar in a strange context. In a business course that we teach at Harvard, we follow this line of reasoning when we define the Alchemy–Technology Continuum in terms of the real-world environment. For example, a scenario that we use entails two students who have no exposure to western cuisine visiting the United States from central Asia. The two are indirectly exposed to an American delicacy—a peanut butter and jelly sandwich and a glass of milk. They both see the meal described in a TV advertisement for milk featuring a small girl enjoying a peanut butter and jelly sandwich while on a picnic with her family. Intrigued, but with only a vague understanding of the meal, the two students decide to recreate the delicacy, but each in his or her own way. The first student, Sam, decides to go with his intuition, while the second student, Jay searches for a recipe.

Brute Force Method. Sam, who isn't very risk averse, but has no experience with western-style cooking, heads directly to a grocery store on his way home from school. In the store, he finds the aisle lined with jars of peanut butter, jellies, jams, and other spreads, and is temporarily immobilized by the number of choices. In the peanut butter section, there are fat-reduced, crunchy, smooth, salted, unsalted, and natural peanut butters. There are even jars of pre-mixed jelly–peanut butter swirls, with grape, honey, and strawberry flavors. Dismayed by the assortment, he asks a clerk for advice. The clerk comes over and indicates his favorite brand of strawberry jelly and then shows Sam the creamy peanut butter that is on sale. Sam thanks the clerk and heads over to the bakery section of the store, where he finds a loaf of soft, sliced white bread.

Back at his apartment, Sam brings the bag of ingredients into the kitchen. He finds a plate, opens the bread wrapper, takes out two slices, and places them on the plate. Next, he finds a spoon, opens the peanut butter, and takes a big scoop of peanut butter out of the jar. Because the bread is soft and fresh, it tears as he pulls the lump of peanut butter across the spongy face. Undaunted, Sam takes another slice of bread out of the wrapper and, this time holding the bread carefully in his hand, slowly and gently pulls the peanut butter across the face of the bread. After the operation, the slice of bread is more or less covered with peanut butter, in a thickness that varies from less than an eighth of an inch to almost a half-inch.

Next, Sam opens the jar of strawberry jelly, dips the peanut butter smeared spoon into the jar and adds a dollop of jelly on top of the peanut butter-covered slice of bread. Because the jelly cannot adhere to the bread, it runs off of the sides of the peanut butter and onto the plate. Sam licks the spoon, covers the jar of jelly, and cleans the cabinet top. He pours himself a tall glass of milk, takes the sandwich on the plate, and goes off to his room to study. In his attempt to work while eating the sloshing sandwich, he ends up dripping jelly all over his class notes. Sam does not understand how Americans can be so infatuated with such a heavy, gooey mess.

A Recipe. Jay, who is more risk averse than Sam, but has the same burning desire to experience a peanut butter and jelly sandwich, searches for a recipe at her local bookstore. She finds a simple recipe, similar to the one shown in Figure 1.3, and goes to her local grocery store for the necessary ingredients. Later that night, around dinner time, Jay pulls out the recipe, lays out the ingredients, and uses a spreader to cover one side of one slice of bread with a quarter-inch layer of peanut butter. Next, she distributes the jelly onto one

Figure 1.3   Simple Peanut Butter and Jelly Sandwich Recipe

Peanut Butter & Jelly Sandwich

Ingredients:

Bread – 1 loaf, sliced
Jelly – 16 oz.
Peanut Butter – 16 oz.
Milk – 1 gallon

Preparation:
Spread a $1/4$" layer of peanut butter evenly on one piece of bread.
Spread a $1/4$" layer of jelly evenly on another piece of bread.
Put slices of bread together, matching jelly to peanut butter faces.

Serving:
Cut each sandwich into four triangles.
Serve with cold milk.

Serves: 8 – 12

---

side of the other piece of bread, again to a quarter-inch thickness. Then she puts the jelly-coated slice of bread face down on the slice with peanut butter and uses the knife to make two diagonal cuts, creating four triangle-shaped finger sandwiches. Jay places the four sandwich pieces on the plate, pours herself a glass of skim milk, and retires to the living room to watch her favorite TV show while enjoying her newly discovered favorite treat. She is pleasantly surprised that her first peanut butter and jelly sandwich and skim milk chaser are delightful.

A Comparison.   Sam and Jay, neither of whom has tasted a peanut butter and jelly sandwich before, start with the same goals and the ingredients available to them. However, Sam does not have a detailed process description or recipe and is unable to create a sandwich to his liking on his first attempt. However, through trial and error, and finally by consulting with Jay, Sam becomes much better at creating what most Americans would agree passes for a peanut butter and jelly sandwich. He discovers that he can use much less peanut butter and jelly on the sandwich, and that a spreader is much better at distributing the peanut butter on the bread than a spoon. That is, through experimentation, he manages to improve the process to his liking. Through a process that starts out as *magic*, Sam manages, through trial and error and data gathering from a number of sources, to come to a recipe or *technology* that suits his purposes.

Jay, who takes the time to locate a recipe—a simple process description—achieves her desired results very efficiently and with a known Return on Investment (ROI). The greater the detail in the recipe, the less room for error of interpretation and action. For example, the recipe shown in Figure 1.3 assumes that the reader knows his way around a kitchen. Given the appropriate ingredients, tools, storage and work spaces, and other resources, anyone with experience in making a sandwich of any type should be able to use the recipe to create a reasonable facsimile of a traditional peanut butter and jelly sandwich.

Consider the qualities of a good recipe. It can be reconfigured and applied to variety of other uses (e.g., grape jelly can be substituted for strawberry jelly). There is brisk competition—and therefore a much wider selection—among the jelly and peanut butter brands. The recipe simplifies the entire operation, and the configuration or setup time is low. Assuming the recipes in the book are tried and true, anyone following them can expect to be pleased with the results. By following the recipe, the cost is contained and known a priori, and the result is a commodity, that is, a dish known and understood within the culture. If Jay decides to serve peanut butter and jelly sandwiches at her next house party, she can fairly accurately predict what she'll need in terms of resources in order to feed any number of guests. Her risk of failure is relatively low; most of her guests, who are a mix of Asians and Americans, will instantly recognize and presumably enjoy the peanut butter and jelly sandwiches. Of course, she can add a few Asian delicacies to the mix, but there is a risk that some of her guests may not be familiar with, or like, an unfamiliar food. She'll know whether her efforts at creating an American staple are successful by watching the number of sandwiches that disappear from the table. In the event that demand exceeds supply, she can easily direct a guest to help her create more sandwiches, following the recipe. However, Jay may find that the recipe does not scale very well. At some point, it will make more sense to buy peanut butter and jelly by the 10-pound tub and use special tools or processes, such as canvas pastry bags with a large pore tip, to apply the spreads on slices of bread, or use an assembly-line, self-serve approach.

Sam, who goes about recreating his peanut butter and jelly experience through trial and error, but with a clear idea of what he wanted to create, is initially at the magical end of the process spectrum. Sam's initial process is unduly complex and wasteful in resources and time, and the initial results aren't acceptable. He is involved in a loop of creating prototypes and adjusting the various parameters with each generation until he happens upon a process that he can use to create his dream peanut butter and jelly sandwich. Sam's initial marginal cost for each sandwich is high, in part because he wastes jelly and ruins bread, and in part because the techniques he uses do not result in a homogenous, repeatable distribution of peanut butter and jelly on the bread. His risk of failure is also high, and his ROI from one sandwich to the next is unknown.

If, before developing the recipe, Sam had to create a few dozen sandwiches for houseguests, he would have been hard pressed to determine how much bread, jelly, and peanut butter he would need. In other words, unless he had an explicit recipe, the scalability of his technique would probably be low. What's more, if demand outstrips supply, he would have difficulty instructing a guest on how to make sandwiches quickly and efficiently. At that point, Sam would probably be better off allowing guests to create their own sandwiches with a peanut butter buffet.

Applying Magic Ingredients

As every chef knows, any cooking process involves a bit of art and creativity. A good chef can substitute one ingredient for another on the fly, keep costs low and resource requirements fixed, and yet produce a delectable dish. In fact, a chef who is experienced in the kitchen adds a bit of his own signature—his art—even when he strictly follows a recipe. For example, he may use freshly ground pepper instead of preground pepper; sea salt instead of free-running, iodized salt; fresh basil and mint instead of the dried varieties; and his favorite dinner white wine instead of a generic, white cooking wine. The result, although repeatable at one level, is really a single event. Like a live music performance, it will never be exactly replicated. In other words, a master chef's work fits somewhere in the continuum between magic and technology. This scenario suggests that there are specific personality types and process approaches that are appropriate for every point within the Continuum. For example, both R&D and marketing require a degree of creativity and an ability to focus their art in order to move a product along the Continuum.

THE CONTINUUM

The *Alchemy–Technology Continuum*, referred to henceforth as the *Continuum*, is depicted graphically in Figure 1.4. The model provides a means of tracking and predicting the development of technology within a business and in the marketplace. It consists of five critical decision points and four periods characterized by specific conditions. Ideally, a product progresses unimpeded from inception to the marketplace, but in reality, most products are abandoned before they are fully developed or marketed. In the United States, for example, less than a third of all software-development

Figure 1.4   The Continuum

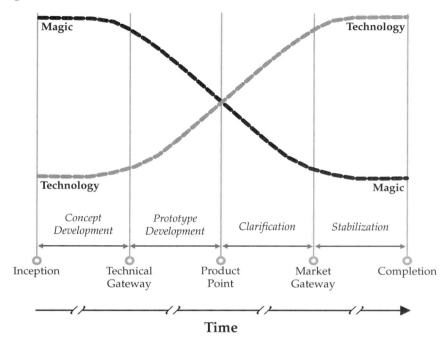

projects—including in-house development in engineering, legal, medical, and financial institutions—make it to completion within specification, on time, and on budget.

A Software Startup Company

To illustrate alchemical transformation of an idea into a product along the Continuum, consider the development of a software product, *The Lean Machine,* the first commercial desktop microcomputer-based nutrition and weight-loss prescription program. The program was developed and marketed in 1982 by Home Health Software, Bryan Bergeron's first software company.

Background.   As a bit of background, the microcomputer hardware and software environment of the early 1980s was characterized by volatility, uncertainty, and, like the more recent eCommerce boom, rapid growth. For home computer users, Apple, Commodore, and Tandy vied for a rapidly expanding game and home utility market. With the exception of small businesses that used the

VisiCalc spreadsheet on the Apple II, most "serious" computing was performed on mainframe systems run in batch mode. That is, instead of interacting with a display, most users worked with punched cards. However, applications that today would be found in the discount software bins of electronics stores, including several nutrition and exercise tracking and prescription programs, were not yet available, even on mainframe systems.

Market Research.   In the few nutrition systems that were available at major medical institutions in the United States, physicians, dietitians, and other clinicians still could not use the "what-if" analysis common to applications such as spreadsheets. Nor could a person interactively determine how much more time she would need to exercise if, for example, she ate an extra 8-ounce container of sweetened, low-fat yogurt. A clinician setting up an exercise and diet regimen for a patient could not predict the effect on a patient's weight loss if exercise time on a treadmill or swimming was increased from 15 to 25 minutes and caloric intake was increased by 200 calories. What's worse, those who were interested in taking charge of their own nutrition and weight loss were far removed from the system and were dependent on their clinician for solutions.

Because of the limited availability of nutrition and exercise software on any computer platform and the lack of interactivity in the systems that did exist, it seemed that there was an obvious, unanswered need that could be satisfied by software that would run on the new, inexpensive desktop microcomputer technology.

Shareholders.   Bryan's first step was to determine who would use the program, what they would pay for it, what the interactive screens would look like, how they would be used, and what kinds of questions a typical user would need the software to answer. After researching what was available on large systems and the most popular programs available on the new desktop computers—mainly games and word processing, database, and spreadsheets programs—Bryan developed a set of software requirements specifications. By casually interviewing dieticians, physicians, and friends and exploring his own needs, Bryan determined that the ideal system would provide the features listed in Figure 1.5, which appeared on the software packaging. At the time, $40 was the going price for

Figure 1.5   Program Features

Designs a medically safe diet for every member of a family, based on age, sex, build, height, weight, activity level, and rate of weight loss desired.

Displays the calories, carbohydrates, protein, fat, saturated fat, vitamins, minerals, and cholesterol from a file of over 600 common foods, with room for 200 more.

Keeps a record of every family member's weight and plots dieting success with colorful graphics.

Portion size of all foods is easily adjusted to suit your needs.

Displays the nutritional content of a particular item or screens all items by a particular nutrient. For example, you may display the nutritional value of an orange or list all fruits and their sodium (or any of the other nutrients) content.

Analyzes your daily diet and graphically displays how it compares nutritionally to your unique requirements, in order to determine whether you need to take vitamin supplements or otherwise alter your diet.

Allows you to save the nutritional content of over 200 additional items, family recipes, or entire meals easily in the expandable database.

Colorful graphics, audio feedback, and full printer support.

---

microcomputer software, so it was easy to set the price for the nutrition program at the same level.

Process.   The next step was proving that a prescriptive nutrition program of significant capabilities and ease of use could be created on a microcomputer. The three core technologic hurdles to be overcome were database design, case mix analysis, and graphical user interface design. The first challenge was met using a standard file system supported by BASIC, the most popular language for software development on microcomputers at that time. Using data from government publications that listed common foods in standard measures along with over 20 macro- and micronutrients— carbohydrates, protein, vitamins, and minerals—the database was partially populated. Once the operation of the database was verified, the next challenge was to determine if the database and the program code could fit on a floppy disk, while leaving enough space for user-defined foods as well as a record of the user's diet and exercise program. This could not be answered until the size of the program code was determined.

Suspending work on the database, he began working on the case mix analysis component of the program, crafting and recrafting code until it could perform on a microcomputer quickly enough to satisfy users while fitting comfortably in a small amount of disk space. The unknown or *magic*, at this stage of the project was developing a linear algebra routine that could solve multiple equations with multiple unknowns using data from the food database, together with user-defined preferences for food.

Part of the challenge was that the initial development platform, the Apple II, had a processor slower than a PalmPilot™ PDA (personal digital assistant), with only about a tenth of the RAM. Again, using BASIC as a prototyping tool, Bryan developed a set of routines that could solve problems in the following form:

> Weight loss should be 1 pound per week
>
> and
>
> Fat consumption must be less than 30 grams per day
>
> and
>
> Protein consumption must be at least 1 gram per kg of body weight per day
>
> and
>
> What is a medically safe diet for breakfast, lunch, and dinner, based on user-specified ranked preferences for foods in the database, that satisfies the above requirements as well as the recommended daily allowance (RDA) for vitamins and minerals for a patient of specified age, sex, weight, and activity level?

Because the program was originally coded in BASIC, a typical solution required about a minute of processing—too slow for an interactive program. Recoding the algorithms in Assembler was still a possibility. However, before rewriting the algorithms, Bryan decided to explore user interface options, which were linked to the available hardware platforms.

Of the most popular platforms, the Tandy, Apple, and Commodore, the Apple and Commodore were the most popular in the home market. However, because of the Commodore's greater graphical and sound capabilities, popularity, and lower price (than

Apple), he chose the Commodore 64 as the initial development platform. This choice was to prove fatal in the long term. However, he made it because of the graphical and sound hardware in the Commodore that made building innovative user interfaces possible. In 1982, about four years after its introduction in the marketplace, the Apple was still limited in the quality and types of graphics that could be drawn and displayed. The Commodore, by contrast, had routines not available in the Apple line until the introduction of the Macintosh in 1984.

With the hardware selected and specifications clearly defined—the database, mathematical routines, and graphical user interface—Bryan began programming in earnest. In order to provide the speed necessary for the mathematical calculations, he rewrote the original BASIC routines in low-level but highly efficient Assembler code. Similarly, in order to provide a "look and feel" that was less intimidating than a blinking prompt, he wrote the user interface in Assembler, allowing the use of colorful icons, floating menus, 3-D bar graphs and pie charts, and other graphical treatments not available on the Apple. After several months of programming, design, and keying in data for 600 common foods (by hand) the product was ready for beta testing.

Product. As the product coding was coming to completion, with testing and subsequent minor bug fixes underway, marketing and financial issues took on more significance, as did customer support and fulfillment. At the start, most of these activities were done in-house. For example, Bryan found binders made to hold the then standard 5 $\frac{1}{4}$-inch diskettes with slots for inserting product description, and developed a marketing plan that included direct mailings, catalog sales, and several magazine advertising campaigns. A local printer produced an initial run of a thousand packages, complete with documentation, packaging artwork, and customer response cards, bound in a 6×9 three-ring binder with a product description on the front and rear covers. He also designed flyers for direct mailing. Simultaneously, he invested in disk duplication hardware and basic office supplies, and established methods of handling payment.

Bryan also addressed intellectual property issues by registering the software with the U.S. copyright office. To sell this and subsequent

programs, he located a distributor of health-related software for the
Apple and Commodore lines located in Southern California and
negotiated a comarketing agreement that included space in their catalog. In addition, he found a part-time salesperson in California who
worked on a commission basis and was selling directly to the microcomputer centers that were springing up like Starbucks outlets in the
malls on the West Coast.

Outcome. For about a year, sales were good, totaling in the thousands of packages, but demand was dropping for the product, as well
as for two other home health products he subsequently developed on
the Commodore platform. But at the same time, three factors
changed the computing landscape: the increased dominance of the
Apple in the marketplace; the segregation of the Commodore as
more of a game computer, even though its hardware was more
advanced than Apple's; and the introduction of the IBM PC and
Apple Macintosh to the scene. By 1985, demand for Home Health
Software's products on the Commodore 64 was only a few dozen copies a month, and even the sale of major commercial programs on the
Apple was in decline. Like many other software development houses,
the company developed its next product on the increasingly popular
Apple Macintosh, again because of the user interface possibilities.

Moving along the Continuum

The inception, development, deployment, and eventual demise of
The Lean Machine illustrates how the start of the Continuum is characterized by an overwhelming preponderance of magic, with what
may be little more than a scribbling on a paper napkin. At the other
end of the spectrum, there is a product rooted in pure technology
that eventually fades from the marketplace. Between the two
extremes, magic is replaced with technology—a tangible product
with specific benefits—in a predictable way over time. However, the
progress of moving from magic to technology is nonlinear and frequently impeded by factors related to the product, company, or
market. A product might take two months to move from inception
to mature product or fail completely at any point along the way.

The story of *The Lean Machine* is significant in that it illustrates
many of the real-world challenges faced by the typical "garage"

startup: the lack of marketing know-how and resources, that is, incomplete marketing information on the competition, consumer demographics, and optimum selling price. Bryan had no real way to gauge likely customer demand, other than belief that the product would succeed. Although this approach worked for Alexander Graham Bell and other entrepreneurs, their connections to investors and name recognition helped them overcome many of the hurdles faced by other innovators operating blindly. Today, successful entrepreneurs rely on a mix of talents, especially marketing, as they move a product along the continuum.

Points and Periods

The five *key points* in the Continuum are milestone events against which progress can be measured. They are the Inception, Technical Gateway, Product Point, Market Gateway, and Completion. In the world of technology development, although there may be flashes of insight and abrupt changes in the economy, there is nonetheless continuity from one point to the next. Furthermore, the times between each of the five points are periods of variable length. The characteristics of each of the points and periods in the Continuum and their characteristics are outlined in Figure 1.6. The points and periods are named here for reference later; what's important are the concepts embodied in each step from ephemeral idea to marketable product.

Inception. A product may begin as an idea that addresses an obvious need, like *The Lean Machine,* or it may simply germinate from a diagram sketched on a napkin over a lunch discussion with a friend. However, unlike the fate of most marked-up napkins, the ideas that make it to Inception on the Continuum are typically instantiated and clarified by a working document, like a specification or a pitch to investors. Inception is characterized by a preponderance of emotion and magic, and marks the beginning of a working requirements specification, which is a list of features that the product or service should provide—whether formally documented, expressed in a few lines of demonstration code, or embodied in a PowerPoint presentation.

The key issues and decisions at Inception include an assessment of the risks and rewards associated with the dream. The decision makers must ask the questions listed in Figure 1.7. The answer

Figure 1.6   Points and Periods in the Continuum

POINTS	ISSUES/ DECISIONS
Inception	Competition Competitive Advantage Groundwork for funding started (established enterprise) Market Marketing and sales first become involved (established enterprise) Potential markets and customers identified Resource Requirements Revenue Model Time line Validity of the Idea Viability of the Business Plan
Concept Development	Preponderance of Magic Time of Idealization Organizational Structuring Technology Focus
Technical Gateway	Technologically superior solutions in the marketplace Expected Return on Investment Clearly defined Functional Specifications
Prototype Development	Uncertainty Marketing and sales first become involved (new enterprise) Potential markets and customers identified Groundwork for funding started (new enterprise) Customer Focus
Product Point	Composition of the management team Identifying best business opportunities Beta test subjects
Clarification	Increased Certainty and Clarity Technologic enlightenment Rapid innovation Increased technology refinement Customer Focus
Market Gateway	Market Share Technology Lifespan Competing Technologies Positioning for Growth
Stabilization	Preponderance of Technology Emergence of Competition Minor enhancement to the underlying technology Market Focus
Completion	Product Viability Technology Improvement Applications in other markets

to many of these questions may be unknown and unknowable. Some may require guessing, with different levels of certainty associated with each guess, and some guesses will be blatantly wrong. For example, as a typical garage entrepreneur holding multiple jobs and lacking marketing support, Bryan had to guess on the demographic of the typical user. In retrospect, assuming that the typical

Figure 1.7   Issues and Decisions at the Power Point

I.   Product
- Is the idea valid?
- Has something like it been attempted before?
- Is the envisioned product technically and financially feasible with current technology?
- Is there a plan in place to move from the Power Point to a viable product?

II. End Users
- What are the demographics of potential buyers?
- Who are the typical users?

III. Financial
- Is the business plan viable?
- Do the numbers add up?
- What is the revenue model?
- How will the product make money?
- What are the required investments and profits?
- Are the needed resources available in terms of skilled people, capital, and space?

IV. Stakeholders
- Who are the main stakeholders?

V.   Competition
- What are the strengths of the competition?
- Is the major competitor a company with infinitely deep pockets, such as Microsoft, or a startup down the street?
- Does the competition have a similar technology or, perhaps more significant, a more coordinated marketing effort?
- Does the competition increase the risk of failure to an unacceptable level?
- What is the competitive advantage of the company?
- Is the advantage primarily technology?
- What are the barriers to entry?

VI. Legal
- What are the intellectual property issues?

VII. Market Definition
- What is the market for the product?
- What is the time line for introduction?

user of any of the three home health software products was an adult health-conscious male or female was an error. When demographic data on computer use began to be compiled and distributed in the trade magazines, it was clear that male users far outnumbered female users. In this regard, the continuum model should help decision makers identify the challenges along the way to a marketable product and effectively avoid similar, costly mistakes.

Concept Development.   This period, which extends from Inception to the Technical Gateway, marks the time of idealization, when magic significantly outweighs any technology available to match the vision of the developers. This is the time of excitement within a development group, when ideas are quickly generated and short pieces of code or physical mockups are created, testing concepts and trying the limits of thinking out of the box. The concept development ends with the Technical Gateway, which is when a pure R&D effort starts to make use of customer-driven feedback and marketing analysis. As noted earlier, market-driven product development begins at the Inception.

Technical Gateway.   The second major point in the Continuum is the Technical Gateway, a decision point where product development and management determine whether the technology involved in the proposed product is worth pursuing. The Technical Gateway is characterized by the development of a technically viable prototype that demonstrates a subset of the technology involved in the proposed product.

For the peanut butter and jelly sandwich recipe, the inclusion of pastry bags in the process may mark the Technical Gateway because it allows the recipe to be scaled to significant production levels. If hundreds of sandwiches per hour were required, then other technologies would have to be included, such as conveyer belts and automatic dispensers that provide fixed aliquots of jelly and peanut butter, or the use of refrigerated, semisolid blocks of peanut butter and jelly together with slicing equipment. For example, the successful repair of a sheep's aorta with Gore-Tex (and subsequent lack of rejection) marks its Technical Gateway. In the development of *The Lean Machine*, the Technical Gateway was achieved when the first prototype of the system was developed, prior to developing the graphical user interface.

At this point, a company has typically invested significant resources, especially developer time, in achieving the prototype or demonstration stage. As such, the CEO should have a much better idea of exactly what will be required, in terms of development resources, time, and money, to move from a prototype to a demonstrable product. However, if the CEO is a 19-year-old with a promising innovation but no marketing experience, the results may be less than ideal.

Regardless of whether the CEO is a neophyte or a gray-haired, brick-and-mortar company veteran, the issues and decisions that should be reassessed at the Technical Gateway involve asking these questions:

- Are there competing solutions in the marketplace that may be technologically superior?
- What are the capital and other resource requirements relative to the expected ROI?
- What are the results of the break-even analysis (BEA)?
- Is the likely ROI worth the risk of investing resources?
- Is the functional specification—the document that precisely specifies the technical features of the product—clear and complete?

The ease of determining end-user requirements and competition is a function of the maturity of the market. Usually the more mature the market, the easier the information-gathering process. The challenge with assessing the marketplace is that there may be technologies under development by any number of companies that will compete directly with a product. In addition, technical superiority is often difficult to assess because products may excel in some areas and be deficient in others.

Prototype Development.   This period is the time of significant, rapid technologic progress toward the realization of a prototype. This is the time when programmers and other development staff disappear from corporate management's radar and bury themselves in development efforts. If all goes well, Prototype Development ends with the Product Point. If there are insurmountable obstacles along the way, then this period may extend beyond the initial time allotted to creating a prototype, either because the technologies available or selected are incapable of addressing the prototype's needs, or because the resources required to reach the product point are excessive or not available. Most development efforts fail in the prototype development stage because development is out of touch with customer needs. In some cases the development time is simply too long.

The Prototype Development stage is also the time when marketing and sales first become involved in the product in a small, new, or pure R&D-focused company. In a mature enterprise, sales and marketing should be involved from Inception. Assuming corporate management believes in the eventual product, then marketing, public relations, and sales forces—usually a skeleton crew—are established to help identify potential markets and customers for the product under development.

For a new venture, this is also the time when management starts working toward securing funding, either from venture capital in the case of a small business, or from the enterprise in the case of a large corporation. In an established company, not only would funding be secured at this point, but the focus would include strategies for deployment support, customer service, and maintenance strategies.

Product Point.   The third key point along the Continuum, the Product Point, marks a shift in the magic–technology mix from magic to technology. Although this determination is usually based on qualitative measures, a product that can be evaluated objectively also characterizes the Product Point. In getting to the Product Point, it's assumed that limited in-house testing has been performed (alpha testing) and that tests using external subjects in a variety of real-world settings (beta testing) are either scheduled or underway. In *The Lean Machine* project, the Product Point was reached with the completion of coding and testing on the hardware delivery platform.

The key issues and decisions at the Product Point are the following:

- Does the composition of the current senior management team fulfill the organization's plans for product deployment?
- In a new, resource-limited venture, is it time to change from a technology-oriented management team to one focused on the marketplace?

- In a market-driven company, how should resources be allocated between marketing and R&D?
- What is the obvious end-user application for the product that demonstrates the technology and creates a story for potential investors and yet exposes the company to minimum risk?
- Who, and what organizations, should be considered for beta testing?
- Can beta testers be converted to paying customers?
- What are the incentives (political and financial) for the initial beta sites? Are these incentives sustainable over time?

Clarification. Like the historical period following the real Dark Ages in Europe, this period marks the time of technologic enlightenment. There is clarity in what the technology can and cannot do, and during this time customers begin buying the product and providing feedback (problems or new feature requests). This period is characterized by rapid innovation and clarification of the underlying technology. That is, while Prototype Development is a time of mutation and revolutionary change, potentially resulting in a usable technology product, Clarification is the time to increasingly refine the most successful technologies instantiated by the product.

Market Gateway. The fourth point in the Continuum, Market Gateway, is marked by a preponderance of technology. From this point on, only minor advances in the core technology may be realized, in terms of the magic–technology mix. However, major changes in the technology may be realized, as determined by customer needs or structural and necessary market changes. In *The Lean Machine* example, the market shifted from the Commodore 64 to the Apple Macintosh.

Major advances in the magic–technology mix are often ruled out because of time, time to market, cost, or other considerations that typically get earmarked for "the next release" of the product. Even minor advances can be costly in terms of time and resources, so they may be ruled out too. Postponed advances may multiply releases in response to customer complaints or advances made by the competition. At this point, it is important not to get too caught up in maintenance issues or current systems, but to establish a core development team to examine looming technology changes on the horizon. Success then depends primarily on gaining acceptance in the market and only minimally on furthering the technology. The issues and decisions at the Market Gateway involve asking these questions:

- Is the market share sufficient to maintain growth?
- What is the likely life span of the technology?
- Are there competing technologies on the horizon?
- Is market positioning optimum for growth?
- How can the company maintain an R&D effort while resources are consumed by creating product updates?
- Is it time to explore and develop new technologies in order to maintain or gain market share?

Issues in the Market Gateway are typically critical to the success of any product. For example, although there are hundreds of PC manufacturers, the top five companies—Dell, Compaq, Hewlett-Packard, IBM, and NEC—control over 40% of the world market. Even the top manufacturer, Dell, which commands almost 13% of the world market, has a gross margin below 10%. The other manufacturers, especially the off-brand labels that compete on price, are squeezed even more. Compaq, Hewlett-Packard, and IBM all reported losses or breakeven results from PC operations for the first quarter of 2001. As a result, many PC manufacturers are more concerned with surviving than growing. However, even in this environment, the premier microprocessor manufacturer, Intel, must continually update its products, if only to fend off competition from AMD, Motorola, and other microprocessor manufacturers.

Stabilization. The final period in the Continuum, Stabilization, is characterized by efforts to stabilize the current technology offering, with only minute changes or enhancements to the underlying technology. That is, there is very little magic involved in the product. The time of Stabilization may be long or short, depending on changes in the customer base or emergence of competition. For example, toothpicks have not changed much in recent years, nor have paper clips. However, a variety of competitors of the toothpick and basic paper clip have emerged. Although triangular, plastic, and metal-plated clips have appeared, the basic paper clip is a relatively unchanging staple in the business world.

In the case of Home Health Software, the rapidly increasing popularity of Apple computers in the home and classroom, along with the development of the Macintosh, were omens of the eventual fall of the Commodore line. This illustrates the need to keep an eye on products and technologies from within and across market sectors. For example, artificial organs replacing the need for donor transplantation will phase out the need for immunosuppressive therapy.

Completion.   The final point in the Continuum, Completion, marks the end of technical development. The product performs as defined in the functional specification, and there are no dangling "any time now" additions. Completion is stable, but only to the extent that customers' needs do not shift the desired Completion point to satisfy some other perceived or real customer need. However, in time, customer needs always shift. For this reason, it may be necessary to create a mechanism for assessing and responding to changing customer needs.

Examples of products that have reached Completion include the pencil, the ballpoint pen, the paper clip, the spoon, the countertop TV, and the countertop clock radio. In the case of Home Health Software, additions and modifications to *The Lean Machine* were limited because company resources were devoted to developing additional titles for the Commodore and, later, the Macintosh.

The issues and decisions at Completion include:

- How long will the product in its current form be viable in the marketplace?
- How should the technology be modified or improved?
- Can the product be applied to new markets, such as international markets?
- What is the risk of ignoring R&D and focusing solely on marketing and sales?

In progressing from one point to the next, it generally is not possible to skip over a point, at least in the long term. For example, skipping over the Technical Gateway and going directly to the Product Point will undoubtedly result in a product that fails to perform to specification, and the business will suffer. At one extreme, potential investors could interpret this as fraud.

RELEVANCE

Models are of value only insofar as they confer predictive value or are a means of increasing efficiencies or cost savings in a business process. In this context, the Continuum model is relevant to modern business operations because it makes explicit the dynamic tension between magic and technology for the major players or stakeholders involved—product development, marketing, sales, corporate management, and customers. The person who must communicate the company's vision of the product must also address the expectations and interests of all these different groups, each with its own viewpoint and agenda. Here again, the model helps the communicator preserve the original magic through the product actualization process. That is, the Continuum makes explicit the evolution of technology from Inception to Completion. This assumes that someone in the company can determine if a technology has room for refinement. Sometimes this determination requires someone close to the technology, but in some cases, evaluating the need for significant refinement is transparent and obvious to nontechnology personnel. For example, consider the peanut butter and jelly sandwich recipe listed in Figure 1.8, and compare it to the simple recipe in Figure 1.3. In addition to listing resources and processes in business terms, the instructions in Figure 1.8 make virtually no assumptions about the cooking ability of the reader.

Figure 1.8   Peanut Butter and Jelly Sandwich Recipe

Resource Requirements

Ingredients	Tools	Storage Units	Work Space
Bread	Cutting Board	Cabinet	Kitchen Table
Jelly	Glass	Cabinet Top	
Milk	Knife	Freezer	
Peanut Butter	Plate	Refrigerator	
	Spreader		
	Toaster		

Figure 1.8   Peanut Butter and Jelly Sandwich Recipe *(continued)*

Variables

Item	Variables	Example
Bread	Type	Wheat, White, Sliced, Whole
	Brand	Wonder, Sunbeam
	Container	Plastic, Paper Bag
	Location	Freezer, Cabinet Top
Jelly	Brand	Smuckers, Welches
	Type	Strawberry, Grape
	Container Type	Glass Jar, Plastic Squeeze Container
	Location	Refrigerator, Cabinet
Milk	Type	Skim, Whole
	Brand	Dairy Farms, Hood, Bordens
	Container	Glass, Plastic, Paper, Box
	Location	Refrigerator, Cabinet
Peanut Butter	Type	Chunky, Smooth, Natural, Salted, Unsalted
	Brand	Skippy, Jiffy
	Container Type	Glass, Plastic
	Location	Refrigerator, Cabinet
Cutting Board	Type	Wood, Plastic
	Brand	Rubbermaid
	Location	Counter Top
Plate	Size	Large
	Brand	Rose China, Crate & Barrel
	Type	Ceramic, Paper
	Location	Shelf
Knife	Size	6-inch, 8-inch
	Brand	Gerber, Henkel
	Type	Bread
	Location	Drawer
Toaster	Size	Two-Chamber, Four-Chamber
	Brand	Maytag, KitchenAid
	Type	Toaster-Oven, Pop-Up
	Location	Kitchen Table
Glass	Size	Large
	Brand	Dixie
	Type	Paper
	Location	Shelf
Refrigerator	Size	Large
	Brand	Maytag
	Type	Built-in, Walk-in
Drawer	Location	Kitchen
Shelf	Location	Kitchen
Cabinet	Location	Kitchen
Cabinet Top	Location	Kitchen
Freezer	Location	Kitchen
Table	Location	Kitchen

(continues)

Figure 1.8 Peanut Butter and Jelly Sandwich Recipe *(continued)*

Process Description

Setup
Take cutting board from cabinet top and put on kitchen table.
Take plate from cabinet shelf and put on kitchen table.
Take jelly, milk, and peanut butter from refrigerator and place on kitchen table.
Take bread from cabinet top and put on kitchen table.
Take spreader and knife from drawer and put on kitchen table.
Take cloth from cabinet top and put on kitchen table.

Preparation
Open bread container, take two slices, put in toaster and toast.
Put toasted bread on cutting board.
Open peanut butter container; using spreader, put a $1/4$" layer evenly on one piece of toast.
Clean spreader with damp cloth.
Open jelly container; using spreader, put a $1/4$" layer of jelly evenly on the other piece of toast.
Put slices of toast together, matching jelly to peanut butter faces.
Use knife to cut sandwich into four pieces by making two perpendicular cuts, each aligned to the diagonal of the sandwich face.
Place four pieces on plate.
Open milk and fill glass to within an inch of the glass top.

Cleanup
Close bread container and return bread to cabinet top.
Close peanut butter, jelly, and milk containers and put in refrigerator.
Wipe cutting board with damp dishtowel and place on cabinet top.
Put glass, spreader, plate, and knife in dishwasher.

Although it may seem unnecessarily detailed, the recipe in Figure 1.8 fulfills the requirements for a mature process description, since it

- Lists all resources, including the work environment, not simply the ones in the recipe
- Identifies all the variables involved, and provides explicit examples
- Provides details of pre- and postpreparation activities

Not surprisingly, a mature process description has a lot in common with a well-documented computer program. A C++ program, for example, lists the resources required for compilation, in the form of INCLUDE statements at the beginning of the program. Similarly, all of the variables included in the program are explicitly defined.

Of course, even the recipe in Figure 1.8 makes several assumptions. The first is that it will be used in a typical home environment. If the recipe were used in a commercial setting, then some variables would have to be altered to accommodate legal requirements. For example, the cutting board would have to be plastic, not open wood, and the maximum temperature of the refrigerator would be specified. Similarly, the workspace would have to include a three-section sink (wash, rinse, and drain) to fulfill board of health regulations for commercial food preparation areas.

In another application of the Continuum model, consider the flurry in the biotech industry surrounding how to make sense—and money—out of the roughly three billion chemical bases that describe the human genome. Because of the sheer complexity and volume of the data, which encompass one-dimensional gene sequences to three-dimensional protein structures, no one knows yet how to mine the data. However, biotech companies are filling their databases, assuming that someone will develop the technologies needed for data mining, visualization, integration, and computer networking. The CEOs of these biotech companies, including several major pharmaceuticals, are operating in an area of uncertainty. Their success is dependent on identifying companies that promise to deliver workable technologies—not mere displays of magic—in the relatively near future. That is, they need to identify the position of the supplier's technology in the Continuum.

Similarly, in the post-dotCom era, where securing venture capital (VC) money takes more than an idea scribbled on a dinner napkin, potential investors need to critically evaluate the status of a technology, in terms of time and likelihood of a reasonable return on investment. The CEO of the hopeful startup has the challenge of communicating this information to investors in a clear, understandable, and believable manner. In addition to showing the usual criteria—the company's competitive advantage, the financial and intellectual backers of the company, the revenue model, the exact nature of the product or service, the market, and the competition—a CEO has to paint a picture of the road to profitability. That is, she must demonstrate that her company has at least made it to the Product Point and is making headway to the Market Gateway. Using the Continuum definition at each point and period, the CEO can identify the position of her company's product in the Continuum, describing progress as well as expectations for the immediate and foreseeable future.

Consider the need for an easily understood model for communications within a technology development organization. It is often the case, for example, that marketing and sales perceive a need in the marketplace and want product development to add features to address the need, but have no idea of what is involved from a time or process perspective. They typically rely on necessarily vague reports from product development that the desired feature can be added, but to do so will add six weeks to the development process and therefore delay the release date by as many weeks.

Management then checks in six weeks later either to find that the feature set has been added or that it is only a week or two away. If management and marketing are technologically savvy, they may understand the progress limitations and be able to help product development assign weights to the product development options. However, the usual case is that those in management, marketing, and sales have no idea of where the other two groups perceive a product is in development. In this regard, the Continuum provides a common language that all three groups can use to communicate their needs and progress with time. The Continuum also helps product development understand the expectations over time, especially when hard dates are assigned to the key points and periods.

The application of the Continuum model in this and similar situations is detailed in Part Three. Chapter 2 continues to explore the alchemical transformation of idea to marketable product from the perspective of the traditional Product Lifecycle. It examines the relevance of the Continuum as a predictor of success in the marketplace.

SUMMARY

Most technologies begin as an idea or a dream—an apparent bit of magic—that developers hope can do things that customers think impossible through other means. Companies involved in developing technology-based products are charged with the challenge of moving the dream along a continuum to realization as a process or device that delivers value. Selling and marketing the value of the technology involves getting the customer to share the initial magical dream by buying into the actual device or process.

The Continuum describes the evolution of a technology-based product from its conception to its full implementation. There are internal issues that must be addressed, in terms of allocating and focusing resources, and external issues, in terms of knowing what the economic climate has to offer, what customers want, and what the competition is up to. Just as the complementary concepts of yin and yang should be in balance, the ideal situation is to fit the tangle of business transactions and their inherent benefits and risks into a model that makes sense, and that can be of some use in predicting or changing the future. In this regard, the Continuum extends from the magical—the mysterious and inexplicable—to technology—the actual result of applying theory. The various points and periods that compose the Continuum correspond to key decision points and challenges that characterize the development of a product within the organization. The value in the Continuum model is that it provides a dynamic view of a product at every stage of development and deployment. In particular, characterizing any development project as tension between multiple factors—technology, magic, risk, and prospect for reward—can help the decision maker determine how to allocate effort and resources when the company is buffeted by the inevitable pressures to release a quality product as early as possible in a highly competitive market.

A key concept in the Continuum is that there are two types of development. The first is the result of a new venture—a chance discovery in the R&D department of an established company or the result of years of labor in an inventor's basement—that leads to a prototype with unknown market potential. In this scenario, marketing is called in to support the movement of the prototype to product along the Continuum. Marketing is involved in both market research and, later, sales support. Although this is not necessarily the most opportune time to start considering sources of funding, the potential market for the product, price, or other factors related to success in the marketplace, it is a common predicament. The primary value of the Continuum in this situation is as a means of predicting the requirements needed by the startup or established company in bringing the innovation to market.

At the other end of the spectrum, the second type of development is the result of an extensive market research initiative. Only after there is a quantifiable probable demand for a particular product or product improvement does R&D get the go-ahead from upper-level management to invest time, money, and other resources toward realizing the product. Once a prototype is developed and determined to be viable, marketing begins tooling up to support the sales effort. The Continuum model is useful in this scenario as a means of communicating progress among the divisions in the company involved in the project—R&D, marketing, sales, and management—so that product expectations and timing are aligned.

2

Product Lifecycle

Give me your intuition of the present and I'll give you the past
and the future.

Ralph Waldo Emerson

CAVEAT EMPTOR (LET THE BUYER BEWARE!)

The consumer should not always take at face value slogans promulgated by Madison Avenue that products embodying leading-edge technology save time and money. To the contrary, leading-edge technology is not only a time and resource sink, but fraught with risk as well. In this regard, the alchemical conversion of an idea into a product, like the Darwinian adaptation of a species, is rarely perfect on the first iteration. Fresh technology, unlike fresh bread, is not always better.

If new products are at one end of the evolutionary spectrum, at the other end are the dinosaurs—the tired products that have been on the market for years. Whether these products are running shoes, fax machines, or laser printers, there is the ever-present risk of termination of production, like the sudden death of the dinosaurs, with each passing day. For this reason, serious runners buy shoes six or ten pairs at a time in order to avoid the arduous task of finding another make and model that agrees with their particular running style, and prudent office supply managers stock up on laser printer and fax cartridges in anticipation of the discontinuation of product lines.

One of the best models that illustrates this concept is the Boston Consulting Group (BCG) model, depicted in Figure 2.1. The BCG model, which is expressed as a 2×2 matrix plotting market share against market growth, is valuable for assessing a company's position relative to others in terms of its product offerings. That is, it can be used to suggest which products and services in a company's portfolio should be invested in, and which should be dropped. Products can be described as stars, dogs, cash cows, or question marks, depending on where they fall in the model.

Stars represent those products or services for which the company has a high share of the market, and the market is growing. They should be invested in further to maintain growth. Cash cows represent those products in which the company has a high market share but where the market is mature and slow growing or even declining. These products should be "milked" to provide cash for investments in future product areas. Dogs are products where the company has low market share and where the market itself is not growing. These should be dropped from the portfolio to release funds for investment in more attractive opportunities. Question marks are those products in which the company has low share but

Figure 2.1   The Boston Consulting Group (BCG) Model

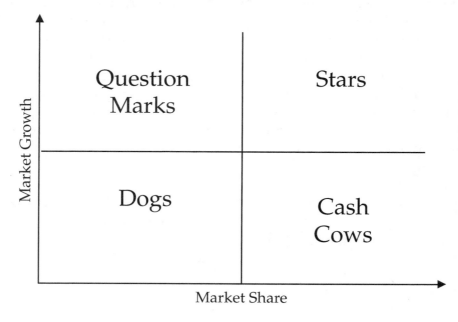

where the market is beginning to take off or has significant growth potential. They need to be watched closely, and the investment should be maintained to keep a presence since they could become tomorrow's stars, but the commitment should not be too high since they could also turn out to be tomorrow's dogs.

The challenge for consumers is deciding when—and if—they should embrace a new product. When the solution must be had at any cost, and time spent learning to use the product is no object, then investing in leading-edge technology makes sense. Conversely, for the marketing executive these adopters of bleeding-edge technologies are hard to find. Most military "investments" fall into this category, whether the product is a Star Wars defense shield or a fleet of stealth bombers. However, for corporate decision makers intent on profit, there is some point between the birth and death of a product where the costs and risks of entering the marketplace are balanced by lost opportunity costs and pressure from the competition. For example, if a competing company successfully uses wireless PDAs to provide service to their customers, and your own company's paper-based organizers and roadside telephones are insufficient to manage customer relations, you will be pressured to invest in wireless PDAs, a young technology, even with its risks. Waiting until the technology is mature could guarantee the competition an increase in its customer base—an advantage that may be impossible to overcome in the future.

Paradoxically, just as in the biological world, the only certainty associated with the birth of a product—the instantiation of an idea into something that can be sold in the marketplace—is death, unless the organization can adapt to change. Although there is no DNA-based biological clock to limit a product's life span, the technology underlying the product, the economic and political environment, the wisdom of the decision maker, and luck all have an effect on the viability of a product over time. Like the fields of medicine, engineering, and physics, the business world is full of models that help the executive team simulate and/or forecast scenarios to support management decisions. The right model can provide an intellectual lever for simultaneously understanding the minutiae and the big picture of what is happening in a complex economy. This chapter explores how the Product Lifecycle model can provide the decision maker with insight into how a product or process can survive in the dynamic, challenging economic environment defined by the Continuum.

A MATTER OF LIFE AND DEATH

In the biological world, the ability to coordinate complex processes under a variety of challenges goes hand-in-hand with survival. Complex biological processes, whether associated with digestion or muscle contraction, must be defined with enough precision to work flawlessly under normal conditions. In addition, the processes must be flexible enough to maintain normal biological functioning while subject to environmental stressors ranging from temperature extremes to invading infectious organisms. In a similar way, technologies, whether products or processes, must be defined precisely in order to provide value to the customer or die in the marketplace.

There are limits, of course, in terms of how much time, energy, and money can be invested in creating and maintaining a viable product. For example, defining every business process as precisely and exhaustively as we did in Chapter 1 with the sandwich-making process, is often impractical. In fact, technological innovation, to a large degree, is about finding shortcuts—whether based on past experience or from accidental discoveries—that provide equivalent results to otherwise arduous processes.

Revisiting a cooking scenario, consider that a great recipe starts with an innovative chef who has an idea and follows it up with experimentation until he gets it right. However, the results of his experiment cannot be considered a scalable recipe until he can describe the process precisely enough for someone to follow it successfully even without firsthand experience of the recipe. The cook's alchemical conversion of his idea into a recipe may initially involve experimentation, that is, using different ingredients in a new combination, by adding a sprig of fresh mint, using homemade bread, or adding a special jelly. The subsequent experimentation and iterative refinement condenses the innovation to an explicit process description—a recipe. From the perspective of the person interpreting the recipe, an element of magic, that is, mystery, remains if anything in the process description is left out.

When it comes to survival, there is no such thing as a perfect organism or product. Conditions change, sometimes instantly, favoring one organism over another. Just as dinosaurs—the most successful life forms in the history of the planet—suddenly died out due to climactic changes, so products can die out as fads and fashion change, or the factors related to macro (political, social) and micro (financial) environment change. Within a few days, demand for a once-popular product may wane to the point that it is not even economically feasible to maintain the product in active inventory. Many recipes and fads come and go, like evolutionary dead-ends, never to return. Other nonessential or luxury items, such as hula hoops and Chia pets, go into a state of hibernation, to be reintroduced to a new generation of consumers every decade or so.

The fate of most products and services over time can be described in terms of a Product Lifecycle that has many parallels with biological systems. As illustrated in Figure 2.2, this model begins with the product ready for introduction, as through a miracle of neogenesis. That is, it bypasses the first half of the Continuum model that includes the product's inception, gestation, and birth, as well as the associated costs and decisions. As such, the classic Product Lifecycle model as depicted in Figure 2.2 has little value for predicting costs and potential barriers associated with premarket introduction. However, the Product Lifecycle is a convenient and compelling model of predicting the course of a product once it is introduced into the marketplace.

Chia Pets and Hula Hoops

The fates of traditional durable goods, such as cars and TVs, roughly follow the typical Product Lifecycle depicted in curve A of Figure 2.2. The hula hoop, Chia pet, and other fads usually have a much steeper curve, as illustrated by curve B.

As described by the classic Product Lifecycle, it is assumed that a product, whether an item on a restaurant menu or pair of Gore-Tex boots, evolves through four discrete stages, beginning with the product offering. An assumption of the model is that different types of products have different time frames for each phase. The predictability of how competition, consumer tastes, and new technological innovations affect these phases is one of the challenges that a CEO or other decision maker faces. The four stages and their characteristics are

1. *Introduction.* The product is offered for sale. The initial price for a product depends on whether an organization wants to maximize revenue or market share. Products may be deeply discounted or even offered for free to obtain market share.

Figure 2.2　Product Lifecycle Curves

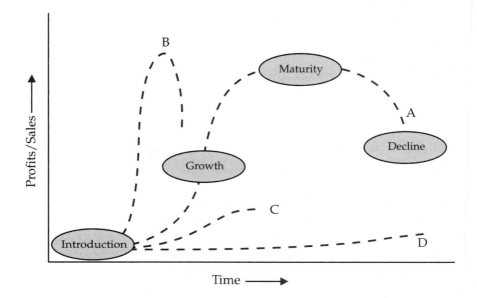

2. *Growth.*　Sales increase after product introduction.
3. *Maturity.*　Demand for the product levels off.
4. *Decline.*　Demand for the product and sales drop off.

Each phase of the classic Product Lifecycle is characterized by marketing conditions and constraints. According to the Product Lifecycle curve, sales grow exponentially immediately after Introduction, continuing in the Growth phase, where the volume of sales becomes significant. Sales stabilize at the Maturity phase due to market saturation unless the product is improved or introduced to a new market. Finally, changing tastes, competing products, or decrease in the quality of components or ingredients results in decreased demand during the Decline phase.

　　The pattern depicted in curve A of Figure 2.2 is typical of traditional products, such as automobiles. Consider the Oldsmobile line, which was introduced in 1899. As illustrated by the Product Lifecycle curve, it experienced brisk growth for the next few years, outselling every other make. Over the next decade, the brand evolved from a 650-pound car with single cylinder engine to an eight-cylinder, 5,000-pound behemoth. The sale of Oldsmobile cars continued to follow the S-curve, and the company was purchased by GM in the 1920s.

Although there were years with less than stellar sales, innovations like the semiautomatic safety transmission in 1938, fully automatic transmission in 1940, overhead V-8 engine in 1949, and front-wheel drive in 1966 continued to drive Oldsmobile sales, with each innovation building up the brand. Toward the end of the 1980s, product innovations ceased, fuel-efficient imports presented stiff competition, and sales declined. Ill-targeted marketing campaigns contributed to dwindling sales in the 1990s. In the end, GM retired the line in 2000.

Many products fail to follow the exponential S-curve illustrated by Oldsmobile, but instead exhibit much slower initial growth rates (Figure 2.2, curve C) or linear growth that is not sufficient in volume to offset the cost of production and marketing (Figure 2.2, curve D). Furthermore, the steepness or flatness of the curve can change, depending upon market conditions. In addition, as the dot-Com products illustrated, simply because a Web site or other product follows the exponential growth curve, there is no guarantee of long-term stability or profitability. Spending millions on advertising campaigns and in some instances even paying customers directly to visit a Web site, simply to maintain the growth rate pattern described by the S-curve, is not necessarily a wise business strategy.

In mid-2001, Apple Computer ended production of its G4 Cube personal computer, only a little over a year after it was introduced. Even though Apple is known for innovative designs and relatively robust technology, the cube failed to achieve a significant customer following. That is, it failed to experience a strong, exponential growth in sales following introduction, but instead had only modest sales, like curve C in Figure 2.2.

Within two weeks of Apple's announcement regarding the demise of the G4 Cube, two online grocery pioneers, Webvan and HomeRuns, announced that they would cease operation. Apparently neither of the online grocery services could attract enough customers to reach profitability. With only about 2% of online shoppers buying groceries online in 2000, the pattern of online grocery sales was similar to curve D in Figure 2.2. Unfortunately for the two online grocers, they ran out of capital before their services had a chance to grow significantly. Although there were several financial issues involved in the failures, timing was also a factor. Just as Bryan's Home Health Software products were introduced at a time when consumers were not yet comfortable with the computer as something other than a game or business machine, Webvan and

HomeRuns were introduced at a time when going to the grocery store was a part of the American culture.

Risky Business

As a descriptive model, the classic Product Lifecycle curve is useful in understanding the position of a product in the marketplace. As a predictive tool, the model has several shortcomings, depending on the underlying assumptions. One is that the eventual decline in sales is built into the model. In addition, the S-curve doesn't recognize that a decline in sales may occur at any time after the introduction of a product. The curve also ignores the contribution that original innovation makes to product success or failure in the marketplace. It is as though the product simply appears on some marketing director's desk, fully developed and debugged. However, such products are just about as common as perfect people, devoid of genetic defects and with perfect childhoods.

It should be noted that the Product Lifecycle is a high-level and generic view of gross product activity in the marketplace, since the forces on the product at critical junctures are hidden from view. Implicit assumptions are that phases of Introduction and Growth are typically customer focused, whereas Maturity and Decline are market focused. In fact, this change in focus from the customer to the competition and other market factors is responsible for the various shapes that the life cycle curve can assume for different types of products. Short-term profitability and survival in the marketplace—not customer loyalty—are usually the focus of business activities once a product achieves maturity.

Another implicit assumption in the Product Lifecycle model is that not only sales, but also the products themselves evolve over time. As the marketing slogan, "Not your father's Oldsmobile" pointed out, the Oldsmobile evolved during its century of production. Of course, what really survived for a century was the Oldsmobile brand, not a particular model of car. Every year, with every model, there was a slightly different process of working through the phases of the Product Lifecycle. Today, computers are especially typical of product dynamics. Even though Gateway, Dell, and Macintosh are viable brands, most models are no longer in production. Some models, especially laptops, are discontinued less than a year after introduction.

Another way to view the Product Lifecycle is that of a dynamic, iterative process that emphasizes the progression from one stage to the next. At any point during this sequence, the product can be discarded or reworked. This perspective is illustrated in Figure 2.3, where the odds of deviating from the traditional Product Lifecycle are high during inception and development, low during introduction and growth, and high again during maturity and decline.

During inception, when dozens or hundreds of ideas are generated, and during early development, it is more likely that an idea will be discarded than reworked. However, toward the end of development, and as the product introduction approaches, there may be so much time, energy, and capital invested in a product that reworking it is the only economically viable alternative to moving forward to the growth phase. Moving forward instead of taking the time to rework a product, either because of resources that have already been invested in the product or simply the tenacity of the decision maker, is usually ill advised. Decisions to move forward to marketing a product should be based on product viability. Customers don't usually respond to the amount of money spent—or wasted—in development, but rather what the product can do for them.

Figure 2.3 Expanded Product Lifecycle Sequence

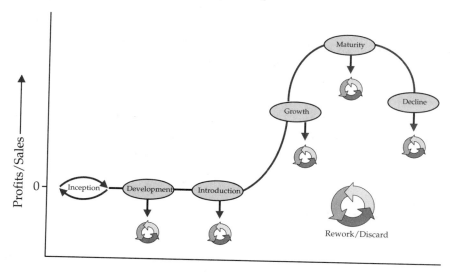

The dynamics change after the growth phase, when the maturity of the product in the marketplace may force reworking of the product to address competition or a drop in demand. Finally, during the decline of a product, the specifics of the product and the market dictate whether to discard the technology in favor of a more advanced technology or to rework it into a form more attractive to customers. For example, the Oldsmobile line survived for a century through almost continuous improvement in its underlying technology.

Sometimes reworking is not necessary, but it may be better to use a period of dormancy long enough so that the product seems new to customers when it is reintroduced. This tactic is somewhat equivalent to adding new features to an existing product in an existing market or introducing the same product into a new market. Exercise equipment seems especially amenable to reintroduction. The abdominal roller—a device with a wheel and a handle for doing abdominal work—and various forms of muscle stimulators, which promise muscle development while the user watches TV, are reintroduced as breakthrough products every eight or nine years. Fad diets are also reintroduced every decade or so, for a new group of customers to discover that fad diets simply do not work.

Decline may be designed in, as in clothing, which undergoes periodic style obsolescence. Decline may also be due to physical obsolescence, where the product is designed to wear out, as typified by American cars, batteries, and prepaid telephone calling cards. Technological obsolescence results in decline when an old technology replaces a new one, such as when digital cell phones replaced analog ones. Many computers seem to follow a path of planned obsolescence, in which demand for existing models declines every six months, just as new, faster, more powerful units are introduced.

The characteristics of the Inception and Development phases, as well as the following four stages of the traditional Product Lifecycle—Introduction, Growth, Maturity, and Decline—are best understood as components of the Continuum.

LIFE AND DEATH IN THE CONTINUUM

Mapping the Product Lifecycle to the Continuum provides a dynamic perspective on the movement of a product from Inception to Decline (see Figure 2.4).

Figure 2.4   The Continuum versus Product Lifecycle

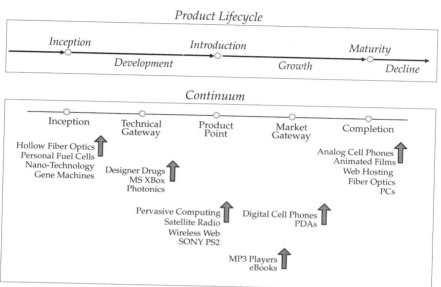

Inception

Inception in the Product Lifecycle model, roughly equivalent to the Product Point in the Continuum, involves coming up with as many ideas as possible, and then discarding the weak ones early to save valuable resources. In this Darwinian approach, the criteria for the survival of an idea include an analysis of the relevant economic, technologic, and political ramifications of the eventual product or service. The criteria for assessing ideas at the inception of a product should inform the decision maker about whether to proceed with product plans, or abandon them. For each product idea, a decision maker must evaluate the

- Likely investment requirements
- Funds available for R&D
- Minimum performance of the product relative to the competition
- Quality and availability of suppliers
- Government regulations and likely support
- Defensibility and scalability of the technologies involved
- Strategies for bringing the product to market
- Qualitative results of focus groups that discuss the product

Many dotCom companies were based on "products" that never made it past the Inception phase of the Product Lifecycle, in part because they did not fulfill the criteria for survival. In particular, many dotCom companies headed by technologists were based on potential products that intended to incorporate innovative technologies that were thought to be "cool," not because they were potentially profitable. Other reasons for failure include the use of flawed financial models based on advertisement dollars and the failure of the consumer-to-consumer approach to selling. In addition, the ability to rapidly prototype untested technologies through newly available Web-enabled development platforms meant that technology was no longer a bottleneck for the enthusiastic entrepreneur. Unfortunately, this did not negate the need to focus on the traditional due diligence required for examining the customer's willingness to pay and the long-term ROI calculations.

Development

Development is about moving a product through the Technical Gateway of the Continuum in preparation for the Product Point. Prior to the Technical Gateway, activities include testing and refining ideas, with the goal of demonstrating proof of practicality from technical and consumer willingness-to-pay perspectives. Figure 2.4 shows products in the Development phase that have yet to reach the Technical Gateway stage as of the fourth quarter of 2001, including personal fuel cells, nanotechnology, hollow fiber optics, and gene machines.

All of these technologies have huge economic potential. Some view fuel cells, which create electricity from hydrogen and oxygen in the air, as the answer to the world's energy crisis. Nanotechnology, the creation of molecule-sized robots that can trigger nuclear bombs today, and perhaps one day can create denser hard drives and smaller integrated circuits or repair heart valves, are similarly relegated to research laboratories. Corning's hollow fiber optics is a very low-loss version of the current generation of fiber optics. If the technical hurdles can be overcome, hollow fiber optics will revolutionize communications, by making possible longer runs of cable without the need to install expensive, power-hungry amplifier electronics. Gene machines, massively parallel supercomputers under development by IBM, Compaq, and others, promise to empower researchers exploring the human genome and proteome.

These potential products are at best demonstrations with significant magical qualities. Even though they are largely unproven and may not be cost-effective in their intended areas of deployment, from an investment perspective, they represent a great potential for gain. That is, the inherent volatility of a totally new product, such as a device based on nanotechnology, means that it has a much greater likelihood of either failing or disrupting entire industries, as compared to mature technologies, such as zip drives and CD-ROM drives.

Once the Technical Gateway has been achieved, activities in the Development phase necessarily include performing business analysis, establishing business partners, identifying and contracting suppliers, creating or contracting production facilities, creating prototypes, and limited test marketing. Examples of products in the Development stage in the fourth quarter of 2001 included wireless digital cameras, photonics, designer drugs, and the Microsoft Xbox computer game console. As noted in Chapter 1, the rate of progress from one phase to the next is product, consumer, and market dependent.

For example, consider photonics, the use of optical switching devices for Internet and voice communications. Because of uncertainties in the post-dotCom economy and layoffs in the high-tech sector, progress in photonics stalled in the Development phase. Microsoft, by contrast, was under intense pressure to debut its Xbox game console for the 2001 holiday season. As a newcomer to the game console market, Microsoft had to enter the market before Sony, the established market leader, had a chance to usurp potential Xbox customers with its newly released PlayStation II console.

Introduction

Introducing a product in the marketplace at the Product Point in the Continuum is the moment of truth. For a company to move a product to the Introduction phase of the Product Lifecycle, the development team has had to successfully address a variety of challenges, from varying and uncertain resource requirements, to unreasonable time constraints, ambiguities in the requirements specification, and unsuccessful budgetary constraints—all of which can hopefully can be avoided or mitigated through a better understanding of the Continuum model.

Assuming that the company created a useful product—that is, one that is functionally working, and where preliminary market research has been conducted, yet is still untested in the mass market—the focus necessarily shifts from technology development to marketing, with a concomitant transitioning of the focus of resources. The balancing of these resources and knowing when to make the critical transition can be achieved through the Continuum model. However, even with a successful refocusing of energy from technology to market research, there is no guarantee that a product, once introduced, will be welcomed in the marketplace. A product can become stuck at the Product Point for any number of reasons, from inferior technology to inadequate production capacity, a limited market, and too high an asking price. Products introducing new technologies to consumers also have to contend with the fear of customers to be first to invest in a technology, inadequate and inept sales and marketing, and a lack of references. While some customers will wait in line for a chance to be the first to own a new technology, most will wait to see if the product is accepted by the marketplace.

Products that are potentially disruptive—that is, with the capability of transforming and redefining entire markets—may also fail dramatically. For example, the iridium satellite system, backed by Motorola and others, was a multibillion-dollar attempt to provide worldwide mobile telephone coverage—as long as the customer was not inside a building. Unfortunately for the backers of the system, in the time it took to design the system, build and launch the 66 satellites, and design, create, and market the handsets, the system became outdated technologically and too expensive compared to the alternatives. By the time the satellite system was debugged, cell phones and services, which worked inside office buildings, were not only cheaper than the satellite services, but the handsets were about one-tenth the size and weight of the iridium handsets. The iridium system was at the point of being dismantled in 2000, when new backers, including the CIA, appeared to provide funding.

Despite the problems with the iridium system, commercial satellite systems are far from dead. For example, in 2001 a nationwide satellite-based digital radio system began operation. Two satellites, "Rock" and "Roll," were placed into geosynchronous orbit above the East and West Coasts of the United States in 2001. Together, they provide 100-channel, nationwide, uninterrupted coverage of

CD-quality digital AM and FM programming. As a start, digital radio receivers will be installed in GM and Honda automobiles sold in the United States, starting with 2002 models, reflecting the belief that long-distance commuters and truck drivers will be the initial customers for the service, in part because they will not have to switch between different radio stations while traveling from one region to the next.

The success of the subscription service depends on the availability of affordable home and mobile receivers that produce CD-quality sound, which in turn depends on the ability of chip set suppliers to keep up with demand for the radio service. Another consideration is the ability of the marketing group to overcome resistance to a subscription model for radio when most listeners consider radio, like Web content, to be free. Competition from a similar service, Sirius Satellite Radio, is another threat to the success of the service.

In each of the preceding examples, timing has a major bearing on eventual success of a company and its products. For these investments to pay off, the period from inception to introduction has to be as short as practically possible. Although the term *Internet Time*, like the dotCom-induced behavior of wearing Polo shirts and jeans at board meetings, has lost favor in corporate America, the Product Lifecycle has shortened since the introduction of PCs and computer technology. Specifically, the incubation time—the time between the instantiation of an idea, as indicated by a patent, for example—and Introduction has shortened from decades to years or months in some cases (see Figure 2.5).

The general trend in incubation time compression predates the computer and reflects the increased efficiencies of the industrial revolution. One major contributor to time compression today is the mix of products. An increasingly larger proportion of products is designed through the manipulation of information instead of physical matter. For example, automobiles are now designed in a matter of months with computer-aided design (CAD) tools instead of years with clay and foam models. Similarly, once hardware infrastructure is in place, Web sites can be designed and implemented within weeks or months—a capability that allowed many dotCom startups to appear virtually overnight. In addition, in the time that it has taken the first PCs to evolve into today's devices, several software

Figure 2.5   Incubation Time Compression

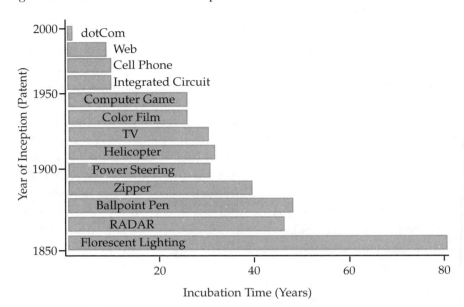

products have evolved through 10 or more generations. In the classic Product Lifecycle model, these and similar differences in the technology development platforms, not the technology product, contribute to the shape of the Product Lifecycle curve.

Growth

From the perspective of the Continuum, the first part of the Growth phase of the Product Lifecycle is about successful transition to the Market Gateway, where the core technology has stabilized and advances are focused on improving marketing. Examples of products in the Growth phase of the Product Lifecycle that had yet to achieve the Market Gateway in the fourth quarter of 2001 include the wireless Web, eBooks, MP3 players, and the Sony PS2 game console. Each of these products has different chances of success and different rates of growth.

For example, consider a wireless modem that enables a PDA or laptop computer to provide access anytime, anywhere to computing power and information. There are several wireless modem technologies and services at various stages of development and with different odds of success. One is wireless ethernet, which provides fast connectivity with a growing coverage area using industry-standard protocols. For high-speed access, there was Metricom's failed attempt at its proprietary Ricochet service, but service was limited to high-density areas, such as Manhattan, Los Angeles, and the San Francisco Bay Area. Metricom failed in 2001 because it insisted on using its own proprietary networking technology, a gamble that did not pay off. The other major players, OmniSky, Wireless WebConnect, and GoAmerica, offer nationwide service, but they are excruciatingly slow.

Although several wireless innovations have obvious potential for market acceptance, from satellites to the use of florescent lighting encoded with information that can be picked up by handheld devices, there are a number of roadblocks to growth. For one, the action of environmentalists and those concerned that new wireless towers are unsightly and interfere with tourism is limiting the growth of wireless computing in many communities. Impending taxation of transactions on the Web may further delay the growth of pervasive computing, as well as other Internet-related ventures.

Many components of the wireless Web, such as products based on the Bluetooth standard that defines short-range wireless communications, were just to the Product Point in the fourth quarter of 2001, with a good deal of *magic* about them, especially in the United States. Unfortunately for U.S. customers, the third generation of cellular infrastructure, G3, will be under development for several years because of legal issues over spectrum rights. Competing standards for wireless text-based communications, such as short messaging service (SMS) and wireless application protocol (WAP), further confused the market. Barring government intervention, the company with the deepest pockets and the greatest political clout typically sets the standards in an industry.

EBooks, the electronic equivalent of printed texts that can be downloaded to and read on portable tablets or PDAs, have been slow to gain acceptance. Thus far, growth has failed to follow an exponential trajectory because of the expense and technical limitations of the quality of portable display devices. In addition, legal limitations and restrictions on distribution turn some customers away. Some publishers now require personal encryption with each download, creating a time barrier between the reader and the act of reading. For example, PeanutPress requires prospective eBook buyers to submit their name and a valid charge card number before they can download an eBook file. The information is stored with the file to discourage the book buyer from freely distributing eBooks via email attachments.

The growth of MP3 players, the solid-state alternatives to cassette and CD players, was crippled somewhat by the restrictions placed on Napster, the free, Web-based service that allowed users of the service to share music. In the area of entertainment, the growth of sales of the Sony PS2 in the United States during the holiday season of 2000 was severely restricted by the scarcity of parts. Unfortunately, this type of problem is inherent in the Japanese model of just in time (JIT) delivery of products from supplier to manufacturer. Companies in Japan rarely keep inventories on hand for more than a few days of activity, and instead rely upon a complex network of well-coordinated suppliers. As the RAM shortage in the late 1990s demonstrated, the catastrophic failure of a parts supplier (in this case, an explosion in a RAM factory in Taiwan) can impede the growth of an entire industry. Despite a strong showing in Japan at the PS2's debut, only a small percentage of the demand for U.S. Christmas sales could be met. As a result, the growth curve for the console was more like curve D in Figure 2.2 for the first year of production.

Just as living organisms depend on a supply of oxygen, water, and nutrients for survival, the sales performance of every product in the Growth phase depends on an infrastructure of other products and technologies. For example, the vacuum cleaner, first a commercial device that ran on gasoline, only became practical for purchase by businesses and home use with the development of affordable electric motors to power the cleaner.

In addition to the interaction of products and technologies, the political climate and public opinion profoundly affects the growth of a product. For example, modern air conditioning was able to grow exponentially in the 1950s and 1960s because of a series of legislative moves and public sentiment, starting with the discovery in the early 19th century that air is composed of several gasses, including waste products of human metabolism. By the late 1800s, there were codes for ventilation, and engineers found it easy to tie heat into the mandatory ventilation systems. The flu epidemic of 1917 served to instill fear of open-air ventilation in the public, pushing the development of closed building designs in public places such as government buildings, theaters, and offices. When tract houses were introduced in the 1950s, they were explicitly designed with central air conditioning. As a result, air conditioning became associated with health, luxury, wealth, and prosperity, and sales of air conditioners skyrocketed.

Product growth may also be kick-started by temporarily coupling it with established, well-performing products. Popular examples of this symbiotic arrangement include meal combos at fast-food restaurants, the bundling of computer games with game consoles, and bundling office software with computer hardware. The relationship is beneficial for the established product as well as the new product because the combination is usually offered at a price that provides customers with proportionally more value for their money.

Maturity

Products clearly past the Market Gateway of the Continuum and approaching the Maturity phase of the Product Lifecycle include PDAs and digital cell phones. PDAs are increasingly popular in higher education and business for everything from keeping track of projects, contact information, and time management. Affordable wireless PDAs have been well received by grade school children, who use them to trade email messages, digital photographs, secret messages, and sometimes even keep track of homework.

The popularity of digital cell phones has reached the point that many producers are entering the Maturity phase of the Product Lifecycle in certain markets. Consider that Japan's NTT DoCoMo cellular phone service, the world's most advanced cell phone system, is expanding its market to other countries in order to maintain growth. The handset suppliers Nokia, Motorola, and Ericsson face stiff competition from dozens of firms, and have even turned to outside manufacturers who can produce handsets more economically. In the maturing market, the handset manufacturers, such as Nokia, are focused on selling brand over technology.

As the digital cell phone market approaches maturity in the United States, some of the supporting infrastructure technologies, such as the fiber optic backbone, are already there. Like the over-built railroads of the 1880s, companies laid down about $90 billion in optical fiber in the United States from 1997 to 2001. However, most of it lies dormant because the projected demand for high-bandwidth Internet access did not materialize. Part of the problem was that customers could not access the high-bandwidth fiber from their homes or offices because of the lack of equipment. This "last mile" dilemma is akin to living next to a six-lane highway with no access ramps. For example, in Bryan's hometown of Brookline, Massachusetts, just across the Charles River from the Massachusetts Institute of Technology (MIT), high-speed wired access is simply not an option. Bryan's only option for high-speed access to the Internet is to purchase a satellite dish and subscribe to a monthly service. The typical customer may have separate telephone lines for telephone and fax, a cable TV hookup, a cell phone, and perhaps a pager—each with an associated monthly subscription cost. Those customers who did have direct Internet access were not willing to pay for yet another subscription service. Because of this, the mature fiber optic backbone began to decline in late 2001.

Decline

A product can start down the slippery slope of decline and eventual death for any number of reasons. The price may be raised to correct for lack of profit, resulting in profoundly decreased sales. The quality of the product may be intentionally reduced as a cost-cutting measure, allowing the competition to move into the market. The product may suffer from technological obsolescence, just as analog phones were displaced by digital models. A limited market may become quickly saturated, stalling sales and sending corporate income into a downward spiral. As the market decline at the start of the new millennium illustrated, the economy may stall, causing demand for nonessentials to drop; the first item on an unemployed consultant's to-buy list typically is not a new PDA. Finally, consumers may simply become bored with the same old product, whether it is an item on a menu or a brand of breakfast cereal.

The declines of some products occur seemingly overnight, whereas others linger on a moribund course for decades. The overnight variety of decline occurred in the "disk farm" market. When dotComs were on the rise, companies erected enormous data centers, or disk farms, for Web hosting. With the dotCom crash and massive overcapacity, these disk farms had no choice but to merge and modify their businesses or else close their doors.

Products in more gradual decline include traditional animation, analog cell phones, and desktop PCs. All-digital films, such as *Toy Story, Antz, Shrek,* and *Final Fantasy,* are challenging traditional, hand-drawn animation, popularized by Walt Disney. Successors to the nearly lifelike synthetic characters in *Final Fantasy* and *Gladiator* will eventually challenge the live actor and actress market as well, replacing and supplementing human actors with digital stand-ins.

The sales of many products ultimately decline because of mistakes made in the Inception and Development phases of the Product Lifecycle. For example, the "Clipit" animated paper clip included in Microsoft Office did not impress users. The software robot, or "Bot," didn't provide the set of features users needed, even though the Bot technology was mature. In other words, simply because a technology is mature does not mean that it will succeed in the marketplace. For this reason, companies like UPS spend months to years testing technologies before they deploy them company-wide. For example, UPS gradually started using wireless scanning technology, testing the scanners, assessing potential problems, and determining the likely return on investment (ROI). Despite this cautious stance, UPS was one of the first companies to incorporate wireless devices corporate-wide, a move dating back to 1992.

RELEVANCE

In the movie *Gladiator,* Oliver Reed's character, Proximo Palindromos, the master and mentor of the former general and supreme gladiator, Maximus, delivers a pre-contest motivational speech in which he announces that the gladiators were all dead men, and the only issues were how and when they will die. In the pep talk, the owner was impressing upon the gladiators that even though they could not control their environment or their adversaries, they could control their focus, make strategic decisions, and act according to their beliefs. So it is with products.

Given that all products will eventually die, perhaps to be periodically reborn, like the abdominal roller and Chia pet, or given a temporary reprieve from death, like the digital stand-in for the deceased actor Oliver Reed in *Gladiator,* how can the Continuum model assist the CEO of a company involved in developing or evaluating a technology-based product? For the answer, consider the battle of two economic and technologic powerhouses, Microsoft and Sony, for the computer game console market of the 2001 holiday season. While sales and margins of PCs were stable or in slight decline, the $7 billion game console market was the fastest growing area of computing.

Sony, the established leader in the game console space, with over $6.5 billion in annual sales, had the benefit of the overwhelming success of its original PlayStation console, which accounts for almost 40% of all game consoles sold in the United States. Despite this early lead, however, PlayStation II (PS2) had only limited success in the U.S. market. As noted earlier, sales volume in 2000 was severely limited because an ongoing parts shortage limited console production. A worldwide shortage of tantalum, a rare mineral mined in the Congo that is used in the production of tantalum capacitors, restricted the production of everything from cell phones to portable CD players. As a result of the capacitor shortage, sales of PS2 consoles during the 2000 holiday season fell far short of Sony's projections by at least 50%. For almost six moths, the situation did not improve much, and PlayStation II consoles were still in limited supply. In addition, there were accounts of numerous hardware glitches, especially related to the DVD drive mechanism, and only a handful of games written expressly for the PS2's architecture were available. Games for the PS2 were in such short supply that Sony shipped demos of upcoming titles with some units, promoting capabilities of games not yet available for sale.

Despite the formal introduction of the PS2 into the U.S. market in the winter of 2000, the supply was so restricted that it had not grown much beyond the Product Point in the Continuum. Sony, which derived about a third of its revenue in 2000 from the sale of PlayStation consoles and accessories, had not demonstrated to the market that it could produce the game consoles in the quantities required. Enough consoles were needed to fulfill consumer demand, support game developers with a viable platform for their products, and fend off sales of competing consoles.

Microsoft announced its *planned* release of the Xbox near the time of Sony's limited introduction of the PS2 (in a similar move, Nintendo, a distant third player in this battle, announced that its less expensive Cube computer would be available three days before the Xbox). Microsoft's announcement of the winter 2001 release of the Xbox caused many potential consumers who would have otherwise upgraded to a PS2—if they could find one—to hold out for the Xbox. This attitude was justified by the expectation of the upcoming availability of Microsoft's own store of popular computer games, such as Microsoft Flight Simulator, as well as multiplayer games distributed over Microsoft's MSN network. In addition, the top game developers, including Activision, THQ, Electronic Arts, and Midway Games, could not ignore the potential market for their games created by the Xbox. In the end, gamers buy consoles for the games, not the hardware. However, until the computer game industry standardizes on a single operating system and hardware architecture, game developers and customers will have to contend with multiple platforms.

Using the Product Lifecycle curve, the PS2 was in the Introduction phase in winter 2000 and on a growth trajectory similar to curve D in Figure 2.2. Examining the curve does not explain the reason for the lackluster growth of domestic PS2 sales. However, the Continuum model explicitly defines the criteria for reaching the Product Point, which is characterized by a product that can be evaluated. However, like any decision support tool, the model involves judgment calls and encompasses certain assumptions—which may or may not be valid. For example, the PS2 must have first made it through the Technical Gateway, which is characterized by the development of a technically viable prototype that demonstrates a subset of the technology involved in the proposed product.

However, a viable process for creating the PS2 was not yet demonstrated by the winter of 2000. The PS2 had a viable design, but it did not have an underlying process of creating the console in sufficient quantities. As a result, the introduction of the PS2 in the United States was more of an implosion. The consoles remained in the magical category; potential buyers could play with the demo models in stores, but could not buy them. Meanwhile, the prerelease marketing campaign of the Xbox included *magical* demonstrations in controlled conference exhibits, as developers made progress toward the Product Point.

In other words, the Continuum perspective provides a view of the underlying mix of magic versus technology that aids in decision

making. It explains why early domestic sales of the PS2 were little
more than a trickle: that is, the process of manufacturing the console was not yet viable or reliable, and there was a risk involved with
committing to a PS2 instead of waiting to evaluate the Xbox or Nintendo's GameCube. For developers, the risk of committing
resources to a product that cannot be manufactured in quantity
means that their sales are stalled until the execution of the manufacturing process can be significantly improved.

Risk Management

The battle for the game console, which will likely continue for several years, suggests that the greatest impetus for using the Continuum model to supplement the Product Lifecycle is to control risk.
As a predictive model, it encourages the decision maker to look
ahead of the current challenges and at least consider the underlying processes that are involved in bringing a product to market.
Because of interdependencies in the economy and uncertainties in
how customers will respond to new technologies, there is always a
certain amount of risk associated with investing resources in a product or development project.

There are also risks associated with interdependencies. For
example, color printers optimized for digital prints are dependent on
the success of digital cameras. The prospects look good for printers,
given that the sale of digital cameras is doubling every year, with 11
million units sold in 2000. By 2003, two-thirds of all cameras sold in
the United States will be digital. As noted above, game console manufacturers depend on exciting game titles to sell their hardware.
Similarly, pervasive computing and wireless PDAs depend on affordable wireless services.

Consider also that scientists at Corning are looking into a new,
low-loss, hollow-core optical fiber for the communications infrastructure. Despite a glut of conventional fiber, the new fiber promises to allow significantly longer cable runs between expensive,
power-consuming amplifiers, resulting in tremendous cost savings
for network infrastructure builders. If its R&D efforts pay off, Corning should be able to maintain its leadership position in the $5 bil-
lion optical fiber market.

It is often difficult to predict how a technology-based product will fare in the marketplace, even when the underlying technology is perfected. In part, this is because of the highly interdependent nature of modern products. Philippe Kahn, the entrepreneur who brought the wildly successful Borland Turbo Pascal to the market in the 1980s, is developing a technology to send images and sound over wireless devices. Whether his company, Lightsurf, succeeds depends largely on the partnerships it can make with cell-phone makers and wireless carriers, as well as on consumer demand.

Regardless of how well Lightsurf's camera system works as a stand-alone prototype, the long-term success of this company hinges on access to hardware and infrastructures built by others, the success of that hardware in the marketplace, and eventual customer demand for wireless imaging. Assuming Corning or Lightsurf excels in the development phase of the Product Lifecycle, its ultimate success still depends on how well its products are received by customers. Fortunately, as described in Chapter 3, customer behavior can be modeled with a degree of certainty.

Sometimes risks are created by government intervention. Celera Genomics was the first to decode the human genome, beating out the government-funded effort in 2000. In this regard, the U.S. government and Celera are equivalent in the Continuum, in that both are past the Product Point. However, the value of Celera's database is eroded by the government's free data, which is posted on the Web and accessed for free. Faced with no revenue stream, Celera started over with a plan to become a drug-development and diagnostic-test company, meaning that it will somehow have to compete with the likes of the pharmaceutical giants Pfizer and Merck. Moving to a new area with tools not yet past the Technical Gateway is a risky proposition for Celera.

Just as there is security in numbers, risk of product failures in the marketplace can be reduced through strategic partnerships, such the one between Cannon and HP. Starting in 1984, Cannon used HP's marketing prowess to introduce its laser printer to European and U.S. markets. In the informal alliance, Cannon produced the insides of the printer, and HP provided the software and marketing. By contributing technologies to the Product Point, Cannon and HP consistently command 70% of the laser printer market.

In another strategic partnership, Simplex Solutions, Inc., is working with Toshiba Corporation to develop next-generation chip architecture. Their new X architecture, in which connections between chip layers are run at right angles to each other (hence the X) is supposed to increase chip density and reduce power requirements over the traditional Manhattan architecture, in which connections are laid in parallel tracks. A consortium of leading semiconductor companies was formed to reduce the risk that manufacturers that are heavily invested in the Manhattan architecture will reject the X architecture.

Risk is not limited to economic and technological considerations, but includes legal issues as well, especially those related to the protection of intellectual property. As the late-night commercials for invention services like to point out, it is not the person who invents something first, but the person who makes it to the patent office first who wins the prize. The invention of the telephone, light bulb, radio, and other everyday devices are attributed to patent holders, not to the first person to invent or even use the technology.

For example, a private practitioner in rural Georgia performed the first administration of inhaled ether for surgery in 1842. However, the creation of the field of anesthesia is attributed to a Boston physician who used inhaled anesthesia in a surgical procedure at Boston's Massachusetts General Hospital (MGH) nearly four years later. The Boston physician reaped the monetary benefits of the technology because he publicized the event and—more importantly—secured patent rights to the technology. In fact, the economic potential of inhaled anesthesia outweighed all other considerations. After the public demonstration in 1846, despite the fact that hundreds of patients could have benefited from the technology, inhaled anesthesia was not used for nearly a year at MGH until after the U.S. Patent Office had processed the patent application.

As another example, even though the inventor Reginald Fessenden was the first to transmit voice over radio, he failed to properly defend his intellectual property rights or create a viable business model (i.e., sustain a revenue stream or define a consumer base that had a "willingness to pay"). As a result, his place in history is overshadowed by Guglielmo Marconi and other radio pioneers who not only secured patents for communications technologies, but developed viable businesses as well.

Winning the Game

In the complex world, total control of the marketplace environment is impossible. Even Microsoft with its billions cannot predict its own destiny. However, any company can better its luck in the game of temporary survival by making the right decisions and timing its moves to coincide with external events. The gamble that every CEO makes is that her models of how the business world works provide her company with a better chance of survival than the models used by the competition. Every acquisition is an unstated declaration that the seller is underutilizing the resource for sale and the acquiring CEO can use it in a way that will generate profits in excess of the purchase price.

A company that has a technology that it considers to be between Maturity and early Decline in the Product Lifecycle may be happy to unload the technology on some other company before the trend becomes obvious. The acquiring company, in contrast, may have a much broader market reach, with hundreds of outlets beyond the relatively small seller's market. As a result, to the larger company, the acquisition should perform as a product in the early Growth phase of the Lifecycle. In addition, the risk is relatively low, since the seller's activities in the market can be considered a realistic test of product viability. When the acquiring company succeeds with its model, the selling company may rationalize that the performance is due to luck.

If *luck* is the result of being prepared to take advantage of opportunities as they arise, then the former street peddler, James L. Kraft, who developed a method of processing and canning cheese so that it could be stored indefinitely, could be considered lucky. Through proper positioning and seizing the opportunity when it appeared, Kraft was able to sell the U.S. military over six million pounds of canned cheese during World War I. Buoyed by the profits of these sales, he was able to patent his cheese-canning and sterilization process in 1916 and then mount an impressive marketing campaign aimed at the U.S. consumer. As a result, by 1930, over 40% of all cheese consumed in the United States bore the Kraft label.

When it comes to winning in the marketplace, an empowering perspective is that the future can be partially created through current decisions; hence the role of wisdom in leading a company.

Business wisdom encompasses the ability to recognize patterns—whether in people, the market, or technologies—and to act accordingly. For example, during the late 1980s and early 1990s, Apple computer virtually owned the kindergarten through 12th grade market, in part because it established the Apple II computer as the standard computer for education. Apple was able to define the early education market for over a decade because it made strategic investments in key educational institutions, established consortia for the sharing of computer courseware, and provided grants to thought leaders in academia. Apple's CEO decided to risk corporate capital to define the future of education by creating demand for its computers in the education market.

Apple was partially successful in the higher education market as well, promoting its Macintosh computer to universities and graduate schools. In the mid-1980s Apple established relationships with Ivy League schools, funded the formation of consortia for the sharing of Macintosh software, and made strategic donations of equipment to high-visibility schools. However, Apple's lack of focus in the late 1980s and the overwhelming popularity of the IBM PC pushed the Macintosh out of many institutions of higher learning.

Few companies have the luxury of having billions of dollars in cash on hand like Apple or Microsoft. If resources are limited, an aggressive CEO may decide to risk an investment in infrastructures so that his company can adapt to a range of future possibilities and capture opportunities as they arise. In this scenario, while the risk and investment are lower and more controllable than for the company that must invest capital in the basic R&D, significant rewards are also possible. For example, the hundreds of PC clone manufacturers in the United States and abroad rely on engineers at IBM, Compaq, Dell, and others to define the hardware characteristics of the standard desktop and laptop PCs.

As soon as the big computer companies define the hardware standards and the price points, the clone manufacturers reverse engineer the systems and offer their products at significantly reduced prices. The clone manufacturers are able to compete in the highly competitive PC market because they create manufacturing infrastructures capable of replicating the standards established by the leading computer manufacturers. A similar situation exists in the auto parts, off-road bicycle frame, and clothing industries.

When Ralph Lauren introduces a new jacket style, the off-name manufacturers create a similar product—sans logo—and offer it at a fraction of the price of the original product.

An option for a more risk-averse CEO of a company with limited resources (a minor player in a market) is to sit back and let another company take on most of the risk. Meanwhile, she can track opportunities and keep open the option of actively adapting to or taking a leadership position in the market. This pattern is seen in the advertising industry, where a market leader introduces a novel approach—a color central image with a black and white background, for example—and other firms immediately follow. Because the copycat ads appear virtually at the same time as the original, it is not clear to consumers who started the trend. As such, the innovator may not get credit for taking the risk on a new approach, and the risk-averse CEO may receive virtually the same benefit with almost no risk.

For example, the trend of translucent, brightly colored plastic computer cases was rekindled by the Apple iMac, and the move was immediately copied by dozens of other firms. Because of the low-risk, copycat behavior, not only were some IBM clones created in Macintosh-like cases, but furniture companies introduced entire lines of translucent plastic desks and chairs. Similarly, discount warehouses and office supply stores carried everything from pencil holders to air conditioners and microwave ovens in matching translucent colored plastic. The challenge for the decision makers of opportunistic companies with limited resources is tracking trends so that they can move into a space quickly before the market leader switches strategies or other opportunistic companies enter the market.

Finally, business perspectives, like religions, color our view of the world. For the decision maker, the value in considering new perspectives is like viewing a scene through different lenses: Previously unrecognized patterns often become apparent. In this context, decision making is synonymous with risk taking. That is, leaders risk corporate resources in pursuing a goal that they deem will provide a significant return on investment. As the most important decision maker in the company, the CEO must have the wisdom to recognize opportunities as they arise and the leadership abilities to direct corporate resources appropriately. CEOs like Bill

Gates, Steve Jobs, Larry Ellison, and Jack Welsh are not only valued
for their personalities, but for their decision-making and leadership
abilities. Although some great leaders have internalized models that
they use for predicting outcomes in the marketplace, most decision
makers use predictive models to minimize risk and maximize likelihood of success.

SUMMARY

The alchemical transformation of an idea to viable product in the
marketplace is in many respects a gamble with significant risks at
every phase of development. And, just as in nature, simply because
a product reaches the mature stage of development there is no
guarantee that the product will continue to thrive. However, even
though risk is an inherent and inescapable component of every
business venture, it is possible to win—generate strong growth
quickly, fending off competition, and create enough profit to support the R&D for the next generation of product—by understanding and recognizing the potential pitfalls at each stage of the
Product Lifecycle. In this regard, the Continuum model focuses the
attention of the decision maker on issues that are key to making
better decisions.

3

Customer Behavior

The better telescopes become, the more stars there will be.

Gustave Flaubert

Technology alone is not enough to guarantee the success of a product in the marketplace. Timing, the political and economic environment, the competition, and customer acceptance are also important. On the surface, assessing the customer acceptance factor seems straightforward. After all, despite the exponentially increasing rate of technologic evolution in the past few centuries, human behavior has not changed much since recorded history. Take status symbols, for example. We walk around with the modern equivalents of face paint and ceremonial weapons, and wear costumes imbued with supernatural powers. The police officer's uniform, attorney's custom suit, and physician's white coat and stethoscope are all instantly recognizable and, to varying degrees, respected.

When it comes to accepting new technologies, some groups of potential customers are more reluctant than others to change behavior even when new products require it. Resistance to change may simply be based on experience with products that fail to perform as promised, but it is usually a reaction to a combination of deep-seated personal beliefs and social issues.

As an illustration of the complex interaction between customers and new technologies, consider the technologic and social evolution of the stethoscope, the device physicians use to listen to a patient's heart and lungs. To many laypeople, the stethoscope is synonymous with medicine. For this reason, medical students, EMS professionals, and clinicians of all types often drape one over their necks just to visit the local Starbucks. However, the stethoscope, which virtually transformed Western medicine, is a relatively new invention, dating back to only 1816.

From antiquity to the beginning of the 19th century, clinicians listened to the chest (*stethos* in Greek) in the most direct way possible—by placing an ear directly against a patient's chest. However, there are a number of disadvantages to this approach. For one, it is difficult to place an ear directly over a specific area of the chest— over a heart valve, for example—without the clinician resorting to a number of contortions. There is also the unpleasant prospect of having to come into close contact with a bleeding, coughing patient (many physicians who treated tuberculosis or consumption in 17th- and 18th-century Europe succumbed to the disease). What's more, in prudish 18th-century Europe, when medicine was an all-male, deteriorating profession, and toxic mercury and bloodletting were in vogue for the treatment of nearly every malady, putting an ear to the breast of a young female patient to listen to her heart was simply taboo.

Although the nature and practice of Western medicine has fluctuated throughout the millennia, from the Hippocratic technique of tasting a patient's urine for the sweetness characteristic of diabetes mellitus to the open and public dissection of executed criminals in Leonardo da Vinci's time, medical practitioners in 18th-century Europe were ignorant of functional anatomy. Lacking any substantive knowledge of functional anatomy, they based medical diagnoses on externally visible signs and patient symptoms. A fever, a rash, or swelling, together with the patient's complaints regarding the frequency, duration, and intensity of pain or discomfort were the basis of most diagnoses. There were no lab tests, no concept of testing for hearing or vision, and no system for understanding the diseases of internal organs, such as the heart and lungs.

Time for Change

However, the world of Western medicine began to change in 1816, when the French physician René-Théophile-Hyacinthe Laennec needed to listen to the chest of a young woman to verify his presumptive diagnosis of heart disease, but could not do so because social restrictions prevented him from placing his ear against her naked breast. Determined to listen to her heart and lung sounds, in a flash of insight he rolled up a few sheets of paper into a tight tube, forming the first chest listening device. He put one end in his ear and the other on the woman's chest and was delighted to be able to hear the heart sounds—much louder and more distinctly than before.

After his discovery, he rushed to the lathe in his workshop and crafted the first real stethoscope, in the form of a hollow wooden tube. He spent the next two years investigating and documenting its use in the diagnosis of various lung and heart conditions. His book on the subject, published in 1819, served to inform other physicians not only how to construct their own stethoscopes, but how to use them in practice as well.

Laennec's invention began a revolution in the very nature of medical practice, shifting it to the objective measurement of phenomenon and placing much less emphasis on the patient's memory of heart symptoms, which tended to be poor. Because of this fundamental change, other physicians did not immediately embrace the stethoscope. However, within about a decade, the new, objective style of medicine had taken root, and a number of other physicians had developed their own improvements on Laennec's hollow wooden tube design. Although the dual-earpiece design was introduced in the 1830s, it did not become popular until the 1850s. The first instrument recognizable as a modern stethoscope—a pair of flexible rubber tubes connecting a set of earpieces to a metal chest piece—was developed in 1855. However, even though the design proved superior in usability and acoustics to other designs, it was not until 1866, when it was endorsed by Austin Flint, an outspoken physician of the time, that it became accepted and soon thereafter came into widespread use.

Today's Market

Today, most chest pieces (the metal, disk-shaped part that is placed on the patient's chest) have two sides, one open to the air and one covered with a thin plastic membrane. The open-ended side, called the bell, accentuates low-frequency sounds, like those of the normal heart. The side covered with a membrane filters out the low-frequencies, allowing high-frequency sounds, like the crackles generated by diseased lungs and the murmurs of abnormal hearts, to be more distinct. Since the introduction of the membrane chest piece around 1910, the stethoscope carried by the vast majority of clinicians has changed very little.

The major players in the stethoscope space are manufacturers such as 3M, Littmann, Tycos, and Welch Allyn. Models range from $20 to $350 to suit the budget—and image—of the user. Although there are some areas of medicine where a special stethoscope design is warranted, such as pediatrics, which requires a smaller diameter chest piece to localize sounds from the heart of a small child, a skilled cardiologist can make a diagnosis with the simplest, cheapest stethoscope. Masters at the stethoscope can use any of the dozens of standardized models available with equal facility, in part because they have a highly developed ability to recognize certain sounds, and because they can use the stethoscope like a sensitive radio receiver—tuning in to certain sounds and blocking out others. A good cardiologist can use the simplest bell chest piece to listen to high frequency sounds of heart murmurs by pulling the patient's skin taut to form a membrane over the chest piece, filtering out the lower frequency sounds just as a plastic membrane would.

Many physicians never actually listen to heart or chest sounds once they leave residency. The use of a stethoscope is either unnecessary, as in radiology or pathology, or delegated to a physician's assistant or nurse who performs the routine blood pressure, pulse, and respiration measurements. However, when a physician first trains her ear to discern particular heart and lung sounds, the experience is inexplicably linked to her stethoscope. The tension in the metal spring pressing the earpieces against the ear canal, the acoustic characteristics of the rubber tube and membrane, and shape of the bell all have an effect on the quality sound. In this regard, listening to the sound produced by the stethoscope is like listening to a musical instrument. Switching to another model—one with a different type of membrane, for example—changes the sound and takes getting used to. For this reason, physicians and other clinicians tend to stay with the brand they first buy or, as is commonly the case, receive as gifts from companies while in training. In addition, since models change very slowly and very little if at all, a lost or stolen stethoscope can usually be replaced within minutes with an identical model sold at any medical supply house.

Lessons Learned

With the invention of the electronic amplifier in 1905, it was inevitable that the technology would be applied to the stethoscope. But acceptance of electronic stethoscopes for clinical use has been very slow. One of the early hurdles was that the first electronic stethoscopes did not resemble traditional stethoscopes, but looked more like a Walkman® radio with headphones. Companies that focused solely on their superior technology were asking physicians to give up their status symbol, even if it did make subtle sounds more discernable. In addition, with the possible exception of specialists interested in specific disease states, an electronic stethoscope has a negative connotation among physicians. After all, a good cardiologist is a master at listening to the heart through a standard stethoscope and doesn't need an electronic crutch.

Manufacturers of the newest models of electronic stethoscopes address the status issue—at least from the layperson's perspective—by encasing their digital signal processing chips and amplifiers in a shell that looks, for the most part, like an ordinary stethoscope. These look-alikes have a disk-shaped chest piece and earpieces connected by what looks like an elastic tube. This new generation of electronic stethoscopes provides a number of features, such as automatic display of heart rate, a variety of filter modes to simulate the bell or membrane of a traditional stethoscope, the ability to store sounds for playback later, and the ability to play sounds back at half-speed to aid in diagnosis. Some even have infrared links for downloading the sound files directly to a PC for teaching and remote diagnosis, or telemedicine.

In spite of the significant technological advances, companies that produce electronic stethoscopes are having a difficult time selling their products. For most students, the issue is price; prices start at around $200, or about five times what a traditional student stethoscope sells for. Another issue is simply tradition and the teaching of stethoscope use. Learning when and how to use the bell versus the membrane, and how hard to press the chest piece against the chest to get a good seal, is still an integral part of medical education. From the perspective of a doctor's public image, the new units can be easily swung over the neck and, to the layperson, look like an ordinary stethoscope. To other clinicians, however, the electronic crutch is clearly visible—and using it to learn medicine is like training to drive a racecar with automatic instead of manual transmission.

Even as electronic stethoscope manufacturers are discovering that changing physician behavior is going to take more than simply improving the electronics, they are realizing that what they think is a better diagnostic tool may not jibe with what physicians actually need. From a technological perspective, the sound that one of these units creates is very different and changes from model to model. "Improved" electronics may sound good in an ad campaign, but to clinicians it means that they'll have to retrain their ears to the subtleties of yet another instrument when it is time to replace a broken or stolen unit. There is currently no standard those electronic stethoscopes ascribe to, such as the standard organ or piano that modern synthesizers use. Beyond the resistance electronic stethoscope manufacturers encounter now in trying to change clinician behavior, the future for their product looks even grimmer.

Medicine is undergoing yet another transformation, like the one started by Laennec's invention. However, instead of evolving from an art based on interpreting patient symptoms into a science concerned with evaluating objective data, today's evolution is about removing the clinician from the low-level data gathering process while constraining costs. DNA sequencing, whole body imaging, and other technologies generate data that cannot be directly perceived in a patient examination, and yet provide additional clinical relevance. Physicians are becoming managers and directors of data gathering—knowledge workers if you will—in an economic environment where good bedside manner and taking time to connect with a patient is not rewarded by the cost-conscious system. It is more likely that clinicians of the near future will be associated, through necessity, more with a medical PDA than with a stethoscope. Like the physicians on Star Trek, modern physicians will use intelligent devices and handheld sensors to gather data they can interpret. Of course, this also presents the physician community with the adoption challenges similar to those originally ascribed to the stethoscope.

The history of the stethoscope exemplifies the need for decision makers to know their customers, and then figure out how such knowledge can maximize the likelihood of success in bringing a product to market. Additionally, this example demonstrates how the initial adoption rate by users of a new technology is constrained by prior experiences and personal beliefs.

THE NEXT NEW THING

Virtual reality, pervasive computing, hybrid gas-electric cars, smart clothes that change to suit the wearer and the environment, and nanobots that perform surgery while patients sit comfortably watching their progress on a computer monitor are all inevitable. However, convincing surgeons to trade their scalpels in for unfamiliar nanobots and motivating style-conscious consumers to give up their sports cars for energy-efficient hybrid sedans is a battle that will take time and energy. Despite the envelopes of technology and high-tech banter, the vast majority of consumers are creatures of habit.

It is certain that society is plunging headlong into a future where information is no longer personal, but is stored and accessed on the net through portable and mobile wireless devices. However, achieving that future in a timely, affordable manner involves a complex technical, political, and social evolution. A prerequisite, but by no means a guarantee, for this evolution is that new technology must provide an incentive for consumers to change their behavior—it must offer a value that is not available any other way.

The inevitable breed of personal appliances with embedded intelligence, from smart refrigerators that track the age of perishables and order replacements online, to medically diagnostic toilets, must, at a minimum, save customers increasingly precious time. A smart microwave oven that recognizes that a frozen dinner taken immediately from the freezer needs to be defrosted with short, intermittent bursts of microwave energy before it can be cooked at full power would seem to have an immediate niche market. For example, a busy professional just home from work may not want to contend with the minutiae of defrosting and then fully cooking dinner. However, for the professional who looks forward to time in the kitchen as a creative outlet and a place to escape from the control of technology, a smart microwave oven has no value.

For a technology to be accepted by potential customers, not only must the customer perceive it as useful, but it has to attract a critical mass of other users as well. A critical mass of loyal users beyond the initial early adopters helps to ensure that a product will not be abandoned and provides the producer with an economy of scale that allows the producer to offer the product at a reasonable price. For example, the fax machine is a valuable business tool by virtue of the number of businesses and customers who use the fax for instant communications. It is only because so many businesses and customers can send and receive faxes that the fax machine, based on a less efficient, pre-email, paper-and-ink technology, is practically indispensable in business. In contrast, the NEXT computer, Apple's G4 Cube, and Chrysler's 1935 Airflow De Soto—all technological and design marvels ahead of their time—appealed to a small number of individuals, but failed to catch on with their target customers. The Airflow De Soto, for example, sported an aerodynamic design at a time when every other model offered square, boxy cars, and had a new suspension design that provided a smoother ride than the competition. Even though the technology was innovative and solid, the look was too different from what people considered normal for a car, and the De Soto was retired.

For a product to be successful, it must be accepted by individuals as well as a population of users of sufficient size to support production, maintenance, and ongoing research and development. These two views of customer behavior—one at the individual or micro level and one at the macro or population level—are discussed in the next section.

INDIVIDUAL BEHAVIOR

A customer's perception of the benefits and risks associated with adopting a new product or service affects the bottom line of every business enterprise. After all, if a customer has a need for a product, then every component and contribution of the value chain of which it is the result—from the stability of the underlying technology to the efficiency of the manufacturing process—is irrelevant.

Predicting individual customer behavior when faced with a new product offering is no trivial task, given the dozens of variables involved. That is, a customer may shun a product because of religious beliefs, political opposition to such technologies as bioengineered foods or nuclear energy, poor product performance and quality, and lack of awareness because of ineffective marketing. A customer may see no clear benefit in using a product; that is, it may seem too expensive, too difficult to use, take too much time and effort to learn, and may not provide an obvious advantage over traditional approaches. A customer may simply be resistant to change and fear the unknown.

However, in today's business environment the executive manager has a variety of tools to help gauge the consumer's purchasing habits. With knowledge of personal styles, it is possible to predict, with a fair degree of accuracy, how a customer is likely to respond, for example, to an offer for a new computer or piece of office equipment. However, getting at that information is still very difficult, even with the large electronic databases that companies compile on U.S. citizens. An alternative approach is to model individual behavior based on accepted psychological models of generic human behavior.

Stages of Change

One way for a decision maker to gain some degree of control over the demand and subsequent purchase of a particular product is to model individual customer behavior change. A popular model of behavior change that is used successfully in everything from dieting to smoking cessation is the Stages of Change Model developed by two clinical psychologists, James Prochaska and Carlo DiClemente, in 1979. It assumes that every customer goes through five discrete, predictable stages when making a major behavior change, such as a purchase and then adoption of a new product. The stages, labeled 1 through 5 in Figure 3.1, are:

1. Precontemplation
2. Contemplation
3. Preparation
4. Action
5. Maintenance

A sixth stage that is often considered part of the model, Termination (of the original behavior), is not included here to simplify the discussion.

Precontemplation. In the precontemplation phase (1 in Figure 3.1), a customer typically has no knowledge of the alternative technologies available, and no plans for changing his or her behavior. At this stage, a customer may selectively filter information that justifies his or her decision to stick with current behavior.

Figure 3.1   Behavior Change Model

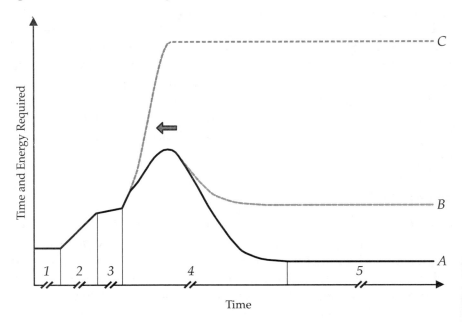

The goal of many marketing campaigns is to move customers out of their comfort zone of precontemplation and create an awareness and desire for new products and services. Because the time and energy for consumers associated with maintaining the precontemplation phase tends to be sporadic and low, it may last for days, years, or, in some cases, a lifetime. Only when the customer becomes aware of a product that promises a time or energy savings is a customer motivated to leave the steady-state condition of precontemplation.

Contemplation.   During the contemplation phase, a customer assesses the investment in time, energy, and money associated with purchasing a product. As depicted by 2 of Figure 3.1, the contemplation phase of behavior change includes a modest, increasing investment of time and energy. The ramp-up in energy expenditure may be instantaneous, as in an impulse buy, or occur slowly over weeks and months, depending on the nature of the behavior change. This stage is often characterized by ambivalence about changing, and a customer may waver between staying in her comfort zone and venturing out into the unknown because of the risks she associates with changing behavior. A customer can contemplate a purchase indefinitely. These first two states of change, with their risk of slowness, can determine the *rate* of behavior change or the pace of product adoption.

Preparation. During the third phase of the Stages of Change model, preparation (3 in Figure 3.1), a customer makes the decision to change and takes steps to prepare for the change. Preparation typically requires only a modest expenditure of time and energy over that already invested.

Action. In the action phase of behavior change (4 in Figure 3.1), a customer is actually making a change. That is, a customer is expending energy and time, throwing aside previous behaviors in favor of the new product. It is during the action phase of behavior change that impediments to change become most apparent and decrease the odds that the behavior change will be long lasting. Impediments to change include:

- Social pressures to maintain the old behaviors
- Uncertainty in the payback of the energy and time invested in the new behavior
- Difficulty in practicing the new behavior
- Extended training requirements
- Significant and unexpected monetary requirements
- Frequency with which the former behavior was practiced
- Disbelief in the efficacy and worth of the new behavior

The challenges of succeeding during the action phase are represented by the left arrow in Figure 3.1. If the challenges associated with taking action are too great, as depicted by the enormous time and energy requirements in curve C, then a customer is likely to travel backward through the behavior change model, that is, revert to old habits.

Similarly, the likelihood of recidivism is greater if the time and energy required to maintain the new steady-state or baseline behavior is not significantly lower than that associated with the initial behavior, as in curves B and C. In this respect, the probability of recidivism is a function of the relative time and energy required to maintain phase 1, or precontemplation, versus the end of phase 4, or action. This relationship, the Recidivism Gradient, is illustrated in Figure 3.2.

Maintenance.   The final phase of behavior change, maintenance, represents sustained behavior change, where the energy and time associated with the behavior is constant. Ideally, energy and time expenditures are along the lines of curve A in Figure 3.1; but the less than ideal expenditures described by curves B and C are also possible. The maintenance phase of one behavior change sequence becomes the precontemplation phase of the next. That is, even if a customer is happy with his purchase, a model that is newer, more efficient, and easier to use may eventually appear on the market. However, the company that is first to market with a new technology product has the opportunity to establish brand recognition, consumer loyalty, and market share, thus creating a market dominance that may be difficult for a competitor to overcome with only a marginal improvement in features.

Figure 3.2   Behavior Change and Recidivism

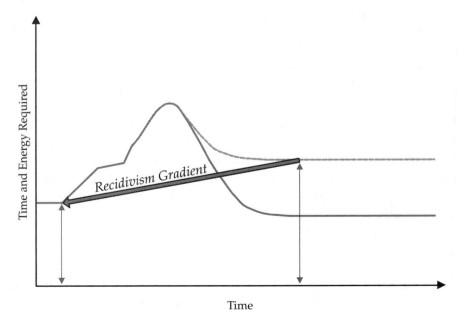

Case Study: PDAs

To illustrate the Behavior Change Model as applied to product adoption, consider the case of Sam, a busy business professional. Up to this point in his career, Sam has ignored the modern status symbol for the technical elite, the PDA. He is happy with the paper-based organizer that he has used since graduating with his MBA a decade ago, and ignores the PDA displays in the office supply stores (precontemplation). However, about a year ago, Sam noticed that the latest model of his organizer binder now provides a free light-weight holster for a PDA. That night, he also noticed an advertisement in the newspaper for a sale on PDAs.

The next morning, Sam spent a half hour talking with cowork-ers about their PDAs, the various options, which brands are the most popular, and other details (contemplation). During his lunch break, Sam read through several PDA reviews posted on the Web, and com-pared prices at the various mail-order centers (preparation).

On the one hand, Sam was ready to make the move to the timesaving technology that his coworkers enjoyed, but on the other, he feared the loss of his personal and business data. In the end, however, the PDA won out because of the prospect of time savings, ease of tracking prospects, the smaller size of a PDA, or simply look-ing cool. That evening, after discussing the purchase with his wife, Sam called one of the mail-order computer companies and ordered a PDA (action).

Although it took more time than he anticipated, Sam began the process of entering his calendar and contact information (his behavior is represented by the upward sloping curve of the action phase in curve A). After a week carrying the PDA and learning to use the stylus, entering and retrieving personal contact information was easier (curve A). Sam no longer took the time to write down everyone's contact information, but simply accepted their contact information beamed through the infrared (IR) link between their PDAs (maintenance). Furthermore, Sam was able to rest assured that the data on his PDA was backed up on at least one PC—a feat that he could not accomplish with the paper organizer that he was constantly in fear of losing.

After about three months, Sam's PDA was fully integrated into his life to the point that it disappeared from his conscious thoughts. His focus turned to other issues at work and home (precontemplation).

About a month ago, a little less than a year since he first purchased his PDA, Sam noticed an advertisement for a wireless version that provided access to email and the Web. He wondered if the wireless unit, which was somewhat bulkier and heavier than his current PDA, would save time (contemplation). Sam went to the Web and looked over reviews, explored monthly service charge options and the extent of service coverage in his area (preparation). He ordered a wireless PDA from the same mail order firm that sold him his original PDA and had it delivered overnight (action). Transferring his contact and calendar information to the new unit was straightforward, and after spending a few hours with the manuals, Sam began using the PDA the next week at work.

Unfortunately, Sam found the email function less than optimal, because he had to continually log in to the device to check for messages. In addition, he found that coverage inside his office building was spotty, and sometimes he could not send emails without going to a window down the hall. Together with the added bulk and weight, the inconvenience of the new PDA simply was not worth the aggravation (curve C of Figure 3.1). He returned the wireless PDA and went back to his old PDA and decided to revisit the wireless PDA in a year, when the next generation of wireless devices should be available (back to contemplation).

POPULATION BEHAVIOR

An understanding of changes in patterns of customer behavior at the population level is critical for the success of any technology-based product in the marketplace. That is, although the market is derived from the actions of individual customers, the ability to predict the behavior of large groups of potential customers is critical in planning and establishing price, product performance standards, and customer expectations.

The technology adoption curve is a common means of modeling customer behavior at the population level as a function of time and the number of customers involved (See Figure 3.3). According to the model, as soon as a product is introduced, a small number of technology-focused *innovators* go to great lengths to acquire it. Often the innovators are price insensitive, and are willing to pay unreasonable sums to be the first in their peer group with the smallest, thinnest, or most powerful gadget. Later, the educated, but less

Figure 3.3   Technology Adoption Curve

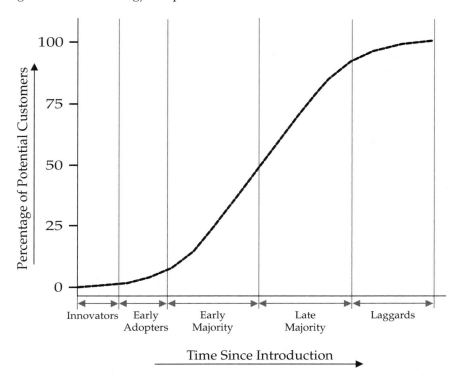

technologically aware *early adopters* follow the innovators' lead and invest in the technology. The major influx of customers constitutes the *early majority*, followed by the *late majority*. Finally, the *laggards*, who tend to be less educated and less economically able, buy into the product.

The Stethoscope

The technology adoption curve describes the history of the stethoscope as well as more recent innovations, such as the PDA. Returning to the history of the stethoscope, after Laennec's original innovation, it took about a decade for the innovators and early adopters to embrace the technology. However, because a fundamental structural change in the nature of medical practice was required for wider adoption of the technology, it was not until a thought leader formally accepted what would now be considered the stethoscope that the early majority of physicians committed themselves to learning the technology and teaching it to their students. Today, every medical school graduate in the United States—even the late majority and the laggards—must demonstrate some proficiency with the stethoscope. However, if the potential population of customers for the stethoscope is extended to physicians and other medical practitioners around the world, then the late majority is still adopting the stethoscope. Many practitioners of Eastern medicine, for example, have yet to accept the stethoscope as a valid instrument in the practice of their healing art.

The PDA

As a more recent example, consider the history of the PDA, typified by the PalmPilot, Visor, Blackberry RIM, or any number of the so-called CE (Microsoft Compact Edition operating system)-compatible units. Throughout the 1980s several manufacturers, including Casio and Sharp, introduced pocketable electronic devices for saving names, addresses, phone numbers, and notes. However, the Apple Newton MessagePad 100, introduced at the MacWorld Expo in 1993, was the first pocket computer that resembled modern PDAs. When the Newton was first released at a MacWorld Expo in Boston, a line of customers stretched the length of the conference center—simply to get the chance to buy an untested Newton at full retail price. The fact that the original Newton was large, clunky, and, by today's standards, slow, did not matter. To these innovators, possession was enough.

Two years later, in 1995, Apple introduced the MessagePad 200, which improved the technology of the 100 with a new version of the operating system. Many innovators again jumped at the chance to own the new Newton model, but additional sales beyond those to early adopters were minimal. In the next few years, despite upgrades and new models with additional features, the Newton still failed to attract the attention of users other than the initial early adopters. There was no champion for the technology and the unit was still too bulky compared to the nearest alternative, a paper calendar system. By 1998, the Newton was officially discontinued.

Despite the Newton's failure, PDAs proliferated. In 1995, the time of MessagePad 100's release, U.S. Robotics, known for their communications modems, introduced The Palm 1000. The Palm 1000 and successors, the PalmPilot series, soon became the overall favorite because of its simplicity, size, and ease of use. By the time the Newton was discontinued in 1998, early adopters were enjoying their PalmPilots. Because the price was right and the technology was readily accessible, Palm, later joined by numerous Windows CE-compatibles and RIM's wireless Blackberry PDA, rapidly gained acceptance in the business world. Today, customers in the late majority are buying into the concept of the PDA for use in grade schools, university classrooms, and the boardroom.

Other Technologies

Few products or categories of products follow the symmetry of the generic curve in Figure 3.1. Most go through periods of different adoption rates, as customer behavior is influenced by depressions, recessions, war, and other external factors. Figure 3.4 illustrates the technology adoption curves for the TV, cell phone, PC, and Internet. Even though the rate of adoption of the PDA over a decade may seem slow, many technologies, even those considered essential for everyday business, can take decades to reach the early and late majority.

The telephone, for example, which was patented in 1876, was initially viewed by most people as a technologic oddity with no apparent practical use. Most of the general public considered it to be an eyesore. This is not surprising, given that the first phone systems consisted of two phones and a private cable—the electronic equivalent of two cans and a string—run from one business to another or from a home to a business office. The result was streets choked with private cables strung directly between pairs of phones, because a comprehensive telephone network had not yet been invented.

Customer service and product choice began to improve for the average consumer when Bell's telephone patents ran out in 1894. From that time onward, new, competing phone services were constructed, and these systems included the working middle class. Even so, the adoption rate hovered around a third of all households until after World War II. With the prosperity of postwar America, adoption rapidly increased to the laggards (nearly 90%) by the 1970s.

Television has had one of the fastest adoption rates. Regular TV broadcasts began just before World War II, mainly showing boxing matches in bars and other commercial establishments. Black-and-white TV was introduced to the working class around 1947, and color TVs, about eight years later. In only four decades, TV had

Figure 3.4 Specific Technology Adoption Curves

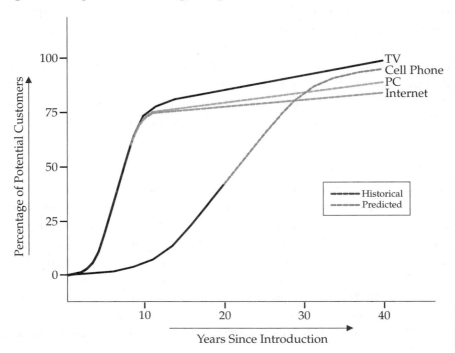

penetrated 98% of households. Most consumers consider TV, like the telephone, a necessity.

As shown in Figure 3.4, the fast growth in adoption of the TV occurred during the first few years after introduction. In the eight years from 1947 to 1955, over 60% of households—the early and late majority—purchased a TV. TV's pattern of adoption is probably a good predictor of how successful the home PC and home Internet connectivity will be, because they are following the same adoption rates relative to their introduction times.

Although population adoption rates reflect group behavior, some of these behaviors are constrained and directed by economics, legislation, and business practices. For example, while the adoption of cell phones is about 40% and growing rapidly, legislation against driving and cell phone use, and health concerns over potential links between cell phone radiation and cancer, may slow the adoption rate.

Similarly, the growth in Internet adoption rates may be limited because of payment options. AOL, the largest Internet service provider (ISP) in the United States, requires users to pay with a credit card, which effectively excludes almost one-third of the population, who do not have credit cards. Although there is a longstanding debate over whether the government should sponsor content development and provide public schools with free Internet access, the current reality is that expansion of the Internet is still very much restricted to the privileged within the United States.

MONEY MATTERS

Of all of the parameters that affect customer behavior, price and value are primary considerations. For example, despite increased use of cell phones worldwide since their introduction a little over two decades ago, rates of adoption of wireless services dropped as part of the worldwide economic technology slowdown in 2001. Even Nokia, the world's largest cellular phone maker, reported its first drop in earnings in five years in 2001. In the tight economy, potential customers simply were not willing to pay the asking price for the new added features. That is, in order for potential customers to change their behavior and become actual customers, price increases must be in line with the incremental value of added features and services.

Hedonic Pricing

When it comes to evaluating the value of added features to potential customers, whether the feature is a larger screen size on a cell phone or racing stripes on a sports car, several methods are available. The traditional method is to have an expert, third-party appraisal of a product with and without the added features. Although this method may be useful for establishing the value of established, large-ticket items such as cars, it is not practical in the real-time, high-technology marketplace, where there may be no recognized experts in a new technology, much less add-ons.

The value of added features and services in modifying customer behavior is often determined with hedonic pricing techniques, in which the characteristics of a product are unbundled and priced separately. Hedonic pricing, which has been used by the U.S. Bureau of Economic Analysis for the analysis of computers and peripherals since 1985, establishes the worth of each characteristic of a high-technology product from RAM to hard disk space. Wireless capabilities add value to a PDA, for example, but the increased price must be in line with the potential customer's perception of the added value in order for the PDA to sell.

Hedonic pricing is especially useful in establishing the value of aesthetic or more ephemeral product features. For example, ease of use has a value that is separate from the underlying technology, a fact that Apple used to its advantage in marketing campaigns in the pre-Windows era. Similarly, compatibility has value that is dependent on, but separate from, the value of the operating system software and computer hardware.

Value and the Continuum

To understand whether the addition of features or value to a product will appeal to customers, it helps to consider the spectrum of customer expectations. As in hedonic pricing, expectations are the result of qualitative and quantitative assessments of features and services, which cannot be completely established by simply measuring the clock speed of a computer or the zero-to-60 acceleration time of a sports car. The minimum functionality that customers are willing to accept from a product at a given price varies. For example, Sam had a minimum set of expectations surrounding his new wireless PDA that were not met, so he returned the unit. Less demanding users might be satisfied by the PDA, especially if they are not concerned with operating within buildings but are content to have any wireless connectivity to the Web, even if it means walking to a window.

Figure 3.5 graphs customer expectations of functionality versus the time since the Product Point in the Continuum, assuming price holds constant. Note that customers expect the functionality of a product line to increase over time, especially with a technology-based product, and potential customer expectations are linked to the technological maturation of a product in the Continuum. This linkage is the result of advertisements, articles, increased competition within the marketplace, and other forms of press coverage. Most potential computer buyers expect, for example, that the clock speed of microcomputers will increase every year, and that processing power will double every year or so, as predicted by the well-publicized Moore's Law.

Figure 3.5   Customer Expectations

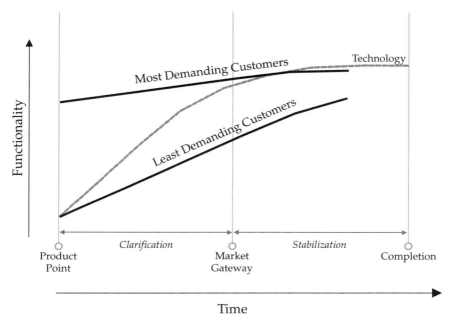

As shown in Figure 3.5, there is a range of customer expectations for functionality. At the Product Point in the Continuum, the least demanding customers are willing to pay the asking price for the functionality provided by product. However, the most demanding customers are not willing to invest in a product that has not proven itself or has a few loose ends that need to be fixed before it is acceptable. For example, Sam will not be satisfied with wireless technology until he can use the PDA anywhere in his home or office. Sam may have to wait until the technology underlying wireless PDAs is nearly at the Product Point in the Continuum. An obvious alternative for Sam is to find a competing wireless PDA product and evaluate the value it provides in terms of functionality and price.

Note also in Figure 3.5 that the spread in expectations narrows as the technology matures along the Continuum. This phenomenon is obvious today in the desktop PC, where all potential customers expect a PC to come equipped with a CD-ROM drive and floppy disk drive, at least 128 MB of RAM, a sizeable hard drive, and a 1 GHz or better processor, regardless of their intended application. The desktop PC is a commodity, and there is increasingly less difference between configurations from one model to the next.

Given the customer behavior illustrated in Figure 3.5, the challenge for the marketing division of a company developing a product from the Product Point to the Market Gateway is to communicate the functionality of the product to those potential customers that fall below the technology curve of the Continuum. For example, it is a waste of corporate resources to market wireless PDAs to customers like Sam, represented by the most demanding customer curve in Figure 3.5. Marketing dollars would be better spent on communicating to less demanding customers (early adopters), and then including the more demanding ones (early and late majority) later in the Continuum.

RULES OF THE GAME

In business, the political, social, and financial climates often dictate customer and corporate behavior that would otherwise seem out of line with the value proposition. For example, stem cell research based on embryonic cells was at least temporarily banned in the United States. Because of the ongoing controversy over whether embryonic stem cell research will be allowed or even actively supported by the U.S. government, many international biotech firms invested their efforts in countries with more politically favorable climates. For example, the United Kingdom's biotech industry, second only to that of the United States, has the full support of the British government. Why should a multinational company fight a national government when it can easily invest its resources overseas?

Similarly, the after-effects of the last energy crisis in the 1970s are still affecting innovation in energy production in the United States. When Congress passed the coal credit in 1980 to encourage businesses to turn domestic coal into a substitute for foreign crude, the effect was to focus innovation on complying with the tax credit stipulations. Paradoxically, the synfuel laws have rewarded companies that use oil as a major ingredient in the coal processing operation, in order to be eligible for the tax breaks. As a result, the public pays about $850 million per year to subsidize energy companies. The supposed intent of the legislation, to foster innovation to create more energy-efficient alternatives to crude oil, has been abandoned. Why should a company invest millions of dollars in R&D for a coal processing plant when spraying coal with waste oil can generate a tax credit of $26 per ton?

As most marketing professionals know, linking emotional issues to otherwise undifferentiated me-too products can often make the difference between product failure and market leader. One of the most obvious examples of this phenomenon is the segment of the U.S. consumer population that responds favorably to "green" products, which are ostensibly friendly to the environment. Energy Star, sponsored by the U.S. Environmental Protection Agency (EPA) and Department of Energy is the modern equivalent of the *Good Housekeeping* seal of approval for energy efficiency. Energy Star labels everything from computer monitors that go into power-saving mode after periods of nonuse to entire buildings. An ad campaign aimed at CEOs that appeared in *Forbes Magazine* through the summer of 2001 emphasized the public relations value of the label because it "tells the world that you are committed to superior energy performance."

Regardless of whether the products are mutual funds that invest in companies that recycle their waste paper or sweaters made from recycled plastic bottles, the green label appeals to many potential customers. Some customers are willing to pay a premium or go out of their way to buy green. That is, the green designation has hedonic value to many customers, above the value of incorporating postconsumer waste in ordinary products such as tissue paper. This value may be derived from peer pressure or the belief that they are doing good. In order for the green value to have a lasting behavior change, the effort required to go green should be minimized, and the value should be comparable to nongreen products. For example, with customers purchasing a new computer monitor, selecting a model that complies with Energy Star should be a simple matter of identifying the appropriate sticker. In all other aspects, the monitor should be equivalent in quality and performance to noncompliant monitors.

Another area where customer behavior is under heavy influence from governmental regulation is that of electronic publishing. Consumers have not yet fully embraced the concept of eBooks, even with the likes of Stephen King contributing to the medium. Part of the issue is economic: consumers are used to free electronic content on the Web, whereas they pay for print materials. There is also the general public's perception that works published through traditional channels have a higher quality than electronic documents. Anyone can post content to the Web and claim to be an expert in any area.

Part of the conundrum facing electronic publishing is the status of eBooks, or books distributed in electronic form and intended to be read on a Web browser, PDA, or dedicated eBook reader. Adding to the confusion are publishers' claims regarding their right to maintain copyright control over books that have been digitized for distribution over the Internet. The court challenge of companies offering electronic versions of books that were originally copyrighted as "books" received center stage attention in July 2001. Within a period of about three weeks, not only did the courts issue a ruling preventing traditional publishers from blocking the electronic distribution of newly digitized works that were not specifically under contract for electronic distribution, but the first full-length eBooks were submitted for electronic copyright registration to the U.S. Copyright Office, and the Library of Congress established a digital book collection. At the same time, the FBI arrested a programmer for selling a program that defeated the anti-copying-protection mechanism built into Adobe's eBook Reader software (one of the most popular eBook reader programs on the market). The illegal software gave customers who had purchased an eBook from the Web the ability to access their eBook on multiple machines—desktop PC, laptop, or handheld PDA. Without the software, customers have to purchase a separate copy of an eBook for each location—a major impediment to the widespread adoption of eBooks.

WATCHED OR SEEN

In all of the preceding discussions, the basis for how customers have and will likely respond to products and services depends on having access to customer data through primary or secondary market research. Customer information has to be immediate and timely to have any predictive value in the marketplace. As such, in today's digital economy companies are investing money into customer relationship management (CRM) programs, data mining, customer profiling, and other automated means of combing through hundreds of thousands of profiles and identifying likely return or new customers.

At issue, from the customer's perspective, is individual privacy—whether they are being watched or seen is of paramount importance. Virtually all customers are averse to the former, and will go out of their way to avoid creating records of their activities for the government or big business to ponder and analyze. If the latter, then most customers are at least willing to provide merchants with access to account balances and similar financial data so that they can make purchases on credit, apply for a home mortgage, and conduct other business transactions without having to produce a box full of documents.

Not surprisingly, one of the impediments to eCommerce is the ease with which customer information can be acquired, collected, traded, and sold. During the collapse of many dotComs, the first asset to go on the table was customer data, in the form of purchase history and demographic information. As a result, it is possible that "trusted" information once part of the customer–client relationship is now in the hands of the government and any number of click-and-mortar companies. The overall effect has been to reduce the trust level of customers who would otherwise engage in eCommerce.

SUMMARY

Regardless of how well an idea is transformed into a product, in the end, customer behavior dictates success or failure of the product in the marketplace. As such, an understanding of how individual customers come to a buy decision, as well as how populations of customers behave, is critical to the economic success of a product. With an appreciation for and understanding of the factors that influence customer behavior—from individual personality styles to government regulations—decision makers can analyze which market opportunities are best suited for their companies' business directions and quickly take advantage of them.

PART TWO

VALUE

4

Alchemy of Entrepreneurship

> Life is pretty simple: You do some stuff. Most fails. Some works.
> You do more of what works. If it works big, others quickly copy it.
> Then you do something else.
> The trick is the doing something else.
>
> *Tom Peters, business speaker*

In the New Economy, as in the old, success is measured the old fashioned way—by wealth. As the dotCom crash illustrated, innovation without income is maladaptive and incompatible with survival in the marketplace. Even the poster children in the New Economy, such as Amazon.com, have been forced to demonstrate to Wall Street that they are capable not only of generating revenue but of long-term profitability. But what is the connection between economic success and a better mousetrap, and where are the customers that are supposed to be beating a path to the company's door? Unfortunately, unlike building the baseball field in *Field of Dreams*, which had generations of baseball fans willing to pay to see an established product, simply creating a new product will not be sufficient to make customers come. It is not enough for a company to come up with a better product or technology for customers to line up to buy it.

Transforming a product (whether it is a better mousetrap or a new wireless communications device) into money is an alchemical event that is often at least as difficult as creating a technologically solid product. Economic alchemy, also known as entrepreneurship, is a form of magic practiced by a CEO or other decision maker wherein capital is created from the innovative manipulation of goods and services, thereby creating value to customers and shareholders.

Sometimes the potential value of a product in the marketplace is obvious to the consumer, for example, less expensive, longer-lasting light bulbs. Other new products are harder to sell, such as a software package designed to support a new type of computer that has yet to command significant market share. Regardless of the innovation, the power of an entrepreneur's magic is measured in terms of the profits yielded by taking that product and properly positioning it in the marketplace.

The CEO as entrepreneur needs the Continuum model because each stage of the alchemical transformation of an idea into a product is associated with different economic pressures, expectations, and challenges. Each of these may positively or negatively influence the transformation of the product into profit. A decision maker, by definition, has the power to choose. This chapter illustrates the alchemy of entrepreneurship in terms of the winners, losers, and the undecided in the economics of commercializing a product, and how decisions based on a working knowledge of the Continuum can increase the odds of economic success.

BASIC PRINCIPLES

Even though a great entrepreneur can transform a mediocre technology into a viable business, there are a few general principles of product development that cannot be ignored if the greatest economic benefit is to be realized.

Customers Expect More

One principle is to focus on customer's requirements, where products are conceived of and created because they address proven needs. In a supplier's market, when a company has little competition, it can begin to dictate what customers can and cannot have. For example, Henry Ford was famous for producing cars in whatever color the customer wanted—as long as it was black. In the recent past, U.S. automobile manufacturers ignored demand for smaller, more fuel-efficient cars and continued to create large, heavy, gas-guzzling models. In the modern global economy, however, where customers are capable of selecting automobiles from any number of global competitors, domestic manufacturers have had to offer models that appeal to customer wants and needs. As competition becomes fiercer, it becomes a buyer's market, where customers can obtain more leverage in the marketplace. For example, customers are now treated to mass customization, whether it means that they can select the interior color of their new car, the color of their pager and cell phone, custom-fit jeans, or their particular view of the news in the online version of their favorite newspaper.

Form Follows Function

Another principle in the commercialization of a product is that form should follow function. Ergonomics and ease of use are not only buzzwords in the computer industry, where Aeron chairs and Microsoft Natural Keyboards are the status symbols of the ergonomic elite, but they permeate every aspect of the work and home environment. Even so, there are numerous examples of business decisions that ignore the basic principles of customer comfort, from ergonomically flawed seating in restaurants to clothing designed to fit svelte models instead of working men and women.

Inventors Are Not Necessarily Entrepreneurs

The history of business is filled with hundreds of examples of innovators who spent their lifetimes perfecting a technology, only to see little or no profit from their activity. Inventions are either ignored by society, or developed by entrepreneurs who, acting as economic catalysts, make a success of bringing products to market. In this regard, entrepreneurs are alchemists—people who can see the future that their technology will help create. They make the decisions regarding commercialization of the product and have access to the necessary capital.

There are examples of single inventors or small teams that develop a new product in their garage and successfully bring it to market. The technical and entrepreneurial duo of Jobs and Wozniak, inventors of the Apple computer, is one such story. However, transforming ideas into a successful product normally requires the help of a team of managers who have access to marketplace experience, industry contacts, and capital to sustain the manufacturing, marketing, and sales effort. The successful entrepreneur can often fill a variety of these roles during an organization's infancy.

Some of the greatest modern *inventors* were actually technologists and entrepreneurs who took innovations created by others and brought them to market. For example, Thomas Edison had little to do with the development of the underlying technology associated with many of the innovations that he is credited with inventing; that work was done by hundreds of researchers and inventors under his employ. Edison's primary contribution was taking the innovations to market in a way that generated profits for himself, his workers, and investors.

Many of the real technological innovators and inventors, in contrast, typically had a hard time making ends meet. For example, Nikola Tesla, who worked for Edison for several years, was directly responsible for dozens of inventions taken for granted today, including the first electric motor to run on alternating current (AC). Unfortunately, he did not have a mind for business and worked as a professional billiard player to support his research. Unlike Edison, the quintessential entrepreneur, Tesla's alchemy worked best at the conversion of ideas to technologies.

In other words, Tesla excelled at the beginning of the Continuum, up to the Product Point, and Edison excelled from the Technical Gateway (proof of concept) to Completion. Even in this regard, Edison was faced with several challenges. For example, the U.S. Patent Office eventually ruled that Edison's patent was invalid because it duplicated the work of another U.S. inventor. Similarly, Edison was forced to make Joseph Swan a partner in his electric company as part of a patent infringement suit. Apparently, the British inventor was granted a patent on the lightbulb a decade before Edison announced his "invention."

Entrepreneurship Is about Increasing the Odds of Success

Failure and success are both part of entrepreneurship. Just as the best batters miss more balls than they hit, even those entrepreneurs considered best at their game make mistakes. When it comes to best, there is no one mold that fits every entrepreneur. Some, like Oracle's Larry Ellison, are sophisticated, traveled, and debonair. Others, like Microsoft's Bill Gates, would still be wearing pocket protectors and horn-rimmed glasses were it not for the sartorial advice of their PR departments. Some have staying power, like Gates and Ellison, whereas others roam from challenge to challenge, like Jobs.

However, regardless of what drives them or how they express their individuality, great entrepreneurs make use of their personal power—charisma—as well as their positional power as leaders of their enterprise. Jobs, Gates, Ellison, and other notable entrepreneurs of the computer industry are not simply the heads of their respective companies. In this regard, great entrepreneurs are Faustian in that they are their companies. For a significant salary and stock options, Jobs is the heart and soul of Apple.

Entrepreneurs can use their personal power as a sort of alchemist's power of magic, molding the corporation into their vision, as if the corporation and everyone in it were clay. Not everyone likes to be molded like clay, however, which probably accounts for the need for some entrepreneurs to move from one challenge—and one group of disgruntled employees—to the next.

The entrepreneur's personal power necessarily extends beyond the company, and normally includes those in charge of capital, the public, and, increasingly, the press. Ellison, for example, is credited with saving Oracle from dire straits several times during the company's history, despite glaring flaws in its underlying database technology. That is, Ellison has been able to consistently sell his vision of where Oracle is going—and where it is taking the employees, stockholders, and customers—to the point that it almost does not matter what the actual product delivers today. However, sometimes the sell does not work.

Every entrepreneur who is not playing it too safe has made at least one blunder. For example, Edison, who was fond of competition, backed the use of direct current (DC) to power factories and homes, ignoring Tesla's work with AC. As a result of this oversight and some political maneuvering by the competition, Westinghouse, a proponent of AC power, won the Current War, and Edison lost control of his power company. Today, AC courses through virtually every home and factory in the developed world.

Often, successful entrepreneurs have several failures along the way. For example, Steve Jobs of Apple and Macintosh fame failed at the Apple Lisa, the immediate precursor to the popular Macintosh. The machine was too expensive and too slow, and it could not compete in the marketplace. In the end, the Lisa was more valuable in a landfill as a tax write-off.

Similarly, despite his initial success with the Macintosh, the somewhat abrasive Jobs was ousted from Apple, and he moved on to NEXT Computing. Although the NEXT Cube provided an innovative, albeit sluggish, platform for leading-edge, object-oriented computing, it failed, despite an infusion of capital from Cannon and others. NEXT devolved into a software company and then, failing at that, disappeared altogether from the marketplace. However, Jobs, like Edison, continued to apply his entrepreneurial skills, and returned to Apple, where he is credited with giving the Macintosh a second life as the popular iMac desktop and iBook laptop systems.

WINNERS

For the entrepreneur, winning in the competitive economic arena is largely a matter of stacking the odds in his own favor. His job is to make the decisions that have to be made, but the conditions are virtually never identical from case to case, and there are always new and often unexpected variables to consider. However, if a model can be used to identify a few variables that have predictive value, then the odds can be shifted in the decision maker's favor. CEOs and other business decision makers have to consider the economy, the current political climate, the characteristics of their company's product, the competition, and their own strengths and weaknesses to increase the odds of success. There are no sure bets and no models, business or otherwise, that can presume to offer a guarantee. At a minimum, however, the decision maker must have a model that captures the richness of a high-tech, fast-paced product that has to evolve with the ever-changing needs of the consumer.

Market-research and product-focus groups are important in shaping the direction of marketing campaigns and predicting how products will be accepted in the marketplace. However, sometimes market research cannot predict the accelerated adoption rate of a new product offering. Examples are the "killer apps," which made a lot of money, were universally adopted, and computerized office practice, such as the VisiCalc electronic spreadsheet, the laser printer, and the Photoshop image-editing program.

The Spreadsheet

The electronic spreadsheet transformed accounting, and put tens of thousands of Apple computers in small businesses throughout the United States virtually overnight. With the introduction of the electronic spreadsheet, the desktop microcomputer was suddenly elevated from its status as hobby and entertainment to serious business tool.

Desktop Publishing

Similarly, Apple's LaserWriter printer, together with the Apple Macintosh with its WYSIWYG (what you see is what you get) graphical interface, started the desktop publishing revolution. The Macintosh's display allowed consumers to preview exactly what the printed document would look like, and the laser printer put affordable, high-quality printing within the grasp of small businesses and individuals. Far from creating the paperless office, the laser printer and desktop computer have created a multibillion dollar business that incorporates technologies from large format displays to specialty papers designed for business, photography, and advertising. Desktop publishing has since evolved to include the Web as well as print media.

Traditional Industry

Products in domains other than computer technology have also made fortunes and transformed industries. The radial automobile tire is another moneymaker. Despite the bad press surrounding the 2000 Ford/Firestone recall, in which catastrophic tire failures of Firestone radials were associated with the Ford Explorer, the radial automobile tire has done more to improve the ride, performance, gas mileage, and safety of the automobile than any other single innovation in the automobile industry.

Digital Image Editing

To appreciate the importance of entrepreneurship in the commercial success of a product, consider the digital image-editing software, Photoshop, which, in retrospect, was a success waiting to happen. The multibillion dollar industry lay dormant until a team of two brothers, John and Thomas Knoll, redefined the field a little over a decade ago. The two developed ImagePro, one of the first digital image-manipulation programs designed to work with digital images from a variety of sources. In parallel with developing the software into a stable product, the Knolls searched for commercial opportunities. Their first success was a license agreement with the slide-scanner hardware company BarneyScan in 1989. The task was to rewrite their ImagePro software to control the BarneyScan, the first commercially available true-color 35mm slide scanner for desktop microcomputers. The modified ImagePro software not only controlled the calibration and operation of the scanner, but it empowered users to make corrections in the resulting digital image. After scanning a slide, users could remove scratches, rotate the image, crop out an area of interest, and modify color balance and contrast—just as they could in a darkroom.

When the slide-scanning system was first released, the software was clearly more technically advanced along the Continuum than the hardware. Although the digitized images were exquisite, there was still a lot of *magic* associated with using the hardware. For example, the scanner required an hour to warm up and stabilize before a slide could be scanned. In addition, the scanner then had to be calibrated to account for variations in intensity of the light source used to illuminate a slide.

Only about 200 copies of the modified ImagePro software were bundled for sale with BarneyScan hardware. However, leading-edge graphic studios and research institutions pushed the software to its limits in a variety of domains. For example, many graphic artists who specialized in photographic work used software for the first time. The same was true for medical researchers. Bryan used one of the first systems manufactured to capture medical images from the 35mm slides that he was creating for educational testing software. Since there was no other affordable means of digitizing slides at the time, word of the system spread quickly through the medical and graphic arts communities.

Demand for the BarneyScan system died out quickly, in part because of the very limited number of potential customers. However, the scanner led the way for an entire industry based on scanners from Polaroid, Nikon, Minolta, Cannon, and others. Today, desktop slide scanners from these and other companies are used to create digital image libraries from slides in only a few seconds. Even though there are digital cameras on the market, scans from 35mm slides are still much higher in resolution and provide the best digital images for critical work.

With more user demand and continued modifications and improvements, ImagePro became more useful as a virtual digital darkroom than as a controller program for the slide scanner. The big break for the Knoll brothers came in 1989, soon after establishing a relationship with BarneyScan. After shopping the software around Silicon Valley, they signed a license agreement with Adobe Systems. ImagePro soon became Photoshop, the leading software on the PC and Macintosh for retouching, color correction, and image compositing.

Thanks largely to Photoshop, Adobe Systems is now the second largest PC software company in the United States, with sales of Photoshop far exceeding that of any of slide scanners on the market. Since version 1.0 of Photoshop shipped in 1990, it has been the single most powerful tool for the creation and editing of graphic images on the PC. Today, most slide and flatbed scanners and digital cameras come bundled with a limited version of Photoshop. Thanks to tools like Photoshop, digital imaging and editing is a multibillion dollar industry, attracting customers who never set foot in a darkroom. By continuing to upgrade Photoshop's core technology, providing training and seminars, and partnering with camera, slide, negative, and flatbed scanner companies, Adobe Systems has been able to continually grow and attract new customers.

The transformation of Photoshop from an idea into the cornerstone of a multibillion dollar industry in less than a decade highlights many of the principles of a winning product. The software was not released until it was stable and near the Product Point in the Continuum. In addition, even though the software quickly went from introduction to maturity and decline in the very small slide-scanner market, the entrepreneurial brothers kept the product alive by extending the technology into other markets. They also generated a loyal following of innovators in the medical and graphic arts communities, which helped drive demand for the software when it reappeared as Photoshop. Similarly, by reworking the software and providing the features requested by the graphic artists, Adobe Systems was able to keep Photoshop ahead of the competition.

Part of the success of Photoshop has been the quality, technical superiority, and usefulness of the underlying technology. However, equally important was the recognition and exploitation of the business opportunity that lay in software for graphic arts and advertising, and the foresight to rework the software to define that market niche. Another component of the success was timing, in that Adobe took over the software product as part of a suite of software products aimed at the graphic artist. In fact, for years Adobe and the Macintosh were synonymous with image work and desktop publishing. Today, Adobe Systems is the market leader of the graphical world in print and video and on the Web.

LOSERS

Because it is less costly to learn from the failures of others than to learn from one's own mistakes, studying failures has value in imparting practical information. Anyone can accidentally fall upon fortune, and that type of luck does not transfer. For example, it is more valuable to determine what went wrong with a dotCom business plan than how market conditions suddenly made it shoot up in value. One of the most frustrating situations occurs when a technology that has the potential to be a clear winner fails in the marketplace because of flawed execution on the business end. For example, introducing a product into the marketplace before it has been thoroughly tested may ruin its long-term business prospects. There have been failures in the areas of wireless technology, computer hardware, the dotCom industry, and biotechnology.

Genetically Modified Edibles

Creating positive emotional associations with products is the cornerstone of a good marketing campaign. Unfortunately, negative emotional associations are often more potent modifiers of customer perception and behavior. One example of the public's rejection of a product is its reaction to genetically modified foods (GMFs). Although the public response to the first GMF approved by the Food and Drug Administration (FDA), Calgene's Flavr Savr™ tomato, was largely positive, worldwide public sentiment toward GM foods has been increasingly negative.

Since the first offering of a GMF in 1994 by biotech startup Calgene, a small but very vocal group managed to heighten public awareness of the potential negative consequences of virus-resistant squash, New Leaf™ potatoes, Roundup Ready® soybeans, Bt corn, and other genetically engineered crops. As a result, many countries require genetically modified (GM) labeling, and most large U.S. corporations, such as Kraft and Kellogg's voluntarily segregate GM and non-GM products.

In a media event that was reminiscent of the near meltdown of the nuclear reactor at Three Mile Island or of beef infected with the virus that causes Mad Cow Disease, the scare in 2000 that genetically modified corn had made it into the human food chain caused public panic. StarLink, a type of corn developed by Aventis CropScience, contains a bacterial gene that produces a protein that kills pests. StarLink, originally targeted for livestock feed, has since been banned as human food by the EPA because of concerns over allergic reactions to the pest-killing protein. However, it may have been inadvertently mixed with nonmodified corn designated for human consumption, forcing the recall of taco shells and other corn products.

The public outcry against contamination of the human food supply by a GMF forced many cereal manufacturers to invest in campaigns to promote the natural source of their products. In an attempt to circumvent a small but vocal public outcry, Kellogg's ran a number of billboard ads touting the natural corn content of their cereal product, and increased the visibility of its Environmental Responsibility in Action program.

In a postmortem analysis of the GMF industry, StarLink corn failed and stalled at the Product Point in the Continuum. Even the product's survival as a crop for livestock feed is uncertain. This is partly because the corn must be handled as a potential biohazard, with absolutely no possibility of contact with grain intended for human consumption.

The status of GMF illustrates the limitations of a purely technology-oriented success strategy. Perhaps the biotech industry would have had an easier time with the introduction of GMF products if they were initially marketed as, say, pest-resistant grains to be planted in third-world countries suffering from food shortages. Additionally, a mass-marketing campaign by the GMF industry to alleviate fears and refute unsubstantiated claims might have mitigated the negative exposure in the press and consumer fears.

Wireless Wonders

Although emotions do not run as high in the high-tech communications and computer industries as they do in biotech, customer attitudes and resultant behavior are just as important to product success or failure. Consider that Motorola was once synonymous with leading-edge cell phone style and technology. Motorola saw its share of the cell phone market fall from 33% to only 14% in the five-year period from 1996 to 2001. Despite early success with its signature flip-phone design, Motorola apparently ignored customer preferences for small, inexpensive, funky phones and instead focused on larger, more expensive phones with complicated features, such as wireless Web access.

In terms of customer behavior, Motorola asked customers to take path B in Figure 4.1, whereas Nokia made it easy for existing customers to stay by providing products that are easy to use, simple, and powerful (represented by path A in Figure 4.1). Motorola's oversight allowed Nokia and other competitors to capture customers.

In addition to misreading its consumer market, Motorola was out of step with its business market as well. The company, which recently witnessed its investment in the troubled iridium satellite

Figure 4.1   Cellular Phone Behavior Change Model

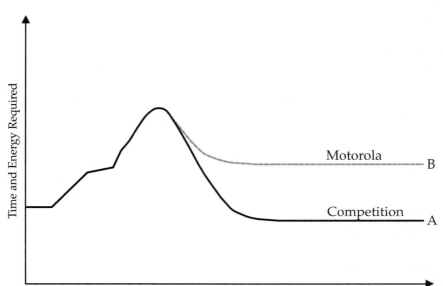

system fail, misread the technical needs of wireless carriers, embracing older analog technology while the competition offered easier digital technology. In the United States, where wireless carriers have yet to provide the coverage and quality anywhere near that of carriers in Europe and parts of Asia, anything that can help make the carrier's work easier and more effective is a boon to customers. Lost calls and busy signals translate to end-user frustration, which in turn results in fewer handset sales.

One of the most notorious mobile carriers is the now-defunct Metricom, known to many subscribers as the Ricochet network, which is deployed in a dozen major markets in the United States. Although the technology was highly praised by the customers who were fortunate enough to live in one of the areas where coverage was available, it was proprietary.

Metricom's microcellular data network used a proprietary technology that went against industry standards, such as the international wireless local area network standard referred to as 802.11b, which is used extensively in corporations and academia. In addition, Metricom ignored the next generation standard for wireless networks backed by Motorola, Ericsson, and Japan's NTT DoCoMo.

Today, manufacturers of all wireless computing and communications devices have the challenge of overcoming customer fears regarding security limitations. Most users of cell phones and wireless handheld devices are aware of the potential threat from hackers and viruses. Although handheld devices have yet to suffer any major attacks like those that erase computer hard drives, the potential—and more important, the fear—is there that such attacks are only a matter of time.

To date, the most egregious acts of wireless terrorism have been the spamming of PDAs with harmless email and causing cell phones to automatically dial specific numbers. Even so, the fear of data loss or eavesdropping will have to be addressed for widespread consumer buy-in outside of the business market. To this end, guarantees associated with charge cards, such as no financial liability to the consumer for charges made through theft, will go a long way to providing comfort in using a wireless PDA or cell phone as a charge card, the so-called digital wallet.

The other emotionally charged concern regarding wireless device usage, especially cell phones, is the possible medical hazard associated with wireless radiation. Most wireless PDAs and digital cell phones transmit and receive signals near the same frequencies used by microwave ovens to cook food. Although the radiation from cell phones has not been proven to cause cancer or brain tumors, it has been shown that parts of the brain increase in temperature because of heating from the microwave radiation. Even though the cell phone industry denies any health risk to cell phone use, virtually all of the major cell phone developers have taken out patents on devices and designs intended to reduce the amount of radiation absorbed by a cell phone user.

Boutique Computer Hardware Manufacturers

As Nokia illustrated, aesthetics, technology, and acceptable price are a winning combination, even against established players in a market. However, even companies experienced in providing this mix can fail to entice potential customers to part with their money. In 2001, just a year after its introduction, Apple pulled its futuristic, diminutive G4 Cube computer from the market. Although the Cube was the pinnacle of Apple's work toward providing the coolest-looking computer on the market, customers were not willing to pay $1,000 more than for comparable Macintosh systems for aesthetics alone—and at a time when complete PCs were selling for less than $1,000. The fate of the Cube illustrates that the value of aesthetics is finite.

This is an example of how marketing research and imperfect information used in a hedonic pricing analysis can overvalue the worth of a proposed design. However, this was apparently not the case with the wildly popular iMac computer. Apple was able to revive its Macintosh line by repackaging its technologically antiquated computer in a translucent, candy-colored case and offering it for a reasonable price.

DotCom Grocery Stores

In recent years, a number of major grocery store chains have experimented with new ways of attracting customers through new valued services. As demonstrated by the demise of HomeRuns and Webvan, which only served a small percentage of the online population, Web-based grocery shopping seems only viable as an extension of brick-and-mortar food stores. Webvan invested $830 million to establish a presence in the marketplace, only to run out of capital in two years.

With the possible exception of Amazon.com and a few other pure dotCom companies, the Web serves as only one of several touch points to a click-and-mortar business. In hindsight, and without the confusion and unproven business models associated with the feeding frenzy that once characterized the Web, Webvan's proposition was obviously flawed. At a time when success was measured in terms of revenue, not profit, here were questionable, huge infrastructure investments in central distribution warehouses and exorbitant contracts for upper management. For one thing, the six-figure, lifetime income guarantee for the CEO was unprecedented. In addition, in order to be profitable, Webvan would have had to have sales almost double that of Kroger, the industry leader with 3,500 brick-and-mortar stores and sales of $49 billion in 2000.

The demise of dotCom grocery stores illustrates the need for CEOs to consider the reality of economics together with customer behavior, especially the typical pattern of technology adoption. Webvan and other pure online grocery services may have underestimated the resources needed to convert traditional shoppers to online consumers. In reality, the service was only used by a few tenths of a percent of its potential customer base, the online community. However, only about 2% of the online users in the United States shop for groceries online. In England, where 90% of consumers have access to the Tesco online service, annual online grocery sales account for about 2% of the country's grocery sales.

In the grocery business, profits are slim, with about a 1% margin in the United States. In England, where margins on grocery items are around 8%, there is enough of a margin to absorb the cost of online operations and still make a profit. For example, Tesco of England is the most profitable and largest of the big online grocers, with a customer base of one million customers. Online ordering, a business with $422 million in annual sales, was introduced as an added service to Tesco's main brick-and-mortar store services, an easy concept to grasp and grow into. Tesco introduced its service in 1996, and slowly but steadily expanded the operation as demand increased, along the path of the typical technology adoption curve.

Figure 4.2 illustrates how Tesco's progress along its adoption curve was slower than that of Webvan, in part because Webvan was giving away its service, bleeding capital in order to attract customers

Figure 4.2   Online Grocery Adoption Curves

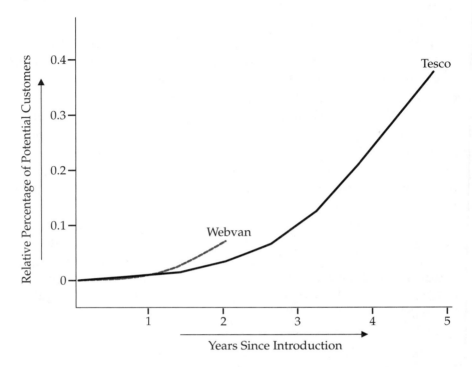

and increase market share. Tesco, on the other hand, charges for its delivery service. The service is profitable because customers pay a fee for delivery in addition to the cost of the groceries they buy over the Internet.

Instead of building central warehouses, as Webvan of California tried to do, Tesco uses its hundreds of supermarket storefronts as bases for its Internet deliveries. Customer service representatives using computers to determine the most effective path in the store to fill an order share aisles with regular shoppers. An additional advantage of online grocers with storefronts, such as Peapod in the United States and Tesco in England, is that they can buy at prices negotiated through the storefront businesses. In contrast, Webvan and other pure eCommerce storefronts with their relatively small volumes paid higher prices for products. Although Webvan's demise was due to a number of factors, the profitability of Tesco strongly suggests that only online grocery stores with a significant brick-and-mortar infrastructure can be profitable in the long term. Unnecessary risk was assumed by senior management in creating a centralized distribution network unfamiliar to the consumer and defocusing financial resources on the critical task at hand—converting new customers through the promotion of an easier and more time-efficient shopping experience.

UNDECIDED

Some industries do not clearly fit the category of economic winners or losers in the world of product development. Technologies such as programmable cars, self-scan shopping, and eBook publishing have the potential to transform entire industries or fail miserably, depending on how the technologies are executed in the marketplace.

Programmable Cars

In the 1950s and 1960s, the ability to work on a car engine was viewed as the modern equivalent of being able to understand and configure a PC. It was a valued skill, if only to have the fastest or more powerful car in the neighborhood. Today, tearing down and rebuilding car engines is a thankless task relegated to a grease monkey working in a hot garage or filling station. Given the difficulty associated with properly disposing of waste oil, few car owners even bother with changing their own oil, but rely on a drive-in, quick-change service.

However, just as Adobe Photoshop reintroduced photographers to the darkroom, without the need to work with toxic chemicals in light-tight rooms, computer technologies are changing the face of auto mechanics. Thanks to the degree with which some modern automobiles are dependent on onboard computers for every aspect of engine function, auto mechanics is taking on a new meaning. This ability to configure the performance of a car may create a new breed of white-collar mechanics.

The computer-controlled Toyota Prius hybrid car, available in Japan since 1998, was introduced into the U.S. market in 2001. The Prius is unique in that it uses a combined electric- and gasoline-powered engine for power, where the battery is charged during braking. There is no need to plug the car into an outlet for an overnight charge, as is required of all-electric cars. However, because of the relative complexity of determining when the electric drive should engage and when the gasoline engine should power the car, the Prius is heavily reliant on an onboard computer system. In addition, unlike the embedded computer systems used in virtually every other make and model of car, the computer is accessible—and reprogrammable—through an ordinary laptop.

Almost immediately, Prius owners in the United States started connecting their laptops to the car's computer system. These white-collar mechanics are able to modify the car's engine control programming to provide custom performance. Although modifying the factory settings to provide enhanced performance in, for example, high-altitude driving conditions is not officially supported or encouraged, the concept may start a new industry.

Assuming warranty issues do not impede progress, tools and utilities for software mechanics may create a new market for automotive suppliers. After all, few baby boomers have the time or resources to tear apart and rebuild their car engines as they did in their teens, but they likely do have the time to alter the fuel injection settings through a graphical user interface on their laptops.

In terms of the Continuum, programmable cars are not yet to the Product Point (see Figure 4.3). Although the Prius has clearly demonstrated the technical feasibility of the technology, Toyota has yet to officially support the concept, and other automobile manufacturers do not yet provide the degree of accessible computer integration found in the Prius.

Self-Scan Shopping

As the short-lived success of the online grocery services demonstrated, standing in line at the grocery store, like doing laundry at a

Figure 4.3   Programmable Cars and the Continuum

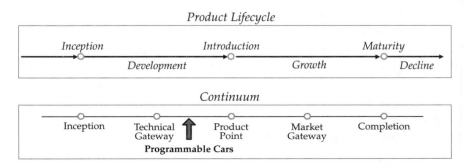

laundromat, is one of the banes of a modern urban existence. In the very low margin grocery business, several major store chains, including Stop and Shop in the northeast, are experimenting with changing the way customers purchase their food, especially those who hate standing in line.

Scan-it-yourself services, in which customers perform their own checkout work at computerized stations, may prove profitable. Customers bring their selections to an automated checkout station, scan each item with a laser barcode reader, and then place the item on a weight-sensing platform. Coupons are read in the same way. The station tabulates the total, verifies that the coupons match the goods purchased, and handles the transaction processing with the customer's charge card.

Because the service is interactive and self-service, stores save money on cashiers, and customers do not feel as bored waiting in line. Typically, one store employee can cover four to six self-service stations. Most studies have not revealed any significant time savings, compared to traditional checkout lines, but because the customers are active and not simply passive observers, they perceive time to pass more quickly.

In terms of the Continuum, self-scan shopping is clearly past the Product Point (see Figure 4.4). The technology is heavily used in the stores where it is installed, and customer response has been positive overall. From an economic perspective, the systems should pay for themselves through increased customer patronage at stores with the systems as well as through cost savings in the number of cashiers that have to be hired.

Figure 4.4   Self-Scan Shopping and the Continuum

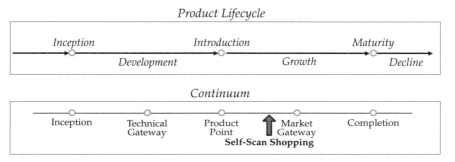

There are several caveats, however. From an ROI perspective, there are issues of installation cost, original equipment cost, maintenance, and support contracts, and how these relate to customer patronage. In order for the systems to be economically feasible in the short term, they have to be used on an almost continuous basis. Installing self-scan stations in a store with insufficient traffic to keep the stations busy would not make sense, which limits the technology to larger stores where the incremental short-term costs of installing the automated systems are less than that of hiring checkout personnel. In addition, because the prices are updated from a central database, the technology is only applicable to larger chains and therefore is not readily adaptable to small, independent stores.

Since margins on most items are only 2 or 3%, any losses, such as those resulting from "shrinkage," or theft, can make or break the system. In this regard, a major component of the computer back-end of the system is concerned with verifying the price and identity of every item that is scanned. For example, if a customer were to scan a can of beans and then place a package of chicken breasts on the weight-sensing platform, the system would detect the difference between the product description from the bar code scan and the actual weight of the system, reject the item, and sound a "soft" alarm to summon an assistant. The system is not foolproof. For example, a customer could scan a 6 $\frac{1}{2}$-ounce can of no-name brand tuna and then place a can of premium albacore tuna of the same weight on the scale, and the fraud would likely go undetected.

Assuming the limitations of the technology can be addressed, the self-scan shopping technology has the potential to transform the grocery industry, just as self-service kiosks or ATMs have changed the banking industry. In this regard, the self-scan technology needs to be thought of as two separate components, product and process. In order for the technology to succeed in the marketplace, the automated checkout units must not only work as designed, but they must improve the current process as well.

eBooks

The traditional paperbound book publishing industry is known for unpredictable cycles of sales and surprise hits. Although best-selling authors are a relatively sure bet, overall buying behavior is highly seasonal and responds to economics and what is available. For example, the lull in book purchases in 1998 was repeated in 2001, with eCommerce titles accounting for at least some of the 12% downturn in hardback sales. Paradoxically, with the downturn in sales, the hottest books in the summer of 2001 were nonfiction. Apparently, in tighter times, readers were more willing to invest in books that may have value for them beyond a few hours of reading on a beach.

One of the challenges of the traditional publishing model is the time required to develop an idea into a product, a process that involves dozens of steps and teams of professionals. The value chain includes authors; editors; graphic artists; designers; copyeditors; production and layout specialists; and marketing, sales, and shipping personnel. As a result, the chain from the printing press to the bookstore warehouses and finally to the bookstore shelves or to Amazon.com's listing requires months and in some cases years. A typical business book on the fast track takes about a year from inception to product, and most novels require an additional six months to a year. As such, many of the dotCom books in production in 2000 were irrelevant before they were halfway through the process—and many of the contracts with authors were cancelled.

One of the technological innovations explored by traditional and online publishers is the eBook, a digital version of a work that bypasses the postediting steps of production. PeanutPress.com, Amazon.com, and other online booksellers offer an increasing number of titles that can be downloaded immediately onto PDAs, laptops, and desktop computers. However, the market for eBooks is as yet unknown and partially dependent on the hardware technologies available for readers. For example, after several false starts, eBook readers, which are liquid crystal display (LCD) panels designed to emulate a hardback book in form and function, are finally getting off to a very modest start. Wireless access to content is another enabling technology that has yet to be developed sufficiently to support large-volume purchases of eBooks from the Web. As such, eBooks are between the Technical Gateway and the Product Point in the Continuum (See Figure 4.5).

As discussed in Chapter 3, one of the economic issues plaguing traditional publishers is the intellectual property rights of older works contracted before the advent of the Web. Although most modern book contracts include the transfer of property rights of all forms, including electronic, from the author to the publisher, many of the contracts for classic works were exclusively for book publication.

Figure 4.5   eBooks and the Continuum

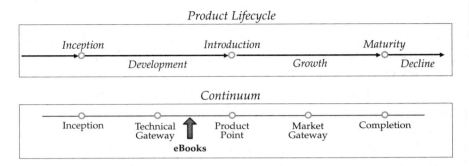

Whether or not the public's appetite for eBooks can be increased depends on the availability of thin, lightweight, inexpensive eBook readers. It also depends on the availability of software that provides rapid, easy access to the content, as well as protection against widespread copying. For example, utilities that disabled Adobe's eBook reader software was available for download on the Web within a few weeks of its debut. Although it seems inevitable that college and high school students will one day soon be toting a backpack with a thin, lightweight laptop to and from school, filled with eBooks downloaded from an online bookstore, publishers will have to first develop a sustainable financial model as well the challenge of converting consumers from traditional reading materials.

TWO CENTS WORTH

The preceding cases illustrate that, although a mature technology must underly a successful product on the market, it is possible to succeed spectacularly in transforming an idea into a technology and fail miserably in the marketplace. As noted in the first three chapters, customer behavior, the concept of Product Lifecycles, and progress along the Continuum all have a direct influence on the challenges that every entrepreneur faces in the transformation of an idea into a product and a product into a profitable business.

In the biological world, even small advantages—an extra half-inch of height for a basketball player, an extra five or ten IQ points for a physicist, or the ability to run the 100-meter dash in 1/100 of a second faster than the competitor—can confer enormous benefits to the individual. Similarly, in business, seemingly minor details can mean the difference between an economic failure and a market leader. Harvey McKay, the CEO of McKay Envelopes and a noted author, makes a point of illustrating this fact by describing how he discovered the difference between profitability and bankruptcy in the envelope business. It turns out that it all depends how the scrap paper is handled. When he first started his envelope business, he threw the scrap paper in the dumpster and paid to have it hauled away. When he learned that the competition was selling their scrap paper, he did the same—and his operation became profitable.

Airports and the entire travel industry is another area where small changes are sufficient to change customer behavior enough to create profit from what could have been loss leaders. Taking the lead from movie theaters, where the majority of profits are generated at the concession stands not from ticket sales, nonairborne extras are responsible for the majority of revenue for the top 20 airports in the United States. For example, Disney World Orlando is a top tourist attraction, in part because airfare is kept artificially low. The Orlando Airport offsets ticket prices with elevated car rental rates. The trade-off works because half of all incoming passengers rent a car.

In the case of Photoshop, the Knoll brothers were successful because they combined technical prowess with entrepreneurial skills. Their affiliation with the BarneyScan slide scanner demonstrated to leaders in the graphics community that their technology was solid and dependable. Adobe Systems continued with the tradition of technical excellence while providing ever-increasing functionality targeted directly at its primary customer base. As a result, Photoshop continues to establish the standards for all other image-enhancement packages.

The sector of the biotech industry associated with genetically modified food is in the same position the nuclear energy industry faced immediately after the Three Mile Island accident. Genetically modified corn is illegal to use in products intended for human consumption, and so the domestic return on investment for GM products seems dim at best, despite advances in the core technology. The wireless industry, like the dotCom grocery industry, has been taking a beating on Wall Street and in the marketplace. However, in the case of wireless, the fault lies primarily with development of the technology, including the inability to provide national coverage with a single standard. Consumer frustration over high monthly charges, compounded by spotty, often poor-quality communications links, and investor reluctance to embrace anything associated with the Web and eCommerce are significant hurdles for the industry to overcome. Wireless remains the next logical step in the evolution of communications and the Web.

In terms of evolution, Apple has been successful in bringing innovative technology, and, more recently, innovatively packaged older technology onto the marketplace. As digital computers have evolved since 1935 from machines designed to code and encode messages for the military to the intellectual levers—automated typewriters and spreadsheets—they are today, their economic value as strictly computational devices has waned. Until computers are powerful enough to act as autonomous thinking machines, there is not much motivation for the average consumer to spend money on a faster processor. The main exceptions are the relatively few specialists who work with computationally intensive applications such as video editing, 3-D image rendering, and voice recognition. Although the computer systems designed to support these high-end applications typically sell with higher profit margins, compared to the millions of PCs sold for word processing, email, and spreadsheet use, the market is comparatively small.

Apple recognized early on that although the "guts" of the personal computer had become a commodity item, there was still considerable hedonic value to be had through proper packaging. The iMac, with its ancient cathode-ray tube (CRT) display, when packaged in a translucent, brightly colored plastic case, is chic. The old Macintosh hardware, wrapped in an envelope of plastic, is capable of outperforming technologically more advanced systems that use lighter, cooler, LCD screen technology.

Programmable cars, self-scan shopping, and eBooks are in their infancy, in terms of both technological and entrepreneurial evolution. For example, although hundreds of titles are available as eBooks, the display hardware and software are still in development. The cost of dedicated readers and the questionable security of the software required to display the content are economic impediments to customers and developers.

SUMMARY

The economics of bringing a product to market and keeping it there involves not only the successful transformation of an idea into a solid technology, but also the entrepreneurial transformation of the resulting product into capital. The magic associated with the latter transformation involves the adherence to several basic principles, such as responding to increasing customer expectations, providing value above and beyond what the customers expect and what the competition delivers. The same genius that can create a technology from a dream is rarely transferable to entrepreneurship in the business environment.

Entrepreneurs, as alchemists, vary in personality and motivation, but share an ability to galvanize the public, investors, and their employees behind a clearly articulated belief or vision. As the winners and losers in the economic space have demonstrated, a multitude of factors, from customer behavior, the political and social environment, funding, adherence to—or failure to adhere to—established standards, and the tenacity of the entrepreneur are all factors that affect the odds of success. In the end, leadership, whether in entrepreneurship or technical development, is about increasing the odds of success in the marketplace. The slight advantage conferred by the Continuum model, like slight evolutionary advantages, can convey a significant benefit to entrepreneurs in their search for the right alchemy.

5

Getting Unstuck

When one door closes another door opens; but we often look so long and so regretfully upon the closed door that we do not see the ones which open for us.

Alexander Graham Bell

In a market characterized by accelerating complexity and increasing customer expectations, moving along the Continuum from idea to market unimpeded is like driving through downtown Manhattan without ever encountering a red light—it never happens. Projects always take longer than expected and cost more than planned, and the development, marketing, and sales teams all periodically loose momentum and motivation. On top of that, the economy is like the flight deck of an aircraft carrier in rough seas, in that a pilot attempting to land a jet can never be quite sure if it will be a soft landing or a spine-jolting slap.

Getting stuck at various points along the Continuum is simply a fact of life. In this regard, a CEO is like a plumber, in that at least part of the job involves locating bottlenecks—structural, process, or organic—in what should be a smoothly operating system. Although every company's problems are different, they tend to cluster in three areas: the underlying technology, the structure and internal functioning of the company, and the capricious marketplace. Figure 5.1 lists the most common sticking points in each of these three areas.

Figure 5.1   Sticking Points

STICKING POINTS
COMPANY
Skilled employees
Employee training
Funding
Focus
Leadership
Legal requirements
Maintaining revenue
Employee morale
TECHNOLOGY
Certification
Production schedule
Training requirements
Specifications and planning
Integration
Maintaining legacy systems
Evolving delivery platforms
Evolving industry standards
Proprietary systems
Technology limitations
Third-party support
MARKET
Advertising budget
Trade press
Competition
Corporate visibility
Differentiation from the competition
Economic downturn
Market Shift
Customer expectations

Product development becomes a sticking point for any number of reasons. Furthermore, despite a business plan and research into the technological requirements, sticking points usually become apparent only after the transformation of an idea into a marketable product has begun in earnest. In this context, sticking does not necessarily mean hitting an impasse, but movement from one phase of the Continuum to the next may simply take more time than the organization anticipated or can afford in the short term. Consider that at the height of the dotCom boom, successfully funded companies evolved new generations of Web-based business innovations every few months. In this period of *Internet time*, laggards were left behind, scratching for the crumbs from the venture capital firms.

Sometimes getting stuck in the process of transforming a seemingly fantastic idea to a demonstrable prototype happens because the infrastructure of the supporting technologies is inadequate. In other cases, components and other technologies may be fully developed but not affordable in terms of capital expenditure or R&D resources.

Typical internal problems that can impede the process of coming to market are inept leadership and a shortage of skilled, motivated employees. These intrinsic components of a business process are usually more significant than any technology in the rate and quality of progress made along the Continuum.

Consider on one extreme how dissatisfied employees can strike for better compensation and improved working conditions. Less obvious, but just as devastating are low employee morale and a lack of willingness of employees to give their full attention to their work. This may be due to the nature of the work—for example, building missiles for a defense contractor that will sell them to third-world countries, which may be difficult for some engineers and technicians to get excited about. More often, however, the fault lies in the corporate leadership.

The situation is like having a professional basketball team saddled with a retired high school coach. Because the coach lacks relevant experience and the energy level to lead a pro team, the players either will not gel into a team or they will do so in their own terms. That is, they will elect their own leader and define their own goals to suit their best interests, which may be at odds with those of the team owner, the league, and the fans.

Conversely, a charismatic, energetic, and intelligent coach can recognize and bring out the latent talent in otherwise average players so that they will perform up to their potential. In business, a great leader can similarly create an environment and the incentives to bring out the best in each employee while achieving the goals of the company. Often, as in sports, bringing in a new leadership team can take a stuck company to the forefront of its industry.

A company can also lose momentum because resources have to be diverted from core technology developments to deal with legacy systems, training, and customer support, which can leave it with insufficient resources to move forward with R&D. When there is an existing customer base that is dependent on a previous generation of a company's technology, it is usually impossible to simply ignore the old customers, if only because they represent the most likely source of future revenue. This pattern is perhaps most obvious in the automobile industry, where companies groom customers to want future models by making certain that they are happy with their current car. Toyota takes care of customers who purchase a Corolla to maintain a positive brand image and ensure that when they buy their next car, it will likely be the higher-priced Camry.

Even with the best internal processes in place, the forward momentum of a product introduced into the market is often at the mercy of external factors, such as the prevailing economic winds. A product may fail because of general customer rejection of an entire market, such as occurred in the worldwide technology slowdown of 2001. The progress of several promising technologies, such as wireless access to the Web, was put on temporary hold because of consolidation in the industry, rethinking of standards, and a general drop in consumer spending.

Bad press (deserved or not), an insufficient advertising budget, or strong competition can also stymie a product's forward momentum in the marketplace. For example, a company may lack a Web site that showcases the benefits and features of a product for prospective customers. On the technical front, movement by industry leaders can spell disaster for smaller companies that have invested heavily in R&D toward achieving industry standards. For example, the short-range wireless standard, Bluetooth, backed by over 2000 vendors over the past several years, is in trouble. Microsoft and other companies that once backed Bluetooth announced products compatible with the increasingly common Wi-Fi or 802.11b wireless standard.

To illustrate the challenges associated with getting unstuck, consider the following scenario of a beleaguered high-tech company that experienced seemingly continuous challenges internally, technologically, and in the marketplace. Despite these challenges, the CEO and management team were able to generate enough momentum to achieve short-term profitability.

A STICKY SITUATION

In addition to an opposable thumb, the trait that differentiates the human species from lower life forms is its ability to recognize, understand, and respond to speech. Not surprisingly, the public consciousness, guided by science fiction visionaries from Isaac Asimov to Arthur C. Clarke, judges the intelligence of any life form—including other humans—in terms of speaking ability. However, despite tales of robots and other machines capable of conversing with their human masters, as in Asimov's *I-ROBOT* series in the 1950s and HAL in Clarke's *2001: A Space Odyssey*, which debuted two decades later, a machine's ability to speak in response to human speech has yet to be realized. The first step in this process will be the machine's ability to understand speech.

The first computer-based speech-recognition systems were developed in the 1950s, using analog computer hardware. Analog systems, which predate the currently popular digital computer architecture, were particularly suited for recognizing the patterns of speech because speech is an analog signal. However, because digital computers could be used for the military purposes of encrypting and decrypting messages before and during World War II, companies backing digital technology received the lion's share of funding from the German and U.S. governments. As a result, analog computing and the scientists who understood the applications of the technology, including analog speech recognition, were put on the fast track of an evolutionary dead end.

Speech recognition reappeared as a commercial product for microcomputers in the early 1980s. Part of the delay in replicating analog speech-recognition techniques in the microcomputer was the inability of early desktop systems to process external analog signals such as speech. The first microcomputer-based speech-recognition systems relied on dedicated, outboard speech-specific computers. These computer peripherals converted analog speech signals into digital signals, which were converted to keystroke equivalents, and then fed to the host microcomputer.

Toward the end of the 1980s, affordable, discrete-word, small-vocabulary, speech-recognition cards and software were available for the IBM PC from COVOX and other companies, which provided an inexpensive means for experimenters to work with speech recognition. Later, audio input and output cards, such as SoundBlaster from

Creative Labs, together with the PC's microcomputer were used to support speech-recognition software. Similarly, Apple tried unsuccessfully to integrate speech recognition and speech generation into its Macintosh operating system. The short-lived experiment failed because of recognition inaccuracies, vocabulary limited to only a few thousand words, and the stipulation that users speak into the system with unnatural pauses between each word. All of these requirements were counterintuitive and went against customer expectations of what speech recognition was all about. As a result, after only about a year on the market, Apple dropped built-in speech-recognition capabilities from the Macintosh operating system.

While the early speech-recognition systems provided limited capabilities for speech recognition, they were nowhere near what science fiction writers—and therefore the general public—considered speech-recognition machines. As in Apple's experiment with the Macintosh, early units worked with discrete words with pauses after each utterance and very limited vocabularies. Normal, continuous speech was simply impossible to deal with. Even so, there were a few areas where discrete recognition of up to a few thousand words was at least partially useful.

The early, albeit limited, successes of discrete speech recognition technology were in medical reporting in specialties such as pathology, radiology, and emergency medicine. Physicians in these specialties used a limited vocabulary to describe findings, making the job for the speech-recognition engine easier. The time it took to transcribe reports and send them to other physicians who needed the findings justified the attempt to use the new speech-recognition technology to try to speed things up. Except for handicapped users and a relatively small number of early adopters in niche areas such as medical reporting, speech recognition of individual words on the microcomputer remained a curiosity at best.

Change Agent

In 1995, Bryan's company was contracted by the CEO of a major speech-recognition development company to help in evaluating and marketing his speech-recognition-based electronic medical reporting systems. At that time, the CEO, who we will refer to as Frank, was in the process of getting his company unstuck from an extremely uncomfortable business situation. Most of the former upper-level management team was incarcerated or awaiting trial resulting from charges of fraud. The Securities and Exchange Commission (SEC) and the company's stockholders were understandably upset that some of the previous managers had artificially inflated sales figures. In order to have a successful public offering, it was necessary to demonstrate several consecutive quarters of profitability. However, the orders counted as filled never materialized. Apparently, shipments of speech-recognition software to customers were actually routed to a warehouse for storage.

Frank, a seasoned turnaround specialist, was hired to make the company profitable, increase shareholder value, and then sell the company for a profit. From his appearance—short sleeves and Rolex—and cramped, unadorned office, it was clear to everyone that he meant business and that he kept a constant eye on the bottom line. Not only were the quarterly employee updates held in the company dining room, where the meals consisted of pizzas, but also visitors to the company were treated to either Burger King or Pizza Hut instead of the former gourmet catering.

From an internal, corporate perspective, Frank faced several formidable challenges. The company had been hemorrhaging personnel for several months from low morale. This corporate-wide attitude was understandable, given the turmoil caused by the acts of the previous management. In addition, the multiple rounds of financing needed to keep the company afloat prior to Frank's arrival had severely diluted the value of the stock options held by the original employees, including the senior research scientists. The original stock options no longer provided the significant incentive that would be needed to turn the company around. On top of that, employee morale dropped because one of Frank's first acts was to reduce operating expenses by firing what he considered deadwood—about a third of the employees.

An additional internal sticking point was that the company was actively engaged in several businesses—speech-enabled electronic medical records, system integration, general-purpose speech recognition, and PC hardware sales and support—all of which diluted progress in the speech-recognition arena. Resources that could have been focused on speech-recognition R&D had to be diverted to other areas. For example, there were hundreds of legacy medical-record-reporting systems that had to be kept running in accordance with maintenance contracts. Most important, fulfilling the maintenance agreements accounted for most of the company's day-to-day revenue stream.

Early on, it made sense for the company to enter the PC hardware business. The speech-enabled medical-reporting systems required a proprietary hardware card that had to be installed and tested by a speech-recognition technician. In addition, to make the purchase decision easier for hospitals and clinics, the company offered a total electronic medical record solution, placing it squarely in the PC hardware support business.

To add to the potential confusion, there were projects in progress that dealt with connecting the PCs configured as medical dictation systems to hospital systems, and these custom connections or interfaces required several weeks of on- and off-site work by integration specialists. The medical division of the company was also charged with maintaining the accuracy and integrity of a variety of medical databases. This work ensured that the reports generated by the speech-recognition system were medically correct and that online resources, such as the formulary—the list of drugs available for physicians to order—were up to date and accurate. Billing codes, a major reason that hospitals and managed care practices invested in these systems, were part of the databases and also had to be regularly updated.

From a technical perspective, the R&D division of the company was stuck as well. The "holy grail" of speech recognition—continuous speech recognition on a standard laptop or desktop PC—still seemed six months to a year away, and yet the word in the industry was that the competition was nearly there. Part of the technological challenge was that the R&D division had been dividing its energies among multiple areas. Legacy medical reporting systems that were based on proprietary hardware cards had to be migrated to a software-only solution that did not require the expensive, custom-made, plug-in cards.

In addition, the new speech-recognition engine, which had been under development for a year, was based on the new Windows operating system. This meant that existing installations had to be upgraded from DOS to Windows. However, since most of the PCs in service were physically incapable of running Windows, much less the new speech-recognition engine, PCs had to be upgraded to units with high-speed processors and as much RAM as the customer could afford. In addition, a liaison from R&D had to work with the documentation division in order to create online and print directions for how to set up and use the new systems.

The R&D department was also under extreme pressure to quickly develop a variety of speech-recognition tools to fit a variety of market niches. The department was tasked with creating a general-purpose speech-recognition system that was tightly integrated with Word, Excel, and other standard applications. For example, a user should be able to say "bold that" to change the format of a selected sentence or word from normal to bold.

The seemingly constant rollout of software taxed the efforts of the core development team, as well as those in support, training, documentation, and marketing. In addition, government contracts for specific applications of speech-recognition technology, from advanced medical-reporting systems to controlling tanks in battle through speech commands, had to be managed. Employees in the medical-reporting division also had to stay current with and actually drive changes to the standards associated with electronic medical records. For example, there were debates in the medical-reporting industry over the image format that should be used to send images from one PC to the next.

From an external market perspective, the company was stuck because of the general public's disinterest with discrete speech recognition. In addition, even in the niche area of medical reporting, the vast majority of physicians did not care for the speech-enabled reporting systems, and many used the system only when they were paid for the extra time it took to dictate a report using speech recognition. This attitude was a reflection of the time and energy investment required to become even partially competent with the systems.

Many physicians required class instruction and individual tutoring to attain proficiency, and even then most found it quicker to hit a key for a command instead of speaking the command. Even worse, if a word was misunderstood, then the correction process was even more arduous and time consuming. As a result, most physicians used some combination of keyboard commands and voice dictation in a talk-and-type interface. Faced with the prospect of impending competition from another company with a continuous speech-recognition system running on standard Windows hardware, Frank sought to attract additional funding to expand the marketing arm.

The key sticking point with marketing and one that Frank could not adequately address, was that in many respects the entire speech-recognition industry was a solution in search of need. Although there were a few key military applications for hands-busy, eyes-busy situations, the civilian market, which included the disabled and dyslexic, was not large enough and did not have deep enough pockets to yield sustainable revenues for the long term.

In addition, the state-of-the-art accuracy limit of one or two errors for every 10 words dictated, and the lack of any real demand for general-purpose speech recognition on the PC, had never been fully addressed. A telltale sign, and one that did not change during Bryan's three-year tenure as a consultant for the company, was that not one of the 120-plus employees used speech recognition in their daily work. Everyone in the company, without exception, preferred to use a keyboard and mouse when work had to get done. Besides, the cacophony that would have been created by a hundred cubicle workers talking to their PCs would have been deafening.

Solutions

At first glance, it is easy to see why a proven turnaround artist like Frank could command a significant salary and stock options. In addition to walking into a company demoralized by corrupt management and having to fire dozens of employees, Frank had to set the tone for the organization by personal example. His focus was the bottom line, and he had to make certain that everyone knew what was expected of them. There was an unambiguous message that those who produced were welcome and would be rewarded for their contributions, and those who were not willing to work would be told to leave. It helped that Frank walked the walk and talked the talk. Although he was a little rough around the edges—a trait no doubt picked up from his decades of turning around companies in the heavy manufacturing industry—he was respected, and sometimes even feared, for his directness.

One by one, Frank addressed the technical, corporate, and market sticking points. For example, each division within the company was held responsible for its own return on the corporate investment. For this reason, the medical division, the major source of ongoing revenue, tried to distance itself from the PC hardware support business and encouraged customers to upgrade to the new

Windows-based solutions. It also aggressively bid on and won several government requests for proposals (RFPs) for the development of a variety of speech-enabled clinical systems.

As part of his makeover strategy, Frank brought in new vice presidents of sales, marketing, and R&D, and shifted the long-term focus of the company from medicine to the general consumer market. Money was allocated for an expanded marketing campaign, and the company issued new stock options to increase employee morale and, by extension, productivity.

To move the technical development along, Frank gave the core technology group extra stock as an incentive to spend nights and weekends working on developing a general-purpose, continuous-speech solution as soon as possible. Frank, working with his management team and advisory board, helped focus the core developer activities on solutions that would make the largest impact on sales. This strategy worked so well that the company was one of the first to market with a general-purpose, large-vocabulary, speech-recognition product.

While getting the company unstuck, Frank also courted prospective buyers while the new marketing group focused on the press. Finally, after demonstrating that the company was in the black by showing several consecutive quarters of profitability, a buyer was found. After a few weeks of intense negotiations, the company changed hands. Like major league ball players with a winning season behind them, the employees saw that the reward for success was, unfortunately, to be traded away. Frank walked away with a handsome portfolio of stock options, and the new owners—a European company with visions of dominating every form of speech technology on the planet—had a viable technology and nationally recognizable consumer product. What's more, only weeks after the agreement, the new management secured a multimillion-dollar investment from a major software company and recouped their investment in speech-recognition technology overnight. The new company, which worked like the Borg in *Star Trek*, acquired and assimilated any and all speech-related companies that it could identify, including the major competitor of their new speech-recognition division.

Although the European conglomerate of speech-related software and services was apparently financially successful, the difference between employee life and morale before and after the takeover became apparent almost immediately. Instead of the usual quick quarterly update over pizza in the company cafeteria, the takeover celebration was a catered event, with lobster and all the extras. Unfortunately, not everyone under the white tent erected on the lawn for the special event would be employed the following week. Instead of Frank's direct manner and open-door policy, the new management team wore an air of European aristocracy, with double-breasted suits and tailored shirts for normal office attire. Employees and consultants no longer had access to management, unless summoned. Corporate culture went from startup to Fortune 500 overnight, and employees were expected to fall in line or fall out. Many employees left the company at the point of acquisition, though the brain trust stayed.

As part of the acquisition, the company moved to a larger building, where management occupied offices with windows and expansive views, and employees shared a central cubicle farm. Instead of Frank's walk-in-closet office, the new CEO's office was large enough to hold a miniature golf course. As employee attrition increased because of dissatisfaction with the company culture, the company retaliated by increasing the stock options for those who remained, but coupled the "gift" with expectations of longer work hours. The new corporate culture became one of endurance; those who could endure the company long enough to cash in on stock options won the game. Camaraderie and pulling toward a common goal took on increasingly less meaning.

Bryan's company terminated its relationship with the new speech company as part of an exodus of employees from the company. Within the next 18 months, as the stock experienced a roller coaster ride of valuation, there was word of possible impropriety in the way profits were being reported. Ironically, in a repeat of what had happened only five years earlier, management was accused of false reporting of sales in order to artificially inflate the price of the stock.

By the end of 2000, upper-level management was behind bars, the company was in Chapter 11, and the stockholders were pressing a class action suit against management. Those employees who held stock in the company were left holding paper of unknown future value. The entire speech-recognition industry was left in turmoil, and tens of thousands of customers were left stranded without support—a major problem for the speech-recognition companies remaining in the marketplace.

Analysis

Today, the use of microcomputer-based speech-recognition software is still limited to a relatively small number of innovators,
despite a tenfold drop in price since continuous speech recognition
was first introduced a few years ago. With the exception of physically challenged workers, including those suffering from repetitive
stress injury, the keyboard is simply an easier, more efficient, and
more effective device for entering data. As illustrated in Figure 5.2,
most users of voice recognition eventually find the return on investment to be negative, in that the effort needed to use a pure speech-
recognition interface is not worth the hassle of learning, and the
end result is less effective and more time consuming than using a
keyboard and mouse alone. Because a combination of speech recognition and a keyboard-and-mouse interface seems to work best,
most speech-recognition products accommodate multimodal use.

Despite lack of progress on the desktop, speech-recognition
technology is making significant inroads in phone-based access
to data, including data on the Web. However, regardless of the
ultimate fate of the technology, the story of the speech-recognition
company illustrates several points about getting unstuck. The

Figure 5.2   Speech Recognition Behavior Change Model

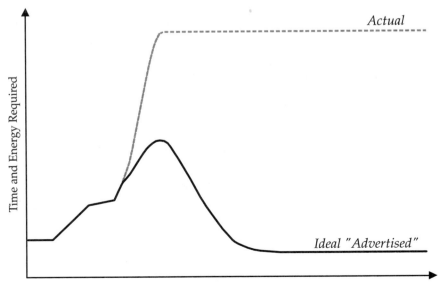

case illustrates how given the proper leadership, it is possible to get unstuck from a seemingly hopeless situation. Conversely, poor leadership is the quickest way to become stuck. In this regard, the personality of the CEO, the chemistry among top-level management and workers, and the culture of the working environment are critical factors in establishing and maintaining progress in the corporate, technological, and marketing components of business.

The case also illustrates how success requires the CEO and other decision makers to communicate a clear, unambiguous vision articulated in concrete terms and reflected in their every-day activities. Getting unstuck is first about managing and understanding customer and employee needs and desires; overcoming technical and market hurdles are secondary.

Although every situation is different, the issues addressed by these axioms are common to most businesses. Depending on the particular business arrangement, other situations might call for identifying a development partner or licensing intellectual property in exchange for operating capital. What does not work is simply throwing money at a problem, as many failed dotCom enterprises have illustrated. If given the choice, most employees would not trade increased working hours and a more stressful work environment for a lobster dinner and the promise of an unknown reward at some later date.

The story of Frank's company illustrates that, unlike fairy tales, companies do not go on to live happily ever after. The remarkably influential Apple II, like the Volkswagen Beetle, has come and gone, replaced by better technology. Similarly, amid what appeared to be great strides in profitability and increased consumer awareness, management of the international speech-recognition company apparently repeated the deeds of their predecessors. Because of insufficient consumer demand, the new management team falsified millions in sales in order to inflate stock prices for personal gain and to stay in business.

They also structured the company in a way that is legal in Europe but illegal in America, a way that allowed them to license technology to holding companies that they themselves started. The holding companies took the voice-recognition company's seed money to get started selling voice-recognition technology, and then the parent company reported the licensing of its technology to its holding companies as income or profits. As a result, the entire microcomputer-based speech-recognition market was thrown into turmoil—a major issue for turnaround CEOs to solve in each of the acquired companies.

Even if the management of the speech-recognition company had stayed on the straight and narrow, it would have faced the major sticking point related to the limitations of the technology. Perhaps it was this realization that the demand for the technology was in decline that pressured management to falsify sales figures.

Although the technologic hurdle from discrete to continuous speech was formidable and costly to overcome, the next technological hurdle is even more formidable. What remains is to create a system that not only recognizes sounds and matches these sounds with commands or words, but that provides some sense of understanding of the sounds. Current systems are little more than lookup tables of sounds, words, and word frequency. The next logical evolutionary step is to provide a degree of artificial intelligence (AI) in the translation of spoken English or other language into text. In theory, doing so should negate the need to correct the one word out of ten or twenty translated words that is mistyped by current systems. The telltale sign that the technology has reached the Product Point is when companies that make speech-recognition software will actually use it internally.

For now, however, the major uses of speech recognition are associated with cellular and wired phone systems. Phone-based speech recognition is commonly used to provide speech-activated navigation commands for telephone users attempting to navigate through speech mail systems. The "say or press one" option is part of most telephone banking and charge card support routines.

The other, more pervasive but less publicized application of speech recognition in the phone system is the monitoring system established in the 1990s by the FBI. The mainframe-based system scours the nation's phone lines, at a rate of thousands of lines per second, searching for specific words, such as "bomb," "assassination," "President," and "kill." When one of the trigger words is detected, the FBI flags the phone line for follow-up action.

STICKING AND THE CONTINUUM

Frank's makeover of the speech-recognition company illustrates many of the potential sticking points in developing and then bringing a product to market that are listed in Figure 5.1. There are unlimited opportunities to lose momentum, sacrifice profitability, and succumb to the temptation to deviate from the central goal while chasing distractions. The specific sticking points illustrated by the voice-recognition company include numerous instances of internal process failure. The established process of recording and verifying sales was fundamentally flawed in that it prevented detection by those employees outside of top management.

Without a failsafe mechanism in place, management, through its mistakes, was able to lead employees and stockholders over a virtual cliff. It is also clear that the company suffered from a communications failure at every level. Amid the turmoil, employees did not know what was happening with the company or what was expected of them to improve the situation. Similarly, the board of directors apparently had no indication of wrongdoing and did not question the figures on which they based their recommendations.

The case also highlights how once self-motivated employees can become suddenly demoralized and disenfranchised because of inept leadership. The original management group confused the mission of the company and minimized the rewards employees could expect for their efforts. Even though employees were helping to make a change in society by providing tools to physicians and hand-disabled users, not simply making money for stockholders, the defocused mission and lack of a broader market for the technology played predominant roles in the initial downturn for the organization. Additionally, after the fraud was uncovered, most of the otherwise idealistic employees lost focus and productivity.

Finally, the case illustrates how external factors, from the SEC to customer behavior, can have a profound influence on the trajectory of a company. Obviously, the legal proceedings paralyzed corporate management, at least temporarily leaving employees directionless and unproductive. Perhaps most important, and at the root of the matter, customers for the original general-purpose voice-recognition products never materialized because of product usability limitations.

In addition to those specific sticking points, each point and period within the Continuum tends to be associated with certain types of sticky situations more than others. The generic descriptions for these stages and periods in the Continuum are described here.

Inception

Getting stuck at the very beginning of the process, when the business plan is being fleshed out and presentations are being made to colleagues, relatives, and anyone else who might be a source of funding or expertise is akin to having writer's block. The process of formulating a defendable business plan that can hold up to the scrutiny of others usually highlights the advantages of a new technology as well as multiple, unanswered issues that may not have been obvious before.

Of course, it is possible to fall upon an idea and even a prototype through serendipity. Researchers looking for something else stumbled upon vulcanized rubber, 3M Post-It™ Notes, and Teflon. A chemist attempting to make a super-strong adhesive, for example, developed the Post-It Note. The semisticky glue, when spread on small sheets of paper, turned out to have far greater value in the marketplace than any super adhesive. Similarly, a graduate student who was looking for a new coolant to use in refrigerators accidentally discovered Teflon. Teflon, one of the top-secret materials used in many military projects in World War II, is still the basis for a multimillion-dollar industry that extends from nonstick cookware to valves and military arms.

Although serendipity is always welcome, having an idea or even a product in hand is not sufficient to bring it to market. Getting stuck at Inception may involve failure to define a competitive advantage for the proposed or discovered product. The time, money, or other resource requirements may be out of line with the potential value of the product. As was the case with Nicolas Tesla, the inventor of several everyday AC devices, many inventors have held multiple jobs in order to pay for their research into building a better mousetrap.

A major potential stumbling block at Inception is dependence on supporting technologies that are not available or accessible. In the case of the speech-recognition software, continuous speech recognition required moving from DOS to Windows, which in turn required a more powerful PC than most potential customers owned. Fortunately, faster, more powerful PCs were only a few months away.

Depending on the market, competition can either spur development or stop it cold. The fact that several companies were working on continuous speech recognition did not impede Frank's determination to be the first to achieve the goal. There was worldwide competition from the other speech-recognition companies, and it was only a matter of time before one of them succeeded at bringing continuous speech recognition to market. As it turned out, one of the competitors was first to market with a continuous speech-recognition product.

However, if Frank's company had not been a close second, the company would have been out of the commercial speech-recognition business. The sticking point of getting from discrete to continuous speech recognition was not over the validity of the idea but rather the timeline; if achieving continuous recognition was a decade—not months—away, then Frank might have decided to halt development and seek to license the technology instead. However, in many instances, the best decision is to simply go with it, especially since so much of the data may be pure speculation and unknowable.

An achievable set of goal-oriented deadlines is just one factor that the formulation of a good business plan should highlight. Since the lack of a clear, realistic business plan with a sustainable financial model and defined marketing strategy can halt progress, input from technologists, experts in the field, and experienced investors can be key to getting unstuck.

Intellectual property issues can slow or halt progress at Inception, especially if patents and other legal instruments have to be filed before real development can begin in earnest. In general, technical limitations are much more easily addressed than are political and social objections to technology. For example, there will be intellectual property, political, legal, and social impediments to human cloning in the United States for years to come.

Concept Development

This phase along the path of transforming an idea into a viable product is normally the time of idealization and acquiring the mental momentum that will be needed to invest the time and energy to create a prototype. The developers in Frank's company, for example, were faced with the task of creating a continuous speech-recognition engine—something that was theoretically possible, but not yet demonstrated in a stable, commercial product.

However, the period of concept development can also be a time of self-doubt, especially with the realization of exactly how much energy and time will be involved simply to prove that the approach will work. This self-doubt may be deepened if the capital requirements are out of line with what could support a business.

Often the main sticking point at this phase of development is the prospect of dealing with a formidable project in a David-versus-Goliath confrontation. Getting unstuck from starting on what may seem to be an impossible task involves basic project-management techniques, such as dividing the project into manageable steps, and delegating components of the steps whenever appropriate. Establishing reporting and work structures to formalize the responsibilities of specific employees can also reduce the sense of chaos associated with a significant project.

Technical Gateway

The Technical Gateway, where the goal is to create a demonstrable prototype, is one of the major milestones of technical product development. It is also the point in development where the probable performance of the planned product in the marketplace may become obvious. For the first time, it may be possible to realistically compare the product under development with competing solutions in the marketplace, and thereby obtain a much better idea of the size of the likely return on the investment. An unfavorable likely return on investment is an obvious sticking point. For example, once a continuous speech-recognition engine had been developed, the developers and marketing staff of the speech-recognition company were able to project the time and resources it would take to commercialize the prototype.

In addition to providing a reality check, getting stuck at the Technical Gateway may demonstrate the development team's inability to define the functional specification clearly and completely enough for an early prototype to be built. Getting unstuck may require partnering with a company or hiring individuals with a proven track record of prototype development in the field, or assigning someone in the development group to research additional development options.

Prototype Development

The period of prototype development is the time when uncertainty predominates, but this lack of certainty need not translate into stagnation. Sticking points include an inability to actually connect with the potential markets and customers identified in the business plan. Getting unstuck usually involves hiring at least part-time marketing and sales professionals. Many companies generate advertisements at this stage simply to gauge initial customer-response rates. A low response rate may suggest that the targeted market is inappropriate for the product, or perhaps that additional features may be required.

Although there usually is not a time when an infusion of additional capital would not be accepted, this period is typically capital intensive because significant funds may be required to create a demonstrable product. Regardless of the promise of the product, the groundwork for funding may be difficult to develop because of external limitations in the economy. Getting unstuck may involve hiring a research firm to resolve some of the uncertainty about the economy and locate additional sources of funding. For example, Frank's company applied for and received several government grants to spur development.

Product Point

Getting stuck at the Product Point is unfortunately very common. One of the major causes is the composition of the management team, especially the CEO. Often, the original inventor with a technology focus does not change from an idea person to a market-oriented manager. When the inventor will not hand over control to an entrepreneurial CEO, the company usually falters. A technology-minded CEO may not be able to recognize the commercial applications for his product, and may be more concerned with deploying the technology that he worked so long to create.

A CEO without a customer focus at this point in product development will not be able to create a story for potential investors. The work-around for the wrong management team is to somehow convince the technologically savvy but entrepreneurially naive CEO that assuming another position in the company, such as chief scientist, exposes the company to lower risk. If the management team fix involves lower-level employees, then they can simply be replaced with more effective employees. For example, one of Frank's first acts was to establish a new management team that understood the focus of the new company was to use speech recognition to realize a profit for shareholders.

Clarification

Once a demonstrable product has been created, the challenge is to refine the technology while keeping the customer's needs and wants in mind. However, it is not always possible to produce the rapid, incremental innovations required to better meet customer needs or reduce costs. Getting unstuck during the Clarification phase of product development may require strategic replacement of management so that the resulting body has more of a customer focus. For example, Frank replaced the vice president of R&D with a more market-minded manager, which seemed to be what was needed at the time to get the company moving.

Market Gateway

Getting stuck in the Market Gateway is possible, though frustrating. Insufficient market share, improper positioning to maintain growth, and lack of resources to maintain an R&D effort—while resources are being consumed by creating product updates—are all possible pitfalls at the Market Gateway. A technology with a very limited life span, such as a tax program designed for a specific year, obviously limits the shelf life of the program. Similarly, competing technologies on the horizon can also break the momentum. Microsoft is famous for stalling the competition in their tracks by preemptively announcing a "killer product" that competes with the company's newly developed product. For example, Microsoft's preannouncement of its Xbox video console cut into PlayStation II sales. Getting unstuck can entail exploring and developing new technologies in order to maintain or gain market share.

In the speech-recognition company, getting stuck with undeliverable product and hiding this fact from investors was the genesis of the problems of the mid-1990s and again in 2000, which resulted in the incarceration of the management teams involved. The pitfall was ultimately consumer rejection of the technology.

Stabilization

Impediments to progress during Stabilization, when the technology is maturing, are usually due to public resistance or some internal event that leaves the company in disarray. Although there is typically an emergence of significant competition and perhaps minor enhancements to the underlying technology, this time is characterized by a market focus. Many genetically modified foods failed at this point in the Continuum.

Alleviating the political, legal, or attitudinal limitations at this phase of development may be much more formidable than overcoming economic limitations. For example, obtaining permission from the EPA to introduce GMFs for human consumption may take years *and* very deep pockets.

Completion

Getting stuck at Completion is associated with uncertainty about what should be done with product on the shelves. If the product is not viable in the marketplace, then at issue is whether the technology should be modified or left alone. For example, although speech recognition promised to increase ease of use of the computer for the average consumer, in its current incarnation, the technology has only served to increase the complexity of operating a computer.

If the product is in a maturing market, then keeping the momentum up may involve applying the product to new markets. With the speech-recognition software fully developed, for example, Frank's company was able to repackage the software and add enhancements so that it could be used by clinicians. The challenge is often balancing the need to keep momentum up with marketing and sales while investing resources in R&D for future products.

GETTING CREATIVE

Getting stuck is not necessarily a bad thing. For a CEO tasked with creating a marketable perpetual motion machine, the sooner the development project is stuck, the sooner the developers can realize that aborting a hopeless project is the best decision. Even with less lofty product development and marketing goals, getting stuck can often point out that there may be a better way to achieve the desired results. Licensing a technology may be the quickest, most economical means of acquiring a particular technology, or of achieving a particular result. In Frank's case, his goal was to bring the company to profitability—not simply by meeting expectations but by defining new ones. From the perspective of the board of directors, how Frank reached that goal was irrelevant, as long as it was done legally.

There is no simple recipe for success based on identifying sticking points, but rather success depends on creativity, that is, thinking of new ways to solve old problems. The challenge of communications, for example, has plagued business since before the concept of business was formulated. Similarly, resolving the multitude of sticking points in the speech-recognition company called for creativity on Frank's part. Knowing that there will be challenges, and knowing that they can all be solved creatively, can help provide the CEO the means needed to deal with the never-ending barrage of challenges inherent in business.

SUMMARY

Getting stuck at various points in bringing an idea to market is inevitable. The challenge is getting unstuck in a timely, economically feasible, and socially and politically correct way. This is where the leadership and visionary qualities of a CEO come into play. Given a CEO with the proper leadership qualities, including the ability to articulate and communicate an unambiguous vision in clear, concrete terms, it is possible for a company to get unstuck from seemingly hopeless situations. In the end, leadership is about motivating people, whether they are employees or potential customers and investors.

As the case history of the speech-recognition company illustrated, getting stuck—and unstuck—often involves the raveling and unraveling of product technology, corporate processes, and the market. The case also illustrates how the most significant issues, and the most difficult to fix, are people-related, especially those charged with defining the direction of the company. The personality and leadership qualities of the CEO, the chemistry between top-level administration and front-line employees, and the culture of the working environment are critical to maintaining momentum along the Continuum.

6

Research and Development

Learn from the mistakes of others—you can never live long enough to make them all yourself.

John Luther

As described in Chapter 4, breathing life into an idea requires a visionary with the energy and resources to make the vision a demonstrable reality. The entrepreneur's motivations for innovation in corporate America and academia may include personal gratification, the thrill of competition, the prospect of fame and fortune, or the simple joy of problem solving. In the arena of human interactions and corporate politics, R&D gives the entrepreneur an outlet for creativity, rivalry, and ambition, constrained only by the economy and the potential consumer base. Regardless of setting, what differentiates entrepreneurs from dreamers is that they act on their visions. After instantiating his vision on a paper napkin or formal presentation to potential backers, the first action an entrepreneur takes who is intent on transforming his vision into a commercial product is to engage in meaningful, focused R&D.

The stereotypical view of R&D activity as the work of some driven inventor toiling tirelessly, closed up in a small work area for weeks and months on end is the stuff of movies. In reality, R&D is the work of *many* men and women, closed up in a work area for weeks and months on end. The lone inventor working away in his garage after her day job simply cannot compete with the resources

147

of the R&D machines backed by the government and industry. Whether it is at the leading business R&D centers, such as Xerox Parc, Lucent Technologies, and 3M, or the academic world of basement laboratories at MIT, Caltech, and the University of Chicago, the work is always challenging, often lengthy, and only rarely economically rewarding. Having a well-financed organization that has a large R&D budget does not automatically guarantee success, but what separates winners from losers is a market-focused R&D effort.

This chapter relates R&D to the Continuum, using the fiber optics communications industry as a practical example. It illustrates that while a successful R&D program by no means guarantees product viability in the marketplace, or even progression beyond the Product Point in the Continuum, it is an unavoidable prerequisite for success. Moreover, it illustrates to the manager the value of approaching the often long and arduous path to innovative discovery with understanding and patience.

As described in the following section, the 150-year process that led to the creation of the fiber infrastructure exemplifies the need for continued innovations in manufacturing, managerial leadership, and R&D efforts.

OPTICAL COMMUNICATIONS

To put modern optical communications into historical perspective, consider that light has served as a mode of communications for millennia. Accounts of the bronze shields used as signaling devices and, collectively focused on the sails of ships, powerful weapons capable of incinerating enemy ships, are described in the *Odyssey*. During World War II, allied ships maintained secure ship-to-ship communications while in formation by flashing narrow-beam lights that were virtually impossible to intercept. Although satellite-based global positioning service (GPS) technology now allows ships to locate their position on a map to within a few hundred meters, lighthouses still signal important landmarks for seagoing vessels.

The first serious R&D focused on the problem of sending and receiving voice over light was performed by Alexander Graham Bell. After Bell made his fortune with the telephone, he spent two years working with Charles Sumner Tainter, a former maker of optical instruments. They were trying to develop the

Photophone. On a good day, the device could transmit and receive sound using a beam of light as the communications medium. The key to the Photophone was selenium, a mineral that temporarily presents a decreased resistance to electrical current when it is exposed to light. Fluctuations in sound were converted into changing light intensity, which could be detected by a selenium-based receiver.

By 1880, Bell was able to demonstrate that he could send a message within a range of about 700 feet under ideal conditions. However, in practice, weather conditions, rain, and other activities limited the range to only a few feet at times. Although Tainter and Bell won prizes and accolades for their inventiveness, their Photophone technology would not serve as the basis for a business. The competition at that time, radio, had a much greater range and relative immunity from local weather conditions.

Although Bell invested two years of his life in the research and development of what he considered his best invention, it was a commercial failure. The Photophone was stuck before the Product Point in the Continuum. In the wake of Bell's invention, a few experimenters in Europe continued R&D efforts of using light as a communications medium, but none was a commercial success.

Today, point-to-point communication over a beam of light is generally restricted to hobbyists and games. For example, we have used a pair of homemade telescopes and a military surplus laser to communicate over a distance of about five miles; the record is nearly 50 miles, established in the dry, clear air of the Arizona desert. In the laser tag game, contestants wear belts that signal an alarm if they detect the laser light from a competitor's laser "gun." Because of the realism and lack of danger from projectiles, the U.S. Army routinely conducts battle games using laser tag equipment.

But the vicissitudes of the atmosphere (dust, rain, birds, and passersby) can disrupt free-space light communications. This realization led to the development of a closed communications path for light. A parallel situation exists between broadcast TV, which tends to be limited and subject to weather conditions, and cable TV, which provides interference-free access to hundreds of channels. The light-frequency equivalent to the coaxial cable used by virtually all cable TV companies to carry radio-frequency signals is glass fiber cable, known as fiber optics.

A Case Study: Fiber Optics

The telecommunications industry is by far the largest user of fiber optic technology. However, there are a variety of consumer products as well. For example, most high-end DVD players and better stereo tuners use optical cables to transfer digital data from one stereo component to the next because they allow a much higher bandwidth and signal-to-noise level than copper cables would, especially in an electrically noisy environment. Although fiber optics are commodity items today, they have been a long time in coming.

Fiber optics are key to broadband communications primarily because they support low-cost, high-bandwidth, secure communications over long distances. The cost savings, relative to standard copper wire cable, is partly because amplifiers or "repeaters" are only required every 50 miles, instead of every few thousand feet. Since the major cost for a network is the amplifier circuitry and associated power, fiber is especially attractive for use in submerged cables and high-rise office buildings.

Fiber optic cable systems are also durable, corrosion resistant, lightweight, and easy to install. For critical communications in electrically harsh environments, fiber's relative imperviousness to electromagnetic radiation from lightning or the electromagnetic pulse (EMP) associated with a nuclear detonation has obvious military applications. Another advantage of a fiber-based communications system is that it is easily upgraded; transmitter and receiver components can be swapped out as newer, more compact, and more efficient units become available. This is important because the bandwidth or information carrying capacity of fiber is virtually unlimited; the restrictions are due to the bandwidth of the electronics used at either end of the fiber.

Optical fiber is attractive when privacy is concerned. It is much more difficult to tap than a typical copper cable, and each splice or tap has a known and measurable loss. Wire, in contrast, works like an antenna for picking up and radiating signals. Because glass is an insulator, the EMP produced by an atomic blast is not picked up by fiber. For this reason, fighter planes and bombers make extensive use of fiber optic connections between electronic circuitry instead of traditional copper wire cables.

The U.S. military deploys fiber optics for secure, point-to-point communications where sensitive receivers would pick up radio frequency communications. On battle ships, fiber optics can carry video from surveillance cameras, missiles, and torpedo launchers and other signals that would otherwise be compromised by interference from onboard, high-power radar systems. For the same reason, fiber is also useful in hospitals and manufacturing plants where X-ray or welding machines would wreak havoc on conventional copper-wire-based connectivity.

Fiber optic cable is also lighter than copper wire, especially on longer runs between circuit boards, and connections can be made with lightweight plastic couplings instead of heavier solder or screw terminals.

Some Science

In order to appreciate the challenges addressed through fiber optic R&D efforts, it helps to understand what constitutes a fiber optic cable and how it can be used in modern communications systems. At the most basic level, a fiber optic cable is a thin strand of extremely pure glass designed to convey light signals from a transmitter to a receiver. As illustrated in Figure 6.1, an electrical signal—the transmitter, for example—converts data from a Web server to pulses of light, and the receiver performs the reverse operation. For fiber lengths of over about 50 miles, an optical amplifier may be required to counteract the signal losses in the fiber.

Although there is nothing innately digital about optical fiber, most communications systems utilize digital signal, using solid-state light emitting diodes (LEDs) and, more often, Laser diodes for

Figure 6.1   Fiber Optic Communications System

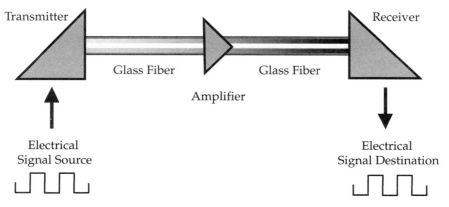

light sources and phototransistors for light detection. As in plumbing, there are fittings for splicing, splitting, and connecting lengths of fiber. Fiber is durable in part because it is very thin and flexible, and in part because the protective jacket—made of polyvinyl chloride (PVC): Kevlar, Teflon, or polyethylene—allows fiber to be used in hostile environments.

Fiber optics work on the principle of *total internal reflection*: light traveling down a length of fiber is refracted or bent back toward the center of a specially constructed fiber. The reflection occurs because the refractive index of the glass decreases toward the periphery of the fiber cladding (see Figure 6.2). The effect of the refractive index gradient is to refract or bend the light, just as a prism does in a set of binoculars. If the glass cladding were of uniform refractive index, light would not be reflected by the cladding but would simply pass through at every bend and be absorbed by the protective jacket.

R&D History

The evolution of fiber optic R&D, shown in Figure 6.3, was by no means a simple discovery followed immediately by a production line. In contrast, the process, which is indicative of most new technologies, spanned 150 years, with many false starts along the way.

The technological basis for the modern fiber optic communication systems from Sprint, MCI, and AT&T that span the United

Figure 6.2   Fiber Optic Construction

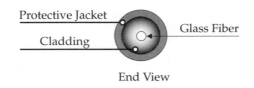

End View

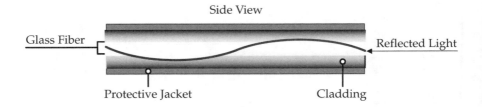

Figure 6.3   Evolution of Fiber Optic R&D

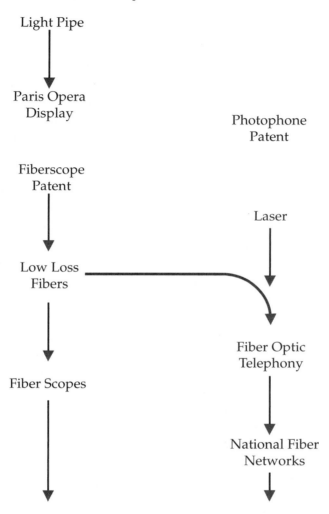

States dates back to at least 1841, when Daniel Colladon, a Swiss physicist, showed how water could be used to "pipe" sunlight along the path of a horizontal jet of water. The effect remained a parlor room trick until 1853 when Colladon used it with electric lighting and color filters for a display for the Paris Opera. More practical applications for the light pipe trickled in over the next three decades; a few patents were granted for medical devices such as microscopes that relied on bent glass rods to pipe light. The activity in the 19th century surrounding the creative manipulation of light culminated with Bell's introduction of the Photophone in 1880.

However, as discussed earlier, despite—or perhaps because of—his enthusiasm for the technology, it was a commercial disaster.

After the failure of the Photophone, the field of optical communications was quiescent for several decades, mainly because of the many breakthroughs in wireless radio frequency work. The status of optical communications changed when, in 1926, Clarence Hansell, an engineer who worked for RCA, and Heinrich Lamm, a German medical student, independently developed fiber optic applications. However, their approaches and motivations were very different. Hansell, the quintessential inventor, proposed a variety of applications for fiber optics, ranging from medical fiberscopes to periscopes and fax machines. After refining some of his ideas, Hansell turned the discovery over to the patent attorneys within RCA and went off to develop several hundred patents in other areas, including long-distance radio, never to return to optics. To Hansell, inventing on paper was reward enough for his work.

Lamm, the medical student at the University of Munich, was more interested in actually seeing the practical applications of fiber optic technology in medicine. After developing a prototype fiberscope he applied for a patent, which is when he learned of Hansell's work. Unable to secure a patent because of Hansell's pending patent application, Lamm went on to recoup some of his investment by publishing papers on the technology. Because of the Great Depression, the impending war in Europe, and Nazi sentiment against Jews, Lamm was forced to flee to America where he practiced medicine, putting an end to his research with fiber optics.

In 1951, after a hiatus of 25 years and on the heels of World War II, fiber optic imaging was rediscovered. As before, multiple investigators were involved, each with a very different motivation and perspective. Holger Hansen, a Danish inventor working at home, focused on developing a fiber cladding that would create the total internal reflection necessary to build a flexible gastroscope—a fiberscope used to view the inside of the stomach. Hansen was partially successful, and created a workable gastroscope using a coating of oil and margarine as a cladding. However, he could not obtain a patent because a patent search by the Danish Patent Office revealed that Hansell had a claim on the technology. Unable to stop others from copying his invention, Hansen moved on to other projects with more potential for profit.

Another experimenter, Abraham van Heel, a Dutch professor of optics, tried to build a new type of submarine periscope using glass fibers with a mirror-like metal coating. However, he discovered that the metal-coated fiber absorbed too much light. Van Heel consulted the director of the Institute of Optics in New York, Brian O'Brien, who suggested the idea of a transparent cladding that would work by refraction, the bending of light. Van Heel experimented with waxes and plastic coatings, but did not find a workable solution. A third experimenter, Harold Hopkins, an optics specialist at the Imperial College of Science and Technology in London, tried to develop a gastroscope using simple, unclad glass fibers, but he was not successful.

In 1953 word of Hopkins's failed attempts at creating a fiberscope reached the highly competitive van Heel, who immediately published a report in an academic journal on the concept of refractive cladding. With the academic community now informed about the challenge of fiber optic imaging, it was not long before several R&D efforts sprang up in the United States and abroad. One of these efforts involved a physics professor at the University of Michigan and his sophomore physics student Larry Curtiss. In 1956, Curtiss developed the idea of a glass cladding with a lower refractive index than the core, but a faculty committee told him that it would not work. Undaunted, he waited until the faculty went away for a conference and then made a cladding using two rods of different glass, one inside the other, melted together and drawn into thin fibers.

The glass cladding was a success, and Curtiss, with the help of his professor, Dr. Wilbur Peters, and Dr. Basil Herschowitz, a physician, quickly made a yard-long gastroscope less than a half-inch thick with 40,000 fibers. However, Herschowitz's supervisor confiscated the instrument because he wanted to be the first to use it. Undaunted, Curtiss built a second fiberscope, which Herschowitz demonstrated to physicians attending the American Gastroscopic Society Conference. The two-year project, run on a shoestring budget, resulted in patents for Herschowitz, Peters, and Curtiss, who licensed the technology to American Cytoscope Makers, who hired Curtiss—still an undergraduate—as a consultant. As a result of Curtiss's work, fiberscope technology went on to evolve into specialized instruments used in a variety of surgical procedures, as well as devices used to examine the insides of engines and even search through rubble to look for trapped earthquake victims.

The 1950s was also the time when radio and television were rapidly expanding. As is true of the cellular industry today, communications companies were constantly pressed to find unused frequencies. In 1960, with the invention of the laser, engineers briefly turned to light as a possible substitute for terrestrial microwave hops of 50 miles or less. Experiments at Bell Laboratories quickly concluded that the same atmospheric limitations that crippled the Photophone 80 years earlier rendered modern laser communications through the air useless as well. Since Curtiss's fibers lost 20% of light every yard, they would not do for long-range communications. In 1965, researchers at Bell Laboratories tried a variety of approaches, from optical waveguides to a series of open-air lenses to keep the laser light focused in a thin beam, but to no avail.

In 1966, Charles Kao, an engineer at the Standard Telecomm Labs in England, proposed that low-loss glass fibers could carry laser signals for communications, and he set out to develop the fiber. Kao turned out to be an evangelist for the concept of optical fiber communications, and sold his vision to engineers in the United States, Asia, and Europe. Interestingly, the infatuation of the general public with light and lasers was evident in laser light shows at rock concerts and even in the comics of the era, which emphasized laser death rays. The soft science magazines, such as *Popular Science*, foretold military laser weapons that would one day be used routinely in combat. In realty, high-powered lasers were being developed by the United States and Russia to disable satellites and temporarily blind enemy pilots.

Light-based toys were popular during that period as well. For example, Hasbro's Lite Brite toy, introduced in 1967, consisted of a grid of holes covering the front of a small box that contained a light bulb. Using plastic pegs of different colors, children created their own pictures or followed the color-by-letter patterns. When the work was done, the bulb was switched on and, through internal reflection of light in the plastic pieces, the artwork came to luminescent life.

The real turning point for fiber optics as a communications medium—the Technical Gateway in the Continuum—came in 1970, when Robert Maurer, Donald Keck, and Peter Shultz from Corning perfected a patented method of making ultrapure, low-loss glass by vaporizing chemicals instead of melting raw silica. Bell Laboratories (the research arm of AT&T) responded immediately by pouring money into fiber optics and the associated electronics—which is where Bell Labs had the upper hand. By 1977, fiber optic telephone systems from AT&T and GE were in commercial operation.

In only seven short years, the progression of fiber optic technology along the Continuum progressed from the Technical Gateway to the Market Gateway. In addition, the rate of progress along the Continuum continued to accelerate for a variety of technical and political reasons. In the wake of the AT&T breakup—a major factor in getting the industry unstuck—MCI laid the fiber backbone of its national long-distance service in 1983. Within five years, AT&T installed the first transatlantic fiber optic cable. Before the start of the new millennium, a single optical fiber and the associated electronics were capable of supporting 100 simultaneous 10-GB signals, equivalent to over 100 TV-quality video signals.

Today, despite what most view as a short-term sticking point because of the economy, the field of fiber optics communications is still growing. This growth is in part because of the hundreds of standards—industrial, military, Bellcore, and International Telecommunications Union (ITU)—that allow worldwide interoperability of fiber optics. These standards range from symbols that may be used to designate fiber optic and laser components, to salt-spray tests for fiber optic components and the construction of optical fiber joints. In addition, there are dozens of societies and trade magazines that focus on the fabrication and use of fiber optic cables and related electronics.

As noted in Chapter 2, Corning is pushing the envelope again by investing in hollow glass fibers. According to Corning, the new fiber has the potential to cut the number of amplifiers needed in long runs in half, totally obviating the need for amplifiers in many installations, which will transform the economics of fiber communications.

ANALYSIS

To the uninitiated, the start-stop course of fiber optics R&D along the Continuum may seem overly circuitous and complex. In reality, it is typical of the development of most technologies in use today, in that the development of inventions and accidental discoveries has to be put on hold until commercial infrastructures and consumer needs can be established. For example, digital cellular phones, although popular in Japan and Europe, took several years to catch on in the United States, in part because coverage was spotty. Similarly, smart cards, which are charge cards with built-in memory chips, are a technology in search of a need in the United States, despite two decades of widespread acceptance by consumers in Europe. This demonstrates that technology is not the only significant issue in making a product launch successful and that the success of a product in one country does not guarantee success in international markets.

General Principles

Even though every R&D project is unique, some general principles can be gleaned from the evolution of R&D in the field of fiber optics communications:

- R&D is a complex, risky business.
- R&D projects can get stuck because of technology, money, politics, or personal issues.
- Patents can harm or help invention and innovation.
- Individuals, not companies, create and innovate.
- Personalities are as important as the process.
- Need drives innovation; creativity drives invention.
- While R&D is necessarily concerned with transforming thought into reality, the trajectory must include practical applications.
- Multiple evolutionary dead ends are common.
- Societal, economic, political, and personal forces affect every aspect of R&D.
- Political infighting can be as detrimental to success as an external competitor.
- Money and a reputation for great execution help, but they do not guarantee success.
- Every invention and innovation builds upon the work of others.
- Identifying the best application for initial product development is not always easy.
- R&D should start with research into what has been done in the past.

R&D is a complex, risky business.   There are no guarantees of success, and it is always a judgment call whether to walk away from a situation or to persevere. Even the IRS treats expenses for corporate

R&D activities differently from ordinary business expenses. In addition, "innovation" is classified as R&D in the corporate arena for both management and tax credit purposes.

In terms of taking risk, Hansell was an exception. Working for RCA, a large corporation, Hansell bore virtually no risk in advancing the original patent for fiber optics, since he was paid regardless of the outcome. In addition, he had other challenges that he wanted to address. Bell, in contrast, had his reputation on the line, and gambled much of the proceeds from his invention of the telephone and two years of his life in a technological and commercial dead end. Aside from winning a modicum of notoriety and an award or two demonstrating the technology, the Photophone was a failure.

Similarly, Lucent Technologies, created in 1996 from Bell Laboratories and AT&T and one of the largest R&D companies in the United States, demonstrated that having innovative ideas was not enough to win in a modern economy. Even though the company's endowment included operations in fiber optic, wired, and wireless communications equipment, less than five years after its inception, Lucent laid off tens of thousands of employees because it could not transform the results of its R&D efforts into revenue.

R&D projects can get stuck because of technology, money, politics, or personal issues. As shown in Figure 6.4, the Photophone was stuck in the Technical Gateway because Bell could not get past a prototype that sometimes worked and sometimes did not, depending on the atmosphere. Lamm could not even make it to the Technical Gateway because of lack of capital. Like many inventors, Lamm was captivated by the technology, but did not

Figure 6.4   Fiber Optic R&D and the Continuum

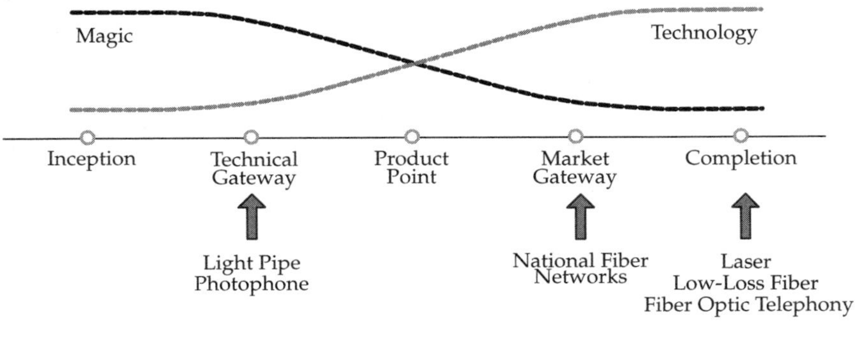

have a view of the Continuum and all of the associated resources required to bring a commercially viable fiberscope to market.

Hansen was stuck at the Product Point in the Continuum because he was not able to secure intellectual property rights for his invention. Like Lamm, he focused on the technology, but did not grasp the legal, economic, and political factors involved in bringing a technology to market. Hansen and Lamm illustrate how different personality types, with different areas of interest and focus, are required for different stages of product development.

Patents can harm or help invention and innovation. Hansell's patent of fiber optics apparently did very little for RCA other than increasing its worth through an enhanced patent portfolio. However, it did serve to stop Lamm from commercializing the fiberscope. Corning invested millions of dollars in optical fiber research, because its leaders knew that it could recoup the expenses by licensing its patented technology.

Individuals, not companies, create and innovate. Hansell, not RCA, was responsible for creating fiber optics. Similarly, Curtiss, not the University of Michigan, was responsible for developing a workable fiber cladding. RCA and the University of Michigan provided the environment and (at least in Hansell's case) the legal resources needed to protect their intellectual property. Hansell's unabated freedom from risk gave him the canvas he needed to create over 300 patents for RCA. Lamm, left to his own resources, made one attempt at commercializing his idea and then went on to other things.

Personalities are as important as the process. Bell's characteristic optimism and tenacity paid off with the invention of the telephone but were liabilities when he tried to develop the Photophone. In retrospect, Bell would have been better off by cutting his losses. Of course, Bell had to consider what the effect of giving up might have had on his career and reputation. Similarly, Charles Kao, the engineer at the Standard Telecomm Labs, was key to enjoining fellow scientists behind the vision of a world in which glass fiber carried the bulk of information.

Need drives innovation; creativity drives invention.   Curtiss's innovation of using two glass rods of different density, one inside the other, was driven by a specific need. Colladon's creative spirit drove his invention of the light pipe, which had no practical value outside of entertaining the wealthy.

Bell's work on the Photophone was apparently driven by his need to create, not by the marketplace. There was no pent-up demand for light-based communications that he was addressing. As a result, the Photophone was stuck at the Technical Gateway in the Continuum. A workable prototype of the Photophone could be used to communicate under just the right conditions, but there was still too much magic involved for there to be a real product. In contrast, later work performed by others at Standard Telecomm and Bell Labs was driven by need for high-bandwidth connectivity.

While R&D is necessarily concerned with transforming thought into reality, the trajectory must include practical applications.   As illustrated by the Continuum model, the evolution of an idea to a prototype and then to a product must include an increasing awareness of the customer. However, a simple awareness is not enough. Inventors may mistakenly view customers as a way to showcase their technology without recognizing the long-term maintenance and support needs.

Multiple evolutionary dead ends are common.   No one who gives their all succeeds at everything they attempt. The winners are not necessarily the ones who refuse to give up, but those who are willing to get into the game the next time. Bell is revered partially because of his ability or drive to keep inventing, despite some failures along the way.

Societal, economic, political, and personal forces affect every aspect of R&D.   In the evolution of fiber optics, a different mix of forces at any point may have significantly impacted the overall result. If Lamm had not had to flee the Nazis, for example, the fiberscope may have been developed decades before Curtiss finally perfected it.

Political infighting can be as detrimental to success as an external competitor.   Horowitz's supervisor, who confiscated the first fiberoptic scope, could have altered the course of fiberoptics in medicine had it not been for Curtiss's willingness to create a second scope in record time.

Money and a reputation for great execution help, but they do not guarantee success.   Bell's reputation and financial prowess that resulted from his invention of the telephone put him in excellent standing for attracting investors and other resources. However, the technology was not sufficiently developed to even approach the Product Point.

Similarly, Bell Labs invested in optical waveguide technology, which failed. Even though the approach showed promise, Corning's success with optical fiber caused Bell Labs to do an about-face with its R&D and pour resources into fiber optics. The demand for bandwidth in the radio frequency spectrum drove money into the expanding optical communications space, while the new laser made longer digital communications possible.

Every invention and innovation builds upon the work of others.   Curtiss's work laid the foundation for low-loss fiber communications, but Curtiss could not have made his innovations without the physics that he learned at the University of Michigan. Similarly, Bell relied on the expertise of his partner and optical expert, Tainter, in developing the ill-fated Photophone.

Identifying the best application for initial product development is not always easy.   Medical applications of the fiberscope seemed like the most lucrative use of fiber optics, but physicians are an extremely conservative group. It took decades for the fiberscope to be accepted as a component of medical practice, much like the case of the stethoscope, as described in Chapter 5. The deepest pockets for leading-edge technology development tend to be the military, as van Heel discovered.

R&D should start with research into what has been done in the past.   As Hansen's dilemma illustrates, the research component of R&D should be performed first. Companies savvy in intellectual property matters file for broad patent rights before investing significant capital in development. If a patent cannot be secured, then developing a product that is covered by an outside patent may not be attractive unless the company holding the patent is amenable to licensing its technology for a reasonable fee.

Implications

Given the general principles of R&D as just described, what are the implications for new ventures? Specifically, what can be done to increase the odds of success in the first few stages of the Continuum? Here are some suggestions to help ensure the success of the first stages:

- Set reasonable expectations.
- Identify potential sticking points—before starting R&D.
- Take care of your company's core R&D brain trust.
- Stay attuned to late-breaking trends and announcements in your industry.
- Stay focused on the goal, but be flexible in the approach.

Set reasonable expectations.   That is, expect some initiatives to fail. As a corollary, learn to recognize the early signs of failure and know when to walk away. Every industry has different failure rates, and these rates should be reflected in your expectations of success and failure. In the software industry, for example, only about a third of initiatives finish on time and within specifications. If a CEO demands 100 percent success on all in-house software development initiatives, then a majority of the company's time and resources will be sunk into projects destined to fail.

Identify potential sticking points—before starting R&D.   For example, the Great Global Grid (GGG) project where anyone can plug into the grid and access processing power and software resources on demand is projected by some as the follow up to the information Web. The initiative seems to have a good chance at making it, given backers like IBM, the DoD, DoE, NASA, and the academic community. However, the issue is not whether it is a good idea—sharing computer resources over a network has been done in academia for years—but whether the approach will be profitable as a business.

Early work with the GGG seems promising. There are standards organizations and nationwide projects in the United Kingdom and elsewhere. However, there are potential sticking points of security, eventual cost, and availability of high-bandwidth connectivity. As noted, despite a national network of high-speed fiber, getting it to the desktop remains a challenge because of the focus of the telecom companies on short-term profitability. In addition, sharing computing power sounds fine until someone's computer slows to a crawl. There are also issues of privacy and, to a lesser extent, security.

For example, when using a small version of the proposed GGG on Sun Microsystems hardware in the mid-1980s, Bryan found it disconcerting that a coworker at the other end of the building could monitor his machine's CPU load. He had a sense of "big brother" watching and also felt somewhat cheated when the program that he was working with slowed in response to the workstation load. The point is that organizations wrestling with the technologic aspects of GGG should consider customer experience as a potential sticking point early on.

Similarly, the pay-as-you-go policy proposed for the GGG, patterned after the power grid and long-distance telephone service, may turn some customers away. The international Internet service provider AOL, for example, discovered early on that more customers were willing to pay a flat monthly fee for unlimited access than for a per-minute charge.

Take care of your company's core R&D brain trust. Creativity and innovation cannot be measured by the amount of time spent sitting at a desk or in meetings. Like other knowledge workers, the company's core R&D group is really being paid for their attention, not their time. Cheating the R&D department of benefits, for example, is likely to result in a false economy of savings.

The in-house juice bars established for the original Apple Macintosh development team, like the pool tables and late-night pizza for programmers and company-issued Razor™ scooters at startups throughout Silicon Valley, help to create an environment that fostered attentiveness to a company's goals. Clarence Hansell was obviously happy with the working conditions at RCA—happy enough to devote his attention to fiber optics and over 300 other patents for the company.

Even today, during what appears to be the nadir of the technology boom, innovative companies do whatever they can to keep their innovators happy. One of Bryan's clients, Kurzweil Technologies, Inc., a high-tech incubator in the Boston area, stocks the company larder with fresh organic fruit, refreshments, and other tokens of gratitude on a daily basis. It also rewards employees with stock options every quarter.

Stay attuned to late-breaking trends and announcements in your industry. Companies move at different rates along the Continuum, depending on available resources, the technology involved and internal and external motivation to produce. However, breakthroughs tend to be clustered in short time frames because innovators share the perception of a need or economic opportunity.

The cyclical advances in fiber optic R&D have been repeated in numerous industries. For example, with the race to create continuous voice recognition, the major players all reached the goal within a few months of each other. In part, this was due to the obvious motivation to fill a perceived market need as well as the knowledge that the competition was working to be first with the breakthrough.

Stay focused on the goal, but be flexible in the approach. Scientists at Bell Labs did not lose the goal of using light for broadband communications, but they were quick to change tactics when Corning announced its achievements with fiber optics. In a fast-paced field where new discoveries are made daily, a CEO has to be able to recognize opportunities and change her approach without losing forward momentum.

SUMMARY

R&D is challenging, lengthy, and only rarely results in a commercially viable product. In many regards, R&D is about taking the mistakes of others and formulating a strategy that has better odds of success. Taken in the context of the Continuum, transforming an idea into a demonstrable prototype necessarily focuses on the underlying technologies.

As illustrated in this chapter, the R&D behind the communications infrastructure was at least a 150-year affair that included several dead ends by prominent inventors. This infrastructure is responsible for many of the gains attributed to modern technology—from the Web to cable TV. Alexander Graham Bell's Photophone demonstrates how failure to move an idea far enough along in the Continuum before attempting to bring it to market can be fraught with problems. Bell's experience also illustrates how R&D is largely a numbers game, and that it is not those who win one and walk away, but those who play regardless of occasional failures who come out ahead in the long run.

The history of fiber optic R&D in the United States and abroad also illustrates how it is people's—not companies'—personal biases, drive, and opinions that drive invention and innovation. The take-home implication for businesses involved in R&D is that virtually every innovation is a rediscovery to some degree, which builds upon knowledge accumulated by others. Unfortunately, many innovators, certain that they have discovered something new, neglect to research what has been done in the past. They need to stay informed through every available information resource.

The R&D history of optical fiber also illustrates that R&D is an iterative process laden with multiple failures. Making it across the Continuum requires being open to alternative approaches and identifying and addressing potential sticking points before starting an R&D effort, whether political, economic, personal, or governmental in nature. Finally, a concerted R&D effort can result in either evolutionary or revolutionary improvements in technology and products. However, successful revolutionary improvements, like viable genetic mutations in biological systems, are extremely rare.

7

Marketing

People may or may not say what they mean . . . but they always say something designed to get what they want.

David Mamet

Bryan's first practical exposure to marketing, including the concepts of product, price, promotion, and place, the laws of supply and demand, the herd mentality, and business ethics was as a stock clerk working one summer for a large dry goods and grocery chain. He was amazed at the accuracy with which the chain's central office could predict the demand for virtually every product in the store. Every Monday morning, the store manager, a wiry man with a constant glower, received a printout from the central office that detailed the number of pallets of products that would be in the day's shipment, where each product was to be placed on the shelves, and expected sales figures, based on national and local promotions. Sure enough, by the end of the week, the aisles were filled with only enough products to make the store seem stocked; rarely was there a pallet of anything left in the warehouse. He learned that soap on the middle shelves outsold the soap on the bottom shelves by two to one, and that items in floor displays outsold competing products on the shelves by three to one, and that these phenomena were highly resistant to fluctuations in sales based on differences in price and brand.

The store manager, a shrewd marketer, entrepreneur, and opportunist, often overrode the suggestions from the central office to reflect local conditions. For example, during that summer, a storm ravaged one of the South American sugar cane farms, and there was talk on the national news about impending shortages of sugar. Even though he was living in Louisiana at the time, and there were cane fields within a few miles of the store, the store manager knew an opportunity when he saw one.

The morning after the newscast, he doubled the price of all of the sugar in stock and put up a sign that limited customers to two 5-pound bags each. As he no doubt expected, the supply of sugar, which would have normally lasted the week, sold out before noon. The sales of other items in the store increased as well, given all of the traffic in the sugar aisle. Not only did customers line up for the length of the aisle to buy two 5-pound bags of sugar, but many brought a friend or a spouse to pick up an additional 10 pounds of sugar. Those who were unable to buy sugar the day after the newscast were more than willing to pay the inflated price the manager set for the next week's shipment of sugar as well. Obviously, no one needed a larder with an extra 10 or 20 pounds of sugar, but fear, greed, and desire are not necessarily logical.

Since the store was located in the hurricane belt, the manager had apparently learned the scarcity mentality from watching customer reaction to the half-dozen storms that passed through every year. At the first mention of a storm, customers eagerly lined up to buy enough provisions for a month, even though a storm might be expected to last only one or two days. There was no need for the special sales designed to lure customers into the store because they flooded in. The manager also discontinued specials. The worst storms, which sometimes resulted in power outages and some flooding, rarely stopped his store from opening the next day. He had backup power generators installed to maintain the banks of flo-rescent lighting and air conditioning that marked the store as a modern addition to the community of 10,000.

A half-dozen years later, as a college student, Bryan continued his exploration of customer behavior by investigating the "Pepsi Chal-lenge," a then-popular marketing campaign in which Pepsi claimed that Coke drinkers actually preferred the taste of Pepsi over Coke. The challenge was supposedly a blind taste test, with subjects given unmarked paper cups containing either Coke or Pepsi. However, when Bryan took the challenge at a booth on campus, he noticed that the area under each cup was labeled with some letter of the alphabet, say B for Pepsi and G for Coke. The booth operator did not bring the labeling to Bryan's attention; it was just there, beside each cup.

Since he had never liked soft drinks and did not care for either Coke or Pepsi, Bryan could not tell any difference in the two drinks. However, he was curious about the lettering. A little research in the library turned up tables of letter pair preferences in experimental psychology literature. It turns out that there are letter and word preferences for a variety of languages. In English, A is more popular than F, and B is more popular than X, for example.

In exchange for a pair of concert tickets, the manager of the university's main dining hall gave Bryan permission to label the two-cup dispensers in the hall and record the results over a one-week period. Controlling for variables such as sex and handedness with several thousand unknowing subjects, he created tables of preferences for cups dispensed from two stainless steel tubes, identical except for a one-inch-high block letter on a white background just above the lip of each dispenser.

As the letter pairing preference charts predicted, students and faculty pulled more cups from the cylinders marked with the more popular letter of the letter pairing. Not surprisingly, given the academic setting, the strongest difference was with the A versus F pairing, with an almost 10 to 1 preference for A cups over F cups. Some of the subjects went so far as to put the F cup back into the dispenser once they noticed the label. As part of his study, Bryan wrote Pepsi and asked about the letter pairings and if their labels were intentional or by chance. Someone from Pepsi's marketing department responded, admitting that they were aware of the letter preferences. So much for truth in advertising.

Marketing, which is concerned with creating and manipulating product demand, is a combination of art and science. In the Continuum, marketing becomes critical once a demonstrable product becomes available (at the Product Point), when a major component of magic is still associated with the product. The shift in focus to marketing at the Product Point is typically more pronounced in a new company bringing its first product to market. Before the product exists, there normally is not enough money to invest in hiring a marketing professional. After all, there may not be a real need for several months—assuming a product is actually created.

In an established company with an existing marketing division, marketing should be busy at Inception, when ideas are crystallized and formally presented to decision makers inside the company. Marketing works with the inventors and innovators to create a requirements specification that codifies the customer needs and wants that the product should address. Although marketing is usually instrumental in defining the target customer population, how the needs and wants are addressed is up to R&D and management.

As Bryan's experience with the grocery store and the Pepsi Challenge demonstrated, marketing is about manipulating a potential customer's perceptions, often at a subconscious level. Although there are obvious ethical issues involved, the fact is that customers act in predictable ways in particular situations, even if the situations exist primarily in the customer's mind. This traditional view of marketing is supported by the behavioral school of psychology, in which human behavior is explained in terms of responses that can be altered or conditioned through experience.

This chapter explores the practical application of viewing marketing and sales as a natural component of the Continuum. In particular, it explores the current challenges facing firms in the wireless space, and the role of marketing in driving product adoption.

WIRELESS WORLD

The wireless market is poised to be the fastest growing phenomenon in the United States, Europe, and Asia since the Web. The potential of mCommerce (mobile commerce), which comprises the use of wireless technologies to access content on the Web and the use of the Internet for voice and data communications, looks especially bright because much of the consumer base is already primed for a wireless Web experience.

It is important to note that in the context of this discussion, wireless refers to a connection without wires among a PDA, cell phone, or laptop and a network of devices. The network could consist of a few PCs, printers, and storage devices; the public telephone network; or the Internet. A cordless device, in contrast, is usually a point-to-point, device-to-device connection without wires. A cordless phone, for example, communicates with its base station; a wireless (cellular) phone can connect to one of thousands of cells, depending on its relative location to each of the cells. Unfortunately, the distinction between cordless and wireless blurs with new wireless technologies, such as Bluetooth, which provide short-range (about 30 feet maximum range) connectivity between a laptop or PDA and printers or other peripherals.

Regardless of the particular wireless technology that is used, applications of mCommerce range from just-in-time or just-in-place information, eMenus, eTickets, eCoupons, and personal simulations, to event previews, instant ordering, eLearning, online auctioning, personal productivity, remote services, financial customer support, and entertainment. For example, people looking for the nearest ATM or car rental agency could initiate a query on their Web-enabled PDAs or cell phones and receive a map or text description of the directions. Similarly, they could review the menu of nearby restaurants, purchase tickets to a movie or concert, or order takeout from a nearby pizza parlor—virtually anything possible from a desktop connection to the Web—all from their cell phones, wireless PDAs, or laptops equipped with wireless modems.

Wireless Web access even has a place for those without a hectic, always-on lifestyle. For example, the ability to email friends and family a digital photo taken seconds earlier from the poolside appeals to many vacationers. Many of these services are already in use in Europe and Asia, and others are under development.

However, the mCommerce market is extremely volatile, with companies coming and going, collaborating, and consolidating. The pace of global and domestic telecom acquisitions and mergers is reminiscent of the competition for dotCom turf in the late 1990s. Furthermore, although the wireless Web is a global phenomenon, Europe and Asia are clearly leading the way.

In the United States, confusion, too many players, and prejudice against products in the technology sector characterizes the wireless space, and there are numerous technical, legal, social, and economic barriers to adoption. In terms of Product Lifecycle, many wireless products, such as smart, Internet-enabled phones, are stuck just after the Introduction stage. Many of these solutions, failing to follow the exponential growth curve, have been discarded, and many more are being reworked (see Figure 7.1).

Given the meltdown of the dotCom industry, there is a prejudice in the investment community against anything in the domestic technology sector. The presence of a countrywide U.S. Internet infrastructure, which is the one supposed advantage of the United States over Europe and Asia, has been overshadowed by lack of end-user hardware, operating system software, efficient microbrowsers,

Figure 7.1   Wireless Product Lifecycle

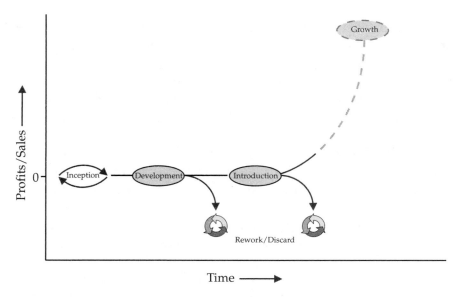

and contentious mobile phone network operators. Also, there are too many domestic players in the enterprise application space for any one to be profitable. Banking, the application the market thought would take off, has proven to be a washout. Mobile operators and carriers that offer data control and other services appear to be regarded as the next great areas of opportunity.

In contrast, within Japan, NTT's DoCoMo cellular service is entrenched and embraced by millions of the populace, and I-Mode (Internet Mode) wireless services are nearly at the point of Completion in the Continuum. Not only does virtually everyone own and use a cell phone for voice communications, but they use special handsets to send and receive email, check the stock market, weather, and even the daily cartoon. With the mature Japanese market nearly saturated, NTT is moving into the overseas market, including the United States, to increase sales and establish DoCoMo as a world standard for wireless voice and data communications.

Similarly, in Europe, the status of wireless technology is somewhere between the Product Point and the Market Gateway. Because there is a single European standard for wireless communications, a businessperson in Germany can fly to Paris and use the same cell phone. In Finland, a woman can walk up to an Internet-aware Coke machine, enter the toll-free number on the machine and out pops a can of Coke—with the charge appended to her wireless phone bill.

Unfortunately for some drivers, a police officer in Finland that pulls a driver over can access his income tax statement and issue a speeding ticket for an amount that is based on his income, so that the ticket bears the same "pain" regardless of income. In this case, custom traffic tickets, like custom airline tickets, are not necessarily cherished. Nevertheless, this level of integration removes many of the barriers to adoption, leaving European countries to fight over less critical technical standards, such as the optimum format for text messages on cell phones and other wireless devices.

Many third-world countries are entering the mCommerce space as well. In rural India, for example, where wired communications are almost as rare as DSL service is in the United States, fishermen use cell phones to contact brokers onshore to determine which port offers the best prices for their catch. A fisherman off of the U.S. coast, in contrast, would be hard pressed to locate a port that supports his digital cellular service. As in many developed countries, U.S. communications are based on a long-standing wired communications infrastructure dating back to the time of Alexander Graham Bell.

The wired legacy in the United States has been and continues to be both a boon and a hindrance. For example, unlike the evolutionary course taken in the United States, where the wired infrastructure is still growing, customers in India did not first adopt a wired phone infrastructure, but bypassed the wired phase altogether. As a result, there is no wired investment to recoup—and therefore no motivation for the voice carriers to drag their feet in providing superior wireless communications. They also benefit from starting off with a modern, high-speed communications infrastructure designed for both voice and data. In contrast, the United States and other developed countries with wired infrastructures have been much slower to switch to a faster communications network. They are slowly cutting back on residential phone lines and are increasingly using digital subscriber lines (DSL) and broadband cable for Internet access and for simultaneous voice and data communications. Even so, this evolutionary change is not occurring overnight.

Although there is a great deal of noise about the lethargic rate at which the wireless carriers in the United States are standardizing on a nationwide wireless solution, wired connectivity fares much worse. Wireless in the United States has been slow to catch on due to the lack of a standardized, nationwide telecommunications carrier, the lack of smart phones and other wireless hardware, and the lack of content on the Web capable of being accessed and displayed by wireless mobile devices. In addition, a quarter of all subscribers change service providers every year because of price, coverage, and quality of service. Europeans, in contrast, have a single wireless standard and much more wireless-compatible content to chose from. One challenge for U.S. marketing firms will be to avoid the overblown hype that could further undermine the move to wireless, especially wireless Web access.

Historical Perspective

To better appreciate the current state of wireless communications, consider the historical developments in wireless from business, technology, and political perspectives, as outlined in Figure 7.2. As noted in Chapter 2, the incubation time for most technology-based products is shortening. However, like the advances in the wired infrastructure, the current status of wireless is based on almost two centuries of technological, business, and political evolution, with technology leading the way.

Figure 7.2   Historical Development of Wireless

Business Milestone	Technological Achievement	Political Milestone
	Telegraph	
Regular Telegraph Service	Transatlantic Telegraph Cable	
Telephone Patent	Manual Switchboard	
	Telex	
Automatic Switching Patent	Marconi demonstrates Wireless	
Marconi Wireless Telegraph Co.		
AT&T buys Bell	Transatlantic Wireless	
	Electronic Amplifier	
RCA buys Marconi	Voice Over Wireless	
	Transatlantic Voice Wireless	
NBC	IMTS	FRC
CBS		FCC
	Digital Computer	SMR
Regular TV Broadcasts	Transistor	
	Comm Satelite	
AT&T Breakup	IC	
	ARPANET	
	Mobile Phone	Experimental Cellular
Cellular Service	Cell Phone	Cellular License
AT&T allows 3rd Party Hardware		Cellular Lottery
Nextel	WWW	PCS
AT&T buys McCaw Cellular		Telecom Act
MCI/WorldCom Merge		EU Deregulation
Verizon		Digital Signature

As with most technological innovations, older technologies are not suddenly replaced by new innovations as soon as they arrive, but follow the typical technology adoption curve. However, simple customer behavior does not account for much of the adoption pattern seen in the United States for communications technologies, in part because of the business (including patents) and political forces at work that have long characterized the communications space. For example, because of inflated costs, a unique licensing arrangement instituted by Bell, and patent protection, the general public was effectively barred from using the telephone.

When Bell received a patent for his telephone invention in 1876, the telegraph business was hardly affected because Bell's customers were well-to-do businessmen in the same town. Instead of sending messages across the Atlantic or the country, these businessmen were interested in having a phone in their home so that they could call their place of business—in the same town—and check on things. Bell's plans for the telephone—a one-way device that would pipe in music and other entertainment from the local theater—were not commercially viable.

The telephone was such a specialized, niche market product when it was first marketed that even a quarter century later, most of the business activity remained in wired and wireless telegraphy. In fact, the business activity surrounding telegraphy around the turn of the 19th century was like the dotCom frenzy in Silicon Valley in the mid-1990s. Within a few years of Marconi's first demonstration of wireless communications, Marconi Wireless Telegraph Company was formed, American Telephone and Telegraph (AT&T) acquired Bell Telephone, and Marconi was transmitting telegraphy regularly across the Atlantic. There was so much competition between the old wired and new wireless telegraphy services, domestically and internationally, for nonvoice communications, that many young radio entrepreneurs became rich and famous overnight.

Time and the technological innovation of the electronic amplifier led to wireless voice transmissions in 1907. In 1919 when voice over a wire became a viable form of communication, RCA acquired Marconi Wireless Telegraph Company. Within the next five years, there were over 500 broadcast radio stations competing for a limited spectrum—not unlike the case today in the mCommerce space. In response to the political pressure of radio station owners who could not sell advertisements in a free-for-all market, Congress passed the 1927 Radio Act, which created the Federal Radio Commission (FRC)—the precursor of the Federal Communications Commission (FCC)—to police the spectrum. The FRC became the FCC in less than a decade.

In the United States by 1946, with the radio spectrum under control of an increasingly powerful FCC, the available spectrum for broadcasting was shrinking. This situation, plus the postwar love affair with the automobile and a barrage of technological advances in electronics, made ripe conditions for the introduction of the improved mobile telephone service (IMTS), which connected a 100-pound, trunk-mounted mobile radio with the public telephone network through a single, central transmitter and receiver. The system allowed customers driving within a 25-mile radius of an IMTS antenna tower to place a phone call, for example, to potential clients to verify meeting time and place. The increasing rate of technological innovation in the next two decades included the first commercial digital computer; the transistor; the first communications satellite; the first integrated circuit (IC); and ARPANET, which would become known as the Internet.

With advances in computing power, miniaturization of components, increased battery performance, and the insatiable demand for communications, it was only a matter of time before IMTS was replaced with something more portable and practical. Motorola was first with a portable and mobile phone prototype in 1973. Within a decade, the FCC authorized several test systems that eventually resulted in the issuance of cellular licenses. Because of incredible demand for spectrum, the FCC immediately imposed the current lottery system of assigning licenses.

Mergers and acquisitions characterized the wireless space in the 1980s and 1990s. NEXTEL was established in 1991, followed by Personal Communications Services (PCS) in 1993. AT&T, the latecomer to the game, came up to speed almost immediately by acquiring McCaw Cellular.

On the political front, the Telecom Act of 1996 was supposed to make it easier for new businesses in the United States to enter the space. However, the United States has been plagued by contention over limited spectrum, eventually involving the FCC, the Supreme Court, companies under bankruptcy court protection, the military, and others fighting over wireless licensing. For example, a federal appeals court decided in mid-2001 that the FCC had violated federal bankruptcy law when it seized wireless licenses from Next-Wave Telecom, which had acquired the licenses in 1996. However, the confiscated spectrum was subsequently sold to companies such as Verizon Wireless, VoiceStream, and AT&T. As a result, the new owners of the spectrum put their service expansion plans on temporary hold until the courts decided the fate of NextWave Telecom's original claim on the spectrum.

In contrast, the deregulation of the European Union (EU) laid the groundwork for a single cellular service standard to be used throughout the union. Instead of contention over which brand of service to use, companies are free to focus on standards such as short text messaging, which allows customers to send and receive email, request movie times from a theater, receive updated stock and weather information, or get driving directions to points of interest on their cell phones. As a result, the wireless developments in Europe, as in Japan, are far ahead of those in the United States.

Today, global issues related to the wireless spectrum are resolved with the help of the International Telecommunications Union (ITU) and corporate-sponsored standards groups. For example, an international Bluetooth consortium of some 2000 companies has agreed to abide by standards for short-range wireless communications. Bluetooth allows, for example, a cell phone to communicate wirelessly with a PDA and extract a phone number from the PDA's database and then make the call. Similarly, the industry-wide, wireless LAN standard known as IEEE 802.11b is making it possible for airports and schools like MIT to offer wireless support for email and Web access to users with handhelds and laptops equipped with the appropriate wireless modem cards.

Expectation Management

While advances in wireless communications in the United States are still limited by an adversarial political and legal environment, marketing's role in establishing customer buy-in is critical for its longer-term success. The potential customer base is already primed for wireless by a wired Web experience. However, getting potential customers to invest the time and energy required to change their behavior involves positioning the wireless experience as something that will eventually save them time and energy—no mean task at this stage of wireless development.

In this regard, there is something to be said for starting from "scratch" (e.g., a third-world country) without a wired infrastructure. For example, consider India. Not only do wireless carriers in India have no wired legacy systems to maintain and no customers to transition from wired to wireless, but customers do not have heightened expectations set by a wired system. To customers experienced with DSL, cable modems, and even 56K analog modems delivering rich, colorful Web graphics to desktop PCs, monochrome text on postage-stamp sized screens do not have much of a "wow" factor. The point is not that it is better to not have a legacy infrastructure, but rather that established economic and political stakeholders strongly influence the adoption of a new technology that threatens their market share.

In contrast, the wildly successful DoCoMo system in Japan offers content on a technically superior infrastructure that not only meets but often exceeds customer expectations of what is available from a wireless handset. It helps that most DoCoMo subscribers have never experienced the wired Web. As such, wireless subscribers are not preconditioned to associate the Web with music, streaming video, and the other eye candy that the typical wired Web user in the United States expects. Instead, many users are impressed with the seemingly infinite amount of information that can be accessed within seconds from virtually anywhere in the country.

Because news of innovations travels rapidly in the global economy, most U.S. citizens have heard of some of the many applications of wireless Web access in Europe and Japan before actually experiencing them first hand. Some of the applications are culture-specific, and others are more general in nature. For example, Finns and Swedes were among the first to purchase gasoline by dialing the toll-free number on a gas pump, and buy and sell securities over their cell phones. Users in England were able to view movie listings, stock prices, news, weather, and sports on their cell phones years before these services were available in the United States. Drivers in France were among the first to access real-time traffic information and navigation services. Japanese commuters were the first to read the morning news and check bank balances, play games, and send email through their cell phones.

Translating the appeal of these European and Japanese services to the United States has been challenging, in part because the needs addressed by some of the mCommerce services are being addressed through other technologies. Many drivers in the United States already have access to specialized wireless services, such as automatic toll payment using wireless systems mounted on cars. Similarly, ExxonMobil's speedpass allows drivers to fill their tanks and then use the diminutive key-ring-mounted device as a radio frequency (RF) ID, and the charge appears on their monthly charge card—without the need to enter a phone number.

One of the potential attractions of wireless for U.S. customers is time management with wireless PDAs that can send and receive email and provide location-specific information on hotels and restaurants, for example. ETicketing for theater, airlines, and other services is a potential use as well. However, the limitations on the adoption of wireless in the United States continue to be access and speed. The United States is behind Europe, Japan, and other parts of Asia in terms of high-speed wireless access. Domestic wireless voice and data networks are slower and much less extensive than those in Europe and Asia.

The only major high-speed wireless service in the United States, Metricom, folded in 2001, in part because it used proprietary and expensive hardware and software, which limited service to only 15 metropolitan areas. About 50,000 customers who paid around $80 per month plus $300 for a wireless modem were left stranded without service. In contrast, wireless subscribers in Europe, for example, can access the cellular network in over 130 countries. NTT DoCoMo cellular system is used throughout Japan, and the optional Internet access feature is subscribed to by over a quarter of its users—making it the largest mobile Internet service in the world.

In addition to the speed limitations, most cellular phones in the United States cannot access the Internet, and those that can must deal with the lack of a standardized, nationwide telecommunications carrier. Cell phone service is expensive, and there is very little content for users to view once they are online. Trust in the infrastructure builders—Cisco Systems and Intel—has waned since the dotCom fall, and yet marketing firms are still continuing to oversell yet-to-be-delivered wireless benefits to potential customers. A key challenge of wireless Web is to avoid the overblown hype that could quash the movement for decades or longer. In other words, the challenges of limited screen size, lack of graphics, slow response times, security, lack of content formatted for mobile phone users, browser incompatibilities, and cost must be addressed from a client relations management as well as from a technical perspective.

Part of expectation management has to do with actual versus perceived adoption of wireless by society. Although the high visibility "corrections"—the Lucents and Ciscos of the world—seem to paint a dour picture of the wireless world, the fact is that wireless products are catching on. Palms beam data back and forth on infrared (IR) beams. Hewlett-Packard (HP) printers connect to laptops through the IR ports. Customer service representatives use featherweight Bluetooth-compliant cordless telephone headsets. A variety of sports watches from Polar, Nike, Reebok, and BodyMedia sense everything from heart rate to shoe acceleration and fitness level, and they download the data to a PC for analysis. Hikers and road warriors use global positioning system (GPS) receivers to find their way out of the forest or into a boardroom meeting in a strange city.

A CEO championing a wireless solution has to tread the fine line between inflating the expectations of customers and creating an air of excitement about her company's wireless Web solution. Expectation management, which encompasses the time before a product is created and the time after it has been released, is often at least as important as the technology.

ANALYSIS

The technical trajectory of wireless in the United States—a seeming comedy of errors on the legal and political fronts that is producing little more than electromagnetic smog in the major wireless markets—illustrates the typical, but not necessarily optimal, shift in focus with progression along the Continuum. As shown in Figure 7.3, the initial focus for a typical wireless gizmo was the idea, the concept of how to create a better communications experience to best exploit the potential market. Heading to the Technical Gateway, where a prototype or proof of concept had to be demonstrated, focus necessarily shifted to developing working prototypes. Next, with the Product Point on the horizon, the point at which an actual product had to be available for testing and limited deployment, the focus shifted to the product.

The predominantly introspective perspective during the early stages of product development, in which the goal is alchemizing ideas into reality, gradually shifts externally to the customer. The reality of

Figure 7.3   Focus along the Continuum

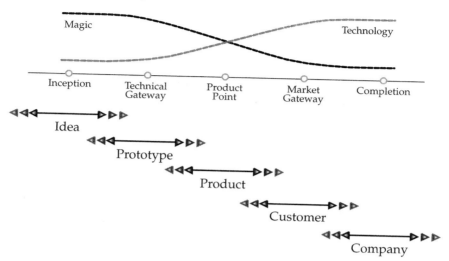

selling customers on the idea of parting with their hard-earned cash in exchange for a product they may not even know they want or need can be overwhelming. This shift of focus to the customer at a minimum should occur around the Market Gateway, when the product must break into the market to be successful. Depending upon the type of organization, the devotion of resources to market research may occur earlier in the Continuum.

In focusing on the customer, technological issues often take a back seat to political and business decisions involved in making the product available to customers and achieving profitability. As described in Chapter 8, the focus typically shifts to the company, especially if the goal is to sell the company to the public in an IPO or position it for acquisition by another company. However, barring significant patent and other intellectual property holdings, making the company as valuable as possible generally requires revenue from customers. As mentioned in previous discussions on marketing, R&D and executive development should be considered as concurrent activities throughout the Continuum. That is, the shift in focus from the customer to the company is only a matter of degree.

Marketing succeeds to the degree that it fulfills the basic principles of product, price, promotion, and place—in other words, offering the right product at the right price with sufficient, targeted promotion, and offering it through the proper distribution channels or place. In addition, along the Continuum the history of the wireless space illustrates how marketing falls apart when the technology is not ready for actual use. Marketing also fails when potential customers do not understand the technology and its potential benefit, which is often because the story of the product is too complex. For example, just about everyone in the United States *gets* the concept of a cell phone, even though less than half of the population owns one. Perhaps they have seen them used on TV, or they own a cordless phone and think of a cell phone as simply more powerful. In other words, it does not take much of a mental leap to go from one type of phone to the other.

However, few domestic consumers get the concept of a smart phone used as an electronic wallet, especially since a simple piece of plastic—the charge card—is more than sufficient for charge transactions. The concept of a secure, wireless phone with an embedded security card containing the user ID is foreign and confusing to most U.S. cell phone users. It is also more time consuming. Why not simply hand a credit card over to a clerk or tell a mail order representative the charge card information over the phone and be done with it?

Marketing also fails when there is no compelling need addressed by the product and consequently no motivating desire for the purchase decision. The established competition—in the case of the electronic wallet, a simple charge card—is also a factor that may undermine market acceptance of a product. In following the customer behavior model described in Chapter 3, it is not simply the relative worth of the smart phone over the charge card, but rather the energy and time required to effect a behavior change.

General Principles

Some general principles of marketing in the Continuum, illustrated by activity in the wireless space, are:

- Marketing is about creating or enhancing a customer's desire for a product or service.
- Technical products can get stuck at the Market Gateway for any number of nontechnical reasons.
- Legislation affects product marketing.
- Hype kills.

- Customers generally buy what they want, not simply what they need—but in down economies, more customers want what they really need.
- Higher risk favors the formation of clusters.
- Success takes time.
- Foreign markets do not necessarily predict domestic markets.
- Identifying the appropriate target audiences is critical in establishing profitability.
- Technological evolution leads political, business, and social evolution.
- Globalization is inescapable.
- Market segmentation is critical for survival.

Marketing is about creating or enhancing a customer's desire for a product or service. Few consumers really need to charge groceries and gas on a smart cell phone when they have a wallet full of charge cards. However, moviegoers may be willing to pay for the privilege of purchasing tickets online while en route to a show to avoid the delays of long lines.

Technical products can get stuck at the Market Gateway for any number of nontechnical reasons. In the wireless space, products are stuck because of product confusion, heightened customer expectations that cannot be met, risk aversion as reflected in a wait-and-see attitude, product divergence, lack of champions, and no compelling need for the wireless product. For example, most consumers do not know the difference between a smart phone (one with a number of features over and above what a standard cell phone provides, including Web access) and a Web-enabled phone (one that provides Web access, but may not provide all of the features provided by a smart phone). What is more, they may not care. Domestic customers generally expect Web-enabled PDAs and phones to be able to access graphics and standard Web pages—but they do not. Similarly, the wait-and-see posture is a common sticking point, especially after customers get burned with a product that did not perform as advertised, as described in the behavior modification model in Chapter 3.

Legislation affects product marketing. Legislation can put a temporary or permanent hold on the marketability of a product, regardless of the status of the technology. For example, the Department of Defense, TV broadcasters, and the satellite industry currently hold the wireless spectrum hostage. Until legislation reassigns the spectrum to the next generation of wireless providers, there is going to be very little movement in high-speed wireless data and voice communications in the United States.

Hype kills.   Marketing a product before it is far enough down the Continuum—that is, while it is still *vaporware*—slows, and may eventually kill, the market for the product. Some parts of the wireless space are being handicapped by the shortage of spectrum. That is, providing wireless access has not yet been transformed from a magic trick into a defined, repeatable process. Instead, there are more questions than answers. For example, assuming higher-speed wireless is on the horizon, what about the added battery drain? Will batteries need to be heavier, making the wireless device less portable, or will the unit simply burn through the battery charge in less time? As a result of all the unknowns, risk-averse customers at every level are turned away by some wireless technologies.

Customers generally buy what they want, not simply what they need— but in down economies, more customers want what they really need. In a weak economy, creating artificial need (wants) is much more difficult than in a strong economy. The concept of a wireless PDA may be intriguing, but for a company faced with the prospect of equipping a 50-person sales force with PDAs that have a $60 per month service charge, there has to be a viable short-term and intermediate ROI strategy.

Higher risk favors the formation of clusters.   Most clinicians in the Boston area use Palms, even when the pager function of the competing Research in Motion PDA is more appealing. Aligning with what an immediate group of potential customers are currently using is usually more important than buying what may be best in the overall market. Clusters of Macintosh users in a sea of IBM clones minimize the risk of having the only machine that is not compatible with the remainder of users in a company.

Success takes time.   Companies must have the resources for an extended battle for the customer's wallet and psyche. As many of the wireless providers have demonstrated, it will take years for wireless to be fully embraced by consumers, and adoption takes time. Success favors those companies with the resources for a long siege.

Foreign markets do not necessarily predict domestic markets. DoCoMo may be great for Japan, but may not be embraced by U.S. customers. Because Japanese users have very little exposure to the wired Web, their expectations are not biased. However, U.S. customers used to multimedia and color on the Internet will be disappointed with postage-stamp-sized monochrome screens and slow access speeds.

Identifying the appropriate target audiences is critical in establishing profitability. Metricom, which offered the Ricochet wireless service that provided customers with access to the Internet at twice the average speed of standard telephone modems, suffered because it targeted only serious Internet users. At about $75 per month, the service was too expensive for the more casual user of the Internet, including businesspeople at home and on the road.

Technological evolution leads political, business, and social evolution. In the case of early broadcast radio, the Federal Radio Commission (later the FCC) was formed in response to the rapidly evolving space. Similarly, public uproar regarding cell phone use while driving delays the introduction of the cell phone. Leading a charge takes time and resources.

Globalization is inescapable. Progress in wireless communications in the United States is based on affordable hand units made overseas. Globalization involves not only where but how companies compete. Barring legal restrictions, communications, information, computation (with the great global grid, or GGG), and decision making are obvious commodities for the global marketplace.

Market segmentation is critical for survival. Wireless includes not only PDAs and smart phones, but wireless LANs, Telematics, and fixed wireless. However, these latter applications are suffering from the negative association with dotComs and the general technology slowdown. That said, extreme product differentiation is detrimental in an undecided and fragmented market. The Visor PDA does well because it is compatible with the Palm and cheaper. For most users, compatibility and familiarity are more critical than packaging and styling.

Implications

One of the implications of the wireless experience is that companies should understand that initial marketing and financial strategies rarely work as originally planned. For example, a company should assume that its initial marketing effort will not succeed in its original written form, and it should be prepared to change strategy. The management of the iridium global satellite-based communications system waited too long before it decided to change the marketing focus from business travelers to professional outdoor workers and others more likely to pay for the system—with nearly fatal consequences.

The fate of the iridium system also highlights the importance of focusing a marketing effort on the right market niche, and the high cost of being off-target. The Motorola-backed iridium satellite system had some technical glitches. For one, the brick-sized, handheld units did not work well inside buildings. However, technical issues aside, the global telephone service was initially targeted at globe-trotting businesspeople. There was virtually no marketing to professional workers in remote areas, or to governments, the military, and other potential customers. By the time the managers of the iridium system realized they were being responsive to the wrong customers, it was too late. Now the customers that would have likely paid handsomely for the iridium services, namely, various sectors of the U.S. government, are major owners of the satellite system, which it bought for pennies on the dollar.

The wireless experience in the United States also illustrates the need to develop strategic alliances, cross-licenses, and joint ventures to reduce the risk of failure and provide access to future products and technology. For example, most large businesses and many groups of smaller companies invest in professional lobbyists to represent their interests at the federal and state levels. In the wireless space, local laws governing the use of wireless devices in restaurants and cars can profoundly affect the marketability of wireless products and services. In many ways, working with standards organizations is akin to developing strategic allies. Standards are important in encouraging innovation and lower prices through competition. More important, from a customer perspective, they reduce the risk of failure due to technology incompatibilities.

However, getting too close to other businesses, or even customers for that matter, can be counterproductive to marketing and R&D efforts. For example, focusing entirely on the customer may cause a company to lose touch with the core product engineering in various ways, such as being too focused on short-term bug fixes instead of longer-term technology product improvements. When other businesses are involved, there is always the potential of guilt by association with substandard performers with a poor track record of client-relations management. This is evident in the eCommerce space where the dotCom experience has had a negative influence on the acceptance of wireless and other product categories in the technology space. Whether the issue is guilt by association or a simple failure to deliver as promised, it is prudent to exercise preemptive damage control. In attempting to hit the mark on expectation management, it is inevitable that someone or some group is going to be disappointed or even offended. Given this reality, it is a good idea for the decision makers to exercise preemptive damage control with customers. Perhaps the needs of a few users cannot be satisfied, even though most end users are delighted with the wireless system.

For example, the national sales force may not be able to work within the constraints of spotty national coverage, even though the much larger local sales force may be happy with the complete regional coverage. The issue might be exacerbated if the national sales force was somehow led to believe or expect that their needs would be met by the wireless solution. Perhaps they were led to believe that national coverage would be available, as the wireless service provider promised, within a certain time period. However, the service provider may have overpromised, and full national coverage may actually be years away.

In exercising preemptive damage control, it is best for management to identify problems and make them known to the stakeholders before others make them known at inopportune moments. Management should decide—based on the politics of the situation, the resources available, and the practical limitation of the current technology—when the system is good enough for release. In other words, the company should know the position of the product in the Continuum.

In the wireless space, preemptive damage control includes planning the long-term evolution of the wireless solution. In some cases, the features that some stakeholders want may simply not be practical, suggesting that plans should be put on hold until new technologies are available. In other cases, an evolutionary path can be laid out, using the Continuum as a guide and with some semblance of a realistic timeline. This may involve identifying collaborators from other departments, companies, or trade associations who are involved in wireless projects that address problem areas in the current product solution. Perhaps partnering can be used to cut expenses, using hardware and software from third parties. It may also be possible to combine offerings with partners within and external to the company.

Another way to improve the odds of success is to be open to a variety of marketing models. For example, Gillette was successful by giving away the razor and selling the blade. Similarly, Adobe gives away its basic Acrobat Reader software as a way of selling its writing tools. By making the PDF format standard for documentation, companies are more likely to create documents with Acrobat's high-margin writing tools. Acrobat Reader, like Gillette's blades, has a low marginal cost. Disposables, such as non-rechargeable batteries and frequently replaced components, are often used as a means of achieving profitability. For example, Hasbro sold its Lite Brite game based on a light bulb and hundreds of clear plastic plugs, and, planning ahead for absent-minded children and/or their slippery-fingered younger siblings, Hasbro offered refill packs of the small pegs, ensuring the future of glowing art for generations to come.

As the Lite Brite game illustrates, customers generally buy what they want and use what they need. The customer's buy decision is based on emotions, not the logic of what they need to survive. As such, marketing is about creating emotions, or at least linking emotions to a product or service. In this regard, marketing is a useful tool in expectation management for existing products or services because it creates and shapes customer expectations. As noted above, part of the challenge of marketing the wireless Web to U.S. consumers is that their concept of the Web has been shaped by prior marketing efforts to be equivalent to large, colorful displays that approach and sometimes exceed TV in terms of multimedia capabilities.

Marketing to the business community can be more challenging for more complex and feature-driven products. Internal business tools tend to be more focused on technology and economics than emotions. For example, if a wireless solution saves the user time and improves the company's bottom line, it will generally be a success, even if everyone is not excited about the technology. However, getting users to the point of feeling that a device is saving them time and money is the longer-term sales and marketing challenge, and hence the importance of expectation management. If a company's potential customers cannot be convinced of a reasonable return for their investment of capital and time, they will not even try a wireless device. In a self-fulfilling prophecy, potential customers will never get to the point of believing a product saves time or money if they did not get to the point of testing the product. Thus the initial expectation is that the wireless solution will be a waste of their time and energy.

Finally, the challenge of internal marketing is to increase expectations in line with what the company and product can deliver, without overpromising. To this end, the Continuum model can serve as a means of communicating the status of product development and market status to everyone in the company. This line of reasoning is continued in the following chapter.

SUMMARY

Traditional marketing is about product, price, promotion, and place, but there is much more to consider than the simple category labels suggest. The volatile yet promising wireless Web and other devices in general provide an excellent example of the challenges that face a modern marketing effort. There is stiff foreign competition, with most of the services well ahead of anything available in the United States. The legal and political aspects of foreign wireless tend to be further along in providing a business environment conducive to sales. For example, the EU has a single standard for wireless so that a handset purchased in France can be used without modification in Germany.

First, from a historical perspective, the wireless space has been in the turmoil that once characterized other industries, such as the automobile industry in the 1920s. Even though wireless seems to be only recently in the news, the technical, political, and business milestones date back over 150 years. During that period, there have been technical advances, which drove business, legal, and political evolution. Given the hype of wireless, expectation management—both internal and external—is key to keeping momentum up along the Continuum.

The predominantly introspective perspective during the early phases of the Continuum, in which the goal is to transform ideas into reality, gradually shifts from an idea that can externally be marketed to the customer. In focusing on the customer, technological issues tend to take a back seat to the political and business decisions involved in making the product available to customers and achieving profitability.

One of the general principles that can be gleaned from the wireless experience is that globalization is inescapable, but foreign markets do not necessarily translate directly to the domestic market. In addition, customers generally buy what they want, not simply what they need, but need is often a function of the economy and amount of disposable income that is available. Another principle is that success takes time, and technological evolution generally leads political, business, and social evolution.

The implications that should be applicable to any business involved in marketing a product include the following: have a "plan B" in the event of an inevitable failure; avoid guilt by association with failed or troubled businesses and market segments; develop allies and abide by industry standards; invest in political infrastructures; focus primarily—but not exclusively—on the right customers; exercise preemptive damage control instead of reacting to the market; be flexible in the use of marketing models; and actively manage customer expectations.

8

The Corporation

There is nothing more difficult to take in hand, more perilous
to conduct, or more uncertain in its outcome, than to take the
lead in introducing a new order of things.

Niccolo Machiavelli

While technical innovation and personal ambition are the engines
that drive ideas to products along the Continuum, operating capital
is the fuel that ultimately determines the extent of influence and success in the marketplace. While personal fortunes have been used successfully to create and nurture small companies, the rate of growth is
limited by the size of personal assets and the willingness of institutional investors to assume not only the risk of losing their investments, but also the possibility of product and service liability related
to the activity of the company. Because a corporation separates the
individual investors from the business, the liability of the corporation
is limited to corporate assets, not the personal assets of the owners
and investors. The financial innovation known as the corporation
dates back to the middle ages, when the construct was used to organize universities, monasteries, and guilds. However, the potential of
using the corporation to exploit personal greed in order to generate
vast sums of capital was not fully appreciated until the early 1700s in
England. Although some reputable English businesses used the corporation as a form of insurance to organize and fund risky voyages,
much of the activity around early corporations was based on somewhat

shady speculation schemes that make the IPO boom of the late 1990s seem tame by comparison. As a government-sanctioned lottery of sorts, unscrupulous promoters used the corporation to raise huge sums of money for business plans that ranged from alchemy—the transmutation of quicksilver into precious metals—to monopolies on trading routes. Before England passed legislation in 1720 to outlaw most of the scams related to public corporations, many unscrupulous promoters offered IPOs, collected their money, and left the country the same day, never to return.

In the United States, where states establish laws that control the use and exploitation of corporate status, New York became the first state to recognize the construct in 1811. As the IPO boom of the late 1990s demonstrated, the potential for a corporation to raise millions of dollars in capital through a speculative stock offering is still possible, despite the legal constraints designed to minimize fraud and abuse. The corporation remains attractive to the public and institutional investors in part because the odds of winning or losing depend on intuition, knowledge, and luck.

For entrepreneurs, the corporation remains one of the best ways to create a sheltered environment for birthing new products and to generate the capital needed to bring them to market. As such, the corporation is the dominant type of business organization throughout the world, accounting for almost 90% of all business income in the United States. This chapter explores how the publicly traded corporation serves as a protective shield for R&D, marketing, and sales.

COMPETITIVE LANDSCAPE

One reason that *The Art of War,* by Sun Tzu (400 BC), has remained a classic in business circles is because in many regards business is a form of warfare. In this context, corporations act as nation-states that either form alliances or compete with each other for limited resources in order to accumulate power and money. While in today's developed world, economic warfare does not necessarily involve physical force, the effects can be almost as devastating for rival companies and their associated communities and countries. For example, throughout much of its history, the British Empire bled economic value from its colonies—including those in North America—often with the assistance of a conscripted military.

Today, many people claim that the United States, which happens to be one of the world's largest arms suppliers and the greatest economic power, is guilty of the same predatory behavior. However, in reality, with today's world of multinational corporations, political borders are often blurred. Not only are the battle lines drawn between competing corporations—FedEx versus DHL for overnight shipping, Sony versus Microsoft for supremacy in the game console market, and Lexus versus Mercedes Benz for luxury automobiles, for example—but between corporations and national governments. Given that many of the Fortune 100 corporations have annual incomes greater than the GNP of some developing countries, it is not unusual for corporations to compete with national and regional governments as well. While governmental compromises on minimum wage and other employee matters may surface in the media, many of the more subtle compromises that governments make to industry—from tax breaks to negotiating the standards for dumping of toxic waste—do not regularly appear in mainstream media stories.

In addition, seemingly unlikely alliances are commonly formed for the mutual benefit of the corporations involved. For example, the U.S. Postal Service contracted with its major competitor, FedEx, for overnight delivery to expand its express mail service while saving about $150 million per year in expenses. Similarly, MGM, Paramount, Sony, Universal, and Warner Brothers have joined to develop a Web-based, video-on-demand system where customers can download films. By combining their resources, Hollywood studios can develop a single encryption standard and distribution method that not only reduces financial risk to any particular studio, but also results in less confusion for consumers. American, Continental, Delta, Northwest, and United Airlines used the same approach in developing the Orbitz Web site that provides customers with a single access point to ticketing and information.

What makes the Western, capitalist system work as well as it does—when it does work—is not the simple set of assumptions as first envisioned by Adam Smith's "invisible hand" of the marketplace or the theoretical laws of supply and demand. Rather, it exists as a complex set of ever-changing rules of engagement that define the social, legal, and economic environments in which corporations and businesses of all sizes operate. In exchange for a degree of economic protection, corporations have to pay local, state, and federal taxes, as well as contend with laws that impose constraints on everything from hiring and firing policies to workplace air quality.

Sometimes the government's form of protectionism is less than appealing to a corporation. For example, U.S. intellectual property laws protect the rights of inventors and the corporations that own or license their inventions in exchange for full disclosure of the underlying technology after a little less than two decades after a patent is issued. However, depending on the nature of the inventions, many corporations opt instead to keep the information out of the public domain and retain the inventions as trade secrets under their own control. In addition, as the Microsoft antitrust case illustrates, it is okay to be successful—to a point. Just as the Roman Empire limited the power of its most successful generals, so do the U.S. antitrust laws limit the power of the economic generals like Bill Gates.

Despite the best efforts of inventors, innovators, and entrepreneurs, even the best technologies often succumb to the perils of the competitive marketplace. There are the obvious issues of competing directly against an entrenched, monolithic empire, such as Microsoft or Toyota. Because of their market prowess, the large companies only allow small niche companies to survive unscathed if they go after small markets that are uneconomical or inconvenient to address. In addition, local and state laws sometimes create pockets of opportunity that only smaller, nimble companies can exploit.

For example, Lee Iacocca teamed up with Western Golf Car Company to create an electric car, the Lido. The car is little more than an oversized golf cart that retails for about $10,000. What makes this unconventional vehicle so attractive is that California's environmental guidelines require automakers to sell at least 2% of their California fleet as zero pollution emitters. In other words, each Lido sold to Californians is worth about $20,000 in electric credits to Toyota, GM, DaimlerChrysler, Mercedes-Benz, and other giant car manufacturers. On their own, each of the major car manufacturers would have a difficult time diverting production facilities to produce a small electric car and have it tested and approved by the relevant state and federal agencies. By allowing—and even encouraging—the Lido to capture the electric car market, the large car manufacturers also minimize their financial exposure to an untested design.

However, usually large, established corporations are in the best position financially and structurally to fully exploit pervasive trends in a timely manner. Take the worldwide energy shortage. In Brazil, where energy costs are soaring, the large appliance companies are enticing customers to replace their current energy-hungry appliances with new, cost-saving, energy-efficient models. No-name appliance manufacturers, regardless of how energy efficient, do not have the same resources and distribution channels to compete globally with GE.

Similarly, entrenched military contractors will likely receive the lion's share of the business of retooling the U.S. armed forces with more energy-efficient weapons. A small startup company that offers to build a more fuel-efficient replacement for the U.S. Army's Abrams tank—which gets 0.2 mile per gallon of fuel—will have to go head-to-head with the original contractor, General Dynamics Land Systems. A smaller, less established company is not likely to land the contract, even if it uses the common tactic of recruiting military-thought leaders as spokespeople and naming ex-Pentagon officers on its board of directors to strengthen its ties to senate budget committees.

David and Goliath

Large, successful corporations like GE, DaimlerChrysler, Sony, Oracle, and Microsoft represent the evolutionary pinnacles of capitalism. However, most companies can only aspire to reach those heights, especially given that so few new business ventures succeed in the United States. As such, the competition for resources and customers can be fierce, especially between small companies. When large and small companies compete, the government has at times stepped in to level the playing field. For example, there are special provisions for small businesses, from inexpensive loans from the Small Business Administration (SBA) to grant programs, such as the federal Small Business Innovation Research (SBIR) Grant fund, among others.

Within the limits imposed by the economy, the amount of capital available for growth and expansion, and the demand for a company's products and services, the trajectory of a company's business is largely a function of the desires and plans of the owners and other decision makers. For example, many small companies in the United States, such as a typical corner convenience store, are lifestyle companies. In other words, the owner-operator has no aspirations other than generating enough capital to live on. Although the owner-operator may eventually either sell the business or pass it on to someone in the family and retire after two or three decades, growing the value of the company for long-term stakeholders is not the usual focus of day-to-day business.

Aside from lifestyle companies, the owners and managers of most small to mid-sized companies fall into one of two camps: those that intend to grow and then sell the company for short-term profit, and those that aspire to continued growth and/or profitability throughout the foreseeable future for current and ensuing generations of owners and managers. The former were especially prevalent in the New Economy, while the latter, more conservative approach to business is typical of most Old Economy businesses.

Old versus New

Regardless of whether the goal of corporate leadership is to grow and then harvest the company profits, or to prepare it for a friendly merger or acquisition, or defend it from a hostile takeover and continue to grow it indefinitely, success is always a function of timing. The relationship between corporate value and the timing of events can be visualized as a value cascade, shown in Figure 8.1, where points A through D represent critical events—such as the installa-

Figure 8.1 Value Cascade

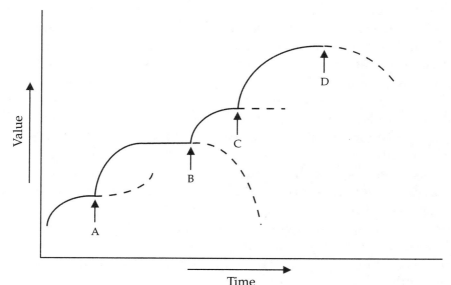

tion of new management, a merger or acquisition, a new business contract, the failure of a competitor, a technological breakthrough, or expansion into a new market. Note that value is not necessarily reflected in profitability; profitability may decrease temporarily due to the immediate cost of an acquisition, for example.

Each time the corporation changes hands through new ownership or the installation of a new management team, there is ideally an added value that was not possible before because of limited resources, or the vision, talent, or motivation of the management team. For example, in smaller companies, the original owner often does not possess the skill or have access to the resources necessary to bring the company to the next level of value and profitability for a larger customer base.

In maintaining the cascading curves that represent increasing value over time, regardless of whether the value is a result of acquisitions or changes in ownership or management, the key issue is timing. If the current owner sells too early, when the company is poised to grow exponentially (point A), then the seller forfeits value. In other cases, the natural evolution of the company without additional investment or changing hands may involve declining value (points B and D), or the value may stay constant (point C). If the company changes hands after its value has peaked (e.g., after point B), then the sellers may not be able to recoup their investment in the company.

Of course, the art of investing is being able to predict when to buy and when to sell, based on likely patterns in the value cascade. The timing of events in the value cascade shown in Figure 8.1 is ideal, in that each successive owner or manager is able to add value to the company, grow it for a period of time, and then sell the company for a profit or pass it on to the next manager. In reality, an ever-increasing value cascade is an anomaly—akin to the short-term dotCom valuation in the late 1990s. Still, successful management is more likely to result in a value cascade like that shown in Figure 8.1 than one that shows a mix of value gains and losses. The figure shows the ideal cascade pattern when management is able to continue a positive value chain through growth in existing product lines, expansion into new markets, and mergers and/or acquisitions.

The increase in value from an acquisition or new management team may result from increased value of the company because of an inflow of new technologies. It may also come about because of access to larger or more lucrative markets, increased efficiencies and economies of scale made possible by new processes, or increased employee motivation and morale because of a new, charismatic CEO. Regardless of how the increase in value occurs, the initial focus traditionally is not on the low-level details of the underlying technology, but is instead on the competition, the employees and other internal resources, and the business and social environments. For this reason, the new owner's speech to employees is usually a vision statement that outlines how to beat the competition, the vastness of the potential market, and how all employees will prosper from their hard work and dedication to the corporation.

A major difference between the New and Old Economies is in the time axis of the value cascade graph. In the New Economy at the height of the dotCom era, each cascade might have lasted a matter of months. In the Old Economy, the time between each point of sale or management change might represent a decade or more. For example, the management team of a company that makes aircraft engine parts that is positioning the company for acquisition by an engine manufacturer must first demonstrate that it is at or near the Performance Point in the Continuum—that is, it has a working, proven process in place for manufacturing parts that is independent of the employees involved in the process. Only then will the engine manufacturer initiate the due diligence in considering acquiring the parts company. Depending upon the amount of debt on the balance sheet of the parts company at the time of acquisition, the value of the engine company should increase if it makes its own parts and saves money overall. What's more, changes in management usually occur through necessity—competition, the retirement of the company's CEO, bankruptcy, or reorganization, for example—not through planned obsolescence.

In the dotCom era, as in 18th century England, the focus was on accruing *apparent* value—and future value through a promised software product, for example—as quickly as possible and then cashing in on that value. What happened to the company in the long term after the IPO was not necessarily understood by, or a primary concern of, employees and administrators holding short-term vesting stock options. The end—quick money, and lots of it—often justified the means. In the traditional or Old Economy companies such as GE, Honda, and FedEx, the focus is more likely to be on building a lasting, self-sufficient, profitable business that can provide capital and contribute to the community over decades, even in trying economic times.

In addition to different target rates of progression through the value cascade, Old and New Economy businesses vary in the relative value placed on their touch points—the points of contact between the company and the customer. Many New Economy companies assign tremendous relative value to their Web touch point—the value of Amazon.com, for example, is primarily its Web site. The fact that it sells books to one customer and CDs or DVDs to the next is not that important. What is more, although Amazon provides a Web touch point for Borders, Toys R Us, and Circuit City, it does not maintain a retail storefront of its own for walk-in customers, and its customer support telephone number is almost impossible to find.

Most Old Economy companies consider their touch points—such as storefronts, salespeople, telephones, customer service, faxes, flyers, and, more recently, Web sites—to be conduits to their core competency. There are exceptions, of course, in that several highly successful Old Economy companies derive their primary value from one or more of their touch points. Consider Domino's Pizza, for example. Although the national pizza company makes a good product, it is not known for quality or innovative ingredient combinations. In fact, there is not much difference between a cheese or pepperoni pizza from Domino's and one from the tens of thousands of small pizza shops throughout the country. What makes Domino's successful is its delivery service touch point—that is, its delivery person. Domino's, like Amazon.com, is about delivering a product quickly and effectively; the product simply happens to be pizza instead of books or music. Still, unlike Amazon, Domino's does deliver a physical product that it manufactures in-house. The key here is identifying the market need and taking advantage of a void. Domino's fills the need for late night and fast delivery service at major universities. Most dotComs fulfill neither a need nor a void.

While few would dispute that the Web has value as a touch point, the issue is quantifying that value. Evaluating the value of the Web as separate from the company's underlying competency—whether that means selling books or cars—can be difficult. Even so, for many companies, the value of their Web touch point is rapidly approaching that of their telephone. In other words, the once extraordinary dotCom touch point—which accounted for much of the tech upswing in the marketplace in the 1990s—has suddenly become very commonplace.

Sudden Death Syndrome

The seemingly overnight resolution of excessive valuation that has accrued over several years is a common, repeating phenomenon in the market. Conglomerates of the 1800s, leveraged buyouts of the 1980s, and, most recently, dotComs, created enormous wealth for corporations as well as many of the first movers in each space. Similarly, the cyclical pattern of actual or perceived scarcity of product, process, or information, followed by a precipitous fall in valuation not only affects corporate investors, but a downturn is often particularly harsh for the workforce, which often takes years to retrain and refocus on the next economic hotspot.

For example, consider the situation that existed in the early 1970s, when electronics technicians were in high demand, much like computer and networking technicians were in the late 1990s. Electronics was the "field of the future." With millions of color TV sets and other consumer electronics in an almost constant state of disrepair and the emergence of a new high-tech military, the demand for technicians and engineers in the commercial and military communications industries could not be satisfied. Projections based on current practices at the time were for an insatiable demand for electronic engineers and technicians for the next 40 to 50 years.

However, unlike the practice of training secretaries to be Web programmers during the dotCom boom, the communications industry's regulatory agency, the Federal Communications Commission (FCC) established minimum standards for technicians. For example, before Bryan could enter the lucrative commercial shipboard electronics field in 1971, he had to pass a grueling test to add a radar endorsement to his electronics license. The endorsement required a demonstrable knowledge of microwave physics, calculus, and low-level electronics, which technicians were expected use to test and repair radar systems. At that time, the typical shipboard radar was an American-made system composed of a roof-mounted rotating antenna, a wall-mounted radar transmitter/receiver about the size of a desktop PC, and a much larger and heavier floor-mounted display that contained all the controls and could be rotated so that the round CRT could be viewed from any angle.

The radar industry changed seemingly overnight when the Japanese company, Furano Radar, introduced a new radar design into the United States. Now, instead of working at the component level, the new design allowed anyone with the slightest physical dexterity to simply swap out cards in the well-engineered, miniature chassis. To repair a unit, all Bryan had to do was swap out cards until the unit passed an internal self-test procedure, and then send the deficient card to Furano for repair. There was suddenly no need for racks of test equipment, stocks of transistors, capacitors, and other components, soldering irons, or even volt-ohmmeters. Within a period of about two years, the electronic radar technician had suddenly been reduced to a cipher.

For the customers, the new, less expensive, innovative radar design meant that they could be up and running within a half-hour or less of making port. This meant that a ship could be on its way as soon as it loaded or unloaded its cargo, resulting in a significant cost savings, since the ship was not taken out of service. Because of the new radar's reputation, ship owners started replacing old units with models from Furano instead of having them repaired. After a short increase in business due to swapping out the old systems for the new Furano Radar systems, radar repair shops suddenly started cutting staff or closing altogether. A single technician could now service a half-dozen radar units in a day, compared to two or three units per week before the change to replaceable cards. Competing U.S. brands at first survived by selling replacement parts, and then quietly faded from the marketplace. Today, Furano Radars are one of the most popular brands for larger private boats, yachts, and large cruise ships, competing successfully with U.S. brands such as Raytheon. In addition, radar is now such an affordable commodity item that even some recreational boats sport the units. Many of the electronics corporations involved in the production of radar components and units in the 1970s still exist today in some form. Radar technicians, in comparison, are virtually extinct.

A similar situation exists in the consumer electronics industry. Early tube-type black and white TVs sets were simple enough for a technician with a minimum of experience to repair. A technician would unplug one of the dozen or so vacuum tubes in the TV receiver, plug the tube in a "vacuum tube checker" and determine within a minute if the tube was good or not. Then, with the advent of the more complex color TV and transistors, repairing a TV suddenly became more involved than simply pulling vacuum tubes and checking them. TVs had to be worked on in the technician's shop, with a volt-ohmmeter, a variety of signal generators, oscilloscopes, and other electronic test gear.

Zenith Radio, once the leading consumer electronics corporation in the United States, and the last fully U.S. owned manufacturer of TV receivers, introduced the replaceable card concept in its TV units in the 1970s. Given that Zenith's founder was an amateur radio enthusiast, it isn't surprising that the company developed the first portable radio receiver, the first FM stereo broadcast system, and the first prototype TV systems. Despite Zenith's innovations, competition from Japanese TV manufacturers quickly supplanted Zenith units with less bulky, less complex, less expensive TVs. In addition, Sony, Mitsubishi, Panasonic, and other Japanese TV manufacturers introduced sets in the U.S. market that were not only less likely to break down and need repair, but when they did need to be serviced, because of their design it was much easier to repair them than working on a domestic TV receiver. In addition, because the imported TVs were relatively inexpensive, many consumers purchased a new imported TV instead of paying to have their domestic unit repaired.

Zenith, now known as Zenith Electronics, is a wholly owned subsidiary of the South Korean firm LG Electronics and few men or women aspire to be a TV repair technician. What is more, with large corporations like Lucent, Sony, Hitachi, and Fujitsu each laying off tens of thousands of employees in the downturn of 2001, work in the technology sector of the economy has lost much of the appeal it once had. Worldwide, the computer technicians, systems analysts, middle managers, and other computer technology specialists who were able to name their salary and stock options a few years earlier were suddenly unemployed. Employees of large corporations, like investors, bear the risk of a corporate downturn.

IN THE TRENCHES

In many respects, the volatility of the electronics corporations in the 1970s pales in comparison to that of the dotCom corporate environment of the 1990s. For example, an established brick-and-mortar software development corporation—let's call it Traditional Software, Inc. (TSI)—hired Bryan's company to perform a post-mortem on one of its failed business relationships. The dream-turned-nightmare described next follows a theme repeated hundreds of times after the dotCom downturn. It also illustrates how although a corporate environment can minimize cost of a failed corporate investment and product development, there is no guarantee of success.

TSI, a medium-sized U.S. corporation, needed a Web-based interface to its new computer-based training (CBT) applications. TSI wanted to get the software into the hands of customers who could not or did not want to invest in the hardware and software for an in-house system. The caveat was that the software was not yet fully developed on a stand-alone computer platform. Furthermore, the company was running low on R&D funds for this particular project and wanted some means to continue to develop what they considered would be the next generation of its product. Lacking internal development resources, the management of TSI initiated a search for a company to whom they could outsource their online CBT development efforts.

Enter the second company—let's call it ETek—an established technology company that was contacted by TSI because of its reputation for leading-edge software development, even though it had no real experience in the CBT market. ETek devised a creative business plan in which it would partner with TSI in the form of a third, jointly owned corporation, which would develop a Web version of the CBT product as well as a plan to sell computer-based learning functionally through the Web. TSI viewed the collaboration as a relatively low-risk source of revenue, and invested $500,000 in the formation of the new company, NewTek. Both TSI and ETek established cross-licensing arrangements with each other and with NewTek. In the licensing agreement, ETek was given a perpetual license to TSI's core CBT technology. In exchange, TSI was given a perpetual license to use anything that NewTek developed during the relationship, including the Web-based technology contributed by ETek. TSI viewed the investment in NewTek as a means of obtaining the interface they needed and making a profit. With the seed money and cross-licensing arrangement from TSI in hand, NewTek set out to raise venture capital (VC) money.

Within about six moths, a high-profile VC firm was convinced to invest about $5 million in the venture, in exchange for 25% of NewTek and a seat on the board. With the money, NewTek hired a PR firm, a head of marketing, and a CBT consultant. Up to this point, all that NewTek had for a product was a prototype that provided a reasonable demonstration of the full CBT program. The CEO of ETek served as the interim CEO for NewTek during a brief search period.

Despite negotiations, TSI never did really transfer its knowledge of the intricacies of the CBT market to the NewTek staff. One issue may have been distance, since the companies were located several hundred miles apart. Another factor may have been the contrasting corporate cultures. TSI was white shirts and ties; ETek was T-shirts and sandals for programmers and polo shirts for the other staff. Technically, there was also a degree of contention between the IS departments of the two founding companies; each department believed that they had a better way to achieve a Web interface that would support NewTek's needs. Then there were the principals in ETek and TSI, each with a clear vision of where they wanted to take NewTek and the best way to get there. These and other differences were easily smoothed over when there was the prospect of fantastic returns on the investment in New-Tek. However, the tension heightened as prospects for huge returns from the NewTek dotCom company became less likely.

Internally, NewTek had troubles as well. For example, NewTek's salespeople did not really understand the product that their R&D department was developing; instead, they crafted a story that talked around the product. However, they were not able to condense the benefits into terms easily understood by potential buyers. In many respects, this inability was due to the ephemeral nature of the product—it did not really exist, other than as a constantly changing demonstration prototype. Furthermore, it was not clear that TSI's stand-alone CBT package was usable. As a result, the NewTek programmers were faced with the challenge of developing a CBT product that worked on the Web, while facing core issues that had not been fully addressed by TSI. In addition, NewTek's sales force had to begin with a market for CBT that did not really exist at that time.

From 1998 to 2000, NewTek developed over a dozen prototype systems for potential clients and investors, but never made a significant sale. Because there was not any further funding for a specific CBT product, a fully functional Web-based CBT program was never developed. Besides, NewTek's programming resources were being used to support the Web site and to create demonstration software for the sales effort. At two years into the relationship, NewTek had developed an impressive Web presence for its CBT owner/investor, but no revenue from the site. As a free reference, it did well in terms of hits, especially since there were no obtrusive banner ads. However, not only was the VC money almost depleted, but the market had started to turn on the dotComs.

With only a few months of cash reserve remaining, NewTek was desperate for more revenue and took on several peripheral projects that pulled in revenue. However, because the projects were so resource intensive, they did not generate a profit. Instead of developing its core technology in CBT, NewTek had developed dozens of PowerPoint presentations and simulations of the final CBT project. However, TSI's fully operational system did not yet exist. NewTek limped along for almost all of 2001, operating from one month to the next.

With cash in short supply, NewTek employees were given additional stock options as incentives instead of salary raises. For the most part, employees were kept in the dark, except for the good news about fund raising. They were not informed, for example, how low the operating funds were each month. However, many employees would have preferred to know the reality of the situation rather than be left wondering if something was wrong, and not knowing the extent of it. The stock incentives helped, especially since the programmers and sales force were busier than ever. However, they were working on small projects generating $50,000 to $100,000 that were detours from the company's mission.

In the end, NewTek's doors closed. NewTek employees, once mesmerized with dreams of a multimillion-dollar IPO, were left holding worthless stock options, the VC company was out $5 million, and TSI was without a Web interface or a means of supporting their costly R&D effort. TSI lost most of its modest investment, but the entrepreneurs that started NewTek, unscathed economically from the failure because of the liability protection afforded by their corporation, went off to start another venture. In the end, the only real losers were the employees of NewTek.

ANALYSIS

The TSI–NewTek story illustrates the value of the corporate shield for companies. Even though the effort failed, TSI's losses were minimal, and its exposure to liability was limited by the corporate structure—and therein lies the rub. Because it was not a matter of life and death for TSI and ETek, their energies were focused elsewhere. For TSI, the formation of another company was a way to compartmentalize the Web-based CBT project. Similarly, for the owners of ETek, forming a separate corporate entity, separate and distinct from their other corporate activities, NewTek was simply one more of a half-dozen projects underway. It only needed one of the six projects—which may or may not have included NewTek—to really take off in order to become successful. As a result, ETek didn't provide NewTek with the care and attention it needed to grow.

The story also shows how, internally, people believe what they want to believe, and how a company can fail through miscommunications and prevalent illusions about a product that does not exist. By failing to exactly track NewTek's progress on the Continuum, both TSI and ETek threw away their prospects for success. To be fair, because of the excitement surrounding the dotCom era and the velocity of decisions being made, it was difficult for NewTek's staff to focus on a static target for developing the product and short-term attainment of profitability for the corporation. At the time, the perceived sizzle was worth much more than the tangible steak.

Of course, from the luxury of hindsight, the predictors for failure were numerous and obvious. For one, TSI's management had unreasonable expectations of what a Web presence would do for their bottom line. In addition, NewTek, a newcomer to the CBT field, had an insufficient depth of knowledge of how to develop a Web-based version of TSI's evolving, untested product, even with a consultant and technology licensed from TSI. Another factor was that the CBT space was too specialized and volatile to provide a reasonable product that would show profit. Companies were not clamoring for CBT applications, Web-enabled or otherwise, and there were numerous competitors from commercial and academic sources.

TSI was clearly unrealistic in hoping to ride the dotCom wave to profitability instead of believing in its own R&D, reflecting the fact that their core technology had not yet reached the Technical Gateway, as shown in Figure 8.2. Finally, given the customer response to product demonstrations, it is likely that customers could see through the shallow sales presentations.

Examining the situation from the perspective of the Continuum, clearly the technology, the perspective of NewTek's R&D group,

Figure 8.2   Perceptions along the Continuum

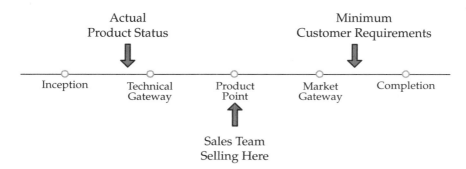

was not at the point where it could be released and supported as a finished product. However, those in NewTek's marketing and sales divisions, which were heavily influenced by pressure from TSI and ETek, had a very different perception, as shown in Figure 8.2. They believed the edict from management that the Web-based CBT package was at least at the Product Point in the Continuum.

In addition, upper-level management at NewTek blamed lackluster sales on the marketing and sales group, and assumed that the technology was far enough along the Continuum to secure a buy-in from customers. Obviously, everyone involved, except perhaps NewTek's management, had a different perception of where the product was in the Continuum.

General Principles and Implications

The TSI–ETek story illustrates the relative ease with which a corporation can provide a protective development environment with the potential to raise capital at minimum risk to the owners. By providing a safety net, the corporate shell can have a detrimental effect on productivity when used with small companies. Conversely, because the larger corporations are such huge employers, small downturns in corporate valuation can dramatically affect the number of employees the corporation can afford to maintain. As a result, employees, like investors, bear the brunt of risk.

The TSI post-mortem also illustrates how surviving in the marketplace is a constant battle. With the possible exception of temporary economic anomalies, achieving the illusive goal of an ever-increasing value cascade does not occur by chance. A corporation that simply maintains its position in the value cascade without defining a clear technology focus risks being overtaken by other corporations that are aggressively pushing their value upward.

A significant component of the battle is understanding the complex set of rules underlying the social, political, and business environment that periodically shifts to favor one business approach over another. Understanding these rules is imperative for a corporation to survive and thrive in a highly competitive market. Part of grasping the complex set of underlying business assumptions is establishing high-quality communications—which is where the Continuum model comes in.

It is imperative that inter- and intracompany communications among R&D, marketing, sales, and management be of the highest quality. Although some degree of information hiding or filtering may be necessary for efficiency and security reasons, poor communications can result in costly misunderstandings and incorrect assumptions.

The scenario above and the history of technology-based upheaval imply that it is possible for a corporation to acquire power and money with any business model—in the short term. A first mover with a novel technology and proven financial model—leveraged buyouts, conglomerates, or dotComs—can extract value from investors and those able to take advantage of the market before it collapses. In this regard, the entrenched, established corporations with a long-term Old Economy view are at risk for missing out on these and other short-term opportunities, but are in a better position to maintain a positive value cascade from one decade to the next.

This chapter ends Part Two, Value. Chapter 9, Making Better Business Decisions, summarizes the concepts covered in this book and illustrates how readers can apply business alchemy with respect to their own companies.

SUMMARY

The popularity of the corporation as a means of moving from idea to successful product along the Continuum stems from the limited liability it affords as well as the prospect of raising vast amounts of capital. The corporation lends itself to analysis as a military entity that forms relationships and maneuvers its resources in order to achieve strategic and tactical advantages over competing corporations. In this regard, the international titans who exercise control over their environments through political and economic force dominate the competitive corporate landscape.

Old Economy strategies, while not necessarily responsive to short-term trends that may provide significant short-term return on investment, are more likely to result in long-term value generation. However, as illustrated by the revolutionary changes in the consumer and commercial electronics industries in the 1970s and the dotCom experience of the 1990s, corporations and entire industries using Old Economy strategies can be disrupted periodically by innovations initiated by competing corporations that do manage to follow the short-term trends. Unfortunately, the corporate model can be inefficiently used, especially with smaller companies that use the corporate shell as a means of partitioning off risk—and focus—while pursuing other goals.

PART THREE

VISION MAINTENANCE

9

Making Better Business Decisions

If necessity is the mother of invention, discontent is the father of progress.

David Rockefeller

One way of looking at the world of business is as an imperfect system ruled by chaos, where chance and fate define the ultimate outcome of any personal venture or enterprise. This view is supported every few decades by the large number of people and companies who profit simply because they seemingly happen to be at the right place at the right time. In the 1970s, for example, investing in real estate in the United States was a sure thing. Anyone with enough money to invest in real estate was virtually guaranteed a return on investment whose rate would beat the prime rate if they held on to the property for a year or two. Early investors in the dotCom companies saw phenomenal returns as well—as long as they did not hold on to the stock too long. It was so easy to make money on tech stocks that many people quit their regular jobs to become day traders. However, this state of affairs was short-lived. The fundamental and underlying understanding of when to invest or divest is the true power of the successful visionary business alchemist. The ever-present question is: When will the next wave of opportunity hit and how can one identify the proper timing to enter a new market?

One way to approach that question is to look at the world as a complex web of cause and effect, where some events can be controlled and other factors cannot—either because of their nature or because we are unaware of their existence. In this view, there are good times and bad times as well, because the economic foundation is continually shifting. What is more, the rate of change in innovation is accelerating in part because of the development of communication technologies. For example, instead of an unaware developer wasting time on an invention only to find out too late that something like it was patented years earlier, anyone can log in to the U.S. Patent and Trademark Office (www.USPTO.gov), search the archives, and even order drawings by fax.

This second view of the world is also compatible with the notion that the conversion of ideas to saleable products is a partially controllable process that replaces variability and uncertainty with known or knowable technology, as described by the Continuum model. In this regard, the Continuum model is helpful in reducing the degree of uncertainty in the conversion process. It shows, for example, how the role of marketing at different points varies as a function of whether the business is newly established and has limited resources or is established and has a marketing division in place to direct R&D efforts. A marketing division also evaluates new and emerging product ideas. The model also illustrates how the chances of a typical garage startup software company succeeding are compromised by an inability to address—or lack of knowledge about—market needs, as opposed to technologic function.

A third view (compatible with the second view) is that businesses, whether lemonade stands or Fortune 500 companies, are fundamentally organic structures and behave in characteristically organic ways. That is, businesses and their products wax and wane with the economic environment. For example, companies rarely stay on top of their market for more than two or three decades, and the few companies that have done so did it by recreating themselves in response to changing customer and economic demands. Although a successful business can be replicated endlessly when a people-independent process is established, someone or some group has to first establish the process. Since these people have a finite career-span, change is inevitable when they retire. It is unlikely that their successors will see a way to do things better—if only to take advantage of a new technology or to create a legacy of their own—unless a successful knowledge transfer is completed between new and old.

This is comparable to the concept of peaking for an athletic event. With an established learning curve that includes understanding the proper training, rest, nutrition, and motivation, it is possible to stay at a moderate to high level of fitness indefinitely. However, for peak performance, it takes planning, mental and physical preparation, motivation, and the necessary skills and aptitude. However, even a professional athlete can only sustain a peak for a limited period. It is unusual for an individual, company, or country to stay in peak state for more than a few decades. Consider that when President John F. Kennedy established the goal of landing a man on the moon, the military (NASA) and hundreds of contractors focused on achieving the goal at any cost, as a means of winning a psychological edge in the Cold War against Russia. As a result, there were more innovations in physics and aircraft engineering in a few years than in the previous two decades, with engineers and scientists devoting long hours and weekends to achieving the goal—akin to the work ethic of the dotCom startups. Of course, it helped that the contractors had a blank check from the Kennedy administration. However, after the illusive goal was achieved, life for the engineers returned to normal, and the rate of innovation slowed as well. Once the dream was achieved, there was no sustained vision or next step in the process.

Similarly, as products mature, they eventually become feature intensive rather than innovation driven, and margins drop. For example, in the high-tech industry, IBM and DEC were the market leaders in the 1980s because they controlled large proprietary systems that were popular with businesses. In the 1990s, with the introduction of the PC, Microsoft, Dell, and Intel dominated the space, displacing the mini- and mainframe computer manufacturers. In the first decade of 2000, wireless handsets, including wireless PDAs, are poised to displace the PC and its associated technical infrastructure in terms of the number of devices used daily for creating and disseminating information.

Continuing with a view that combines the deterministic and organic views of business, this chapter examines how to use the information introduced in the previous chapters to make better business decisions. The discussion begins with a review of the factors associated with success in business, is followed by an examination of some business concepts that surfaced during the New Economy, and finishes with a discussion of how the Continuum model can be useful to startups or established companies with either technology- or market-driven products.

ROLE OF LEADERSHIP

Assuming that the fate of a business is not predetermined and that decisions can define or establish the direction for progress, much of the fate of a business rests squarely on the shoulders of the CEO and other executive decision makers. Through directing the focus of the company, managing risk, creating a shared vision, and determining the proper timing of events, a CEO can create a successful culture or bring a company to a screeching halt.

For example, the new GE simply is not the same without Jack Welch at the helm, just as Intel is still partly defined by Andy Grove's legacy. Similarly, Chrysler would never have succeeded in the same fashion without Lee Iacocca. Great CEOs not only excel at recognizing markers of progress along the Continuum model, but they are keyed into the significance of personal relationships and the business environment. As noted in Chapter 3, the motivation behind exemplary performance as a leader is often difficult to determine, although it is possible to guess in some cases. For example, Lee Iacocca was fired from Ford only to lead Chrysler out of the doldrums. Whether his success at Chrysler was because his failure at Ford motivated him to prove to the world that it was not his fault is debatable. However, what is not debatable is that he managed to pull the company out of a slump. For example, he single-handedly obtained a loan for the company from Congress, and cemented his image as a man of his word by paying back the loan before it was due.

Iacocca also illustrates a characteristic of winning leaders. Success is not about avoiding failure, but about managing failure when it occurs. For example, Iacocca left Chrysler and went on to champion a battery-powered bicycle that flopped. Undaunted, his next move was to a make a battery-powered vehicle that has the potential to do well, especially in California. Whether or not the vehicle is a success, the point is that Iacocca keeps stepping up to the challenge, win or lose.

Another characteristic of successful leaders is the ability to clearly define the focus of the enterprise. Seasoned CEOs are aware of the need to constantly balance resources throughout the Continuum, from product development to marketing, as the technology moves along the Continuum. In addition to external economic factors, customer acceptance of a product in the marketplace is crucial. The odds of success are greater if the customer is considered as early as possible in the Continuum. Moreover, it is critical to appreciate that customer behavior change takes time and energy. A marketing campaign that begins after a product is fully test-marketed may fail in the larger marketplace because the product may sit idle for years before market demand is sufficient to warrant large-scale production. However, the time horizon to build a critical mass of customers to sustain revenue may go beyond the initial seed capital that the company started with. The time required for universal adoption is far greater than the life span of a typical company, suggesting that timing is a major factor in the success of introducing customers to a product. Furthermore, even if the company has the resources and bandwidth to wait for customer willingness to accept the new product, the threat of competition introducing a superior technology at a lower price is ever present.

Success in the marketplace is a matter of timing and accurately communicating a product's benefit to the end user, as well as the creation of a working technology. History is full of great ideas that failed in the marketplace because of timing. The Commodore Amiga, circa 1985, was ahead of its time as a digital video- and audio-editing machine, comparable in many ways to contemporary tools available on Windows and Macintosh. Despite the Amiga's technical superiority, which included video capture and playback hardware and editing software, marketing was not able to save the technology in the marketplace—there simply was not a big demand for digital video editing outside of the small niche professional market. As it was, the Apple Macintosh at that time was pushing the technology adoption envelope in the general consumer market with its grayscale graphical user interface. Conversely, the Apple Newton PDA and the NEXT computer were released into the hands of marketing and sales long before the underlying technology was ready. Apple and NEXT computing apparently failed to follow the Continuum model, hoping that marketing would take care of holes in the technology.

Finally, the role of decision maker carries with it the responsibility of seizing opportunities as they arise. Since opportunity implies risk, a large part of a decision maker's job is to manage risk. In this regard, risk management is not about doing whatever it takes to avoid disaster, but rather making plans to respond to disaster when it strikes. For example, risk management includes setting aside money, time, and other resources to deal with failure. A CEO who is good at risk management can quantify risk so that specific risk-management actions can be instituted to solve the challenges at hand.

MISCONCEPTIONS OF
THE NEW ECONOMY

During the technology bubble of the late 1990s, there were a number of New Economy misconceptions that were thought to be applicable to all present and future business practices. These misconceptions, which were then embraced by at least some of the companies taking part in the dotCom boom, are no longer viable in today's business world. A discussion of these outdated maxims follows.

Early Mover Wins

The advantage of being the first or second company to offer a new type of product in and of itself does not guarantee success over the competition. Being an early mover in a new product space is just as important as being a best mover. Microsoft illustrates this by its late but ultimately successful entry into the Web browser market. Similarly, once Corning demonstrated the feasibility of fiber optics as a communications medium, AT&T responded immediately by pouring resources into the space and soon dominated it.

During the dotCom boom, the belief that simply claiming a catchy URL planted a company flag in the dotCom space was short-lived. Of course, being a first mover with deep pockets and a good long-range financial plan is optimal, as are speed and agility in responding to change in the economic environment, including meeting ever-vacillating customer preferences.

Companies and even countries with vast resources do not have to be first movers to dominate a consumer market space. The second mover has the advantage of watching and learning what does and does not work for a target market. For example, China was a late mover in the wireless space, behind Japan, much of Europe, and parts of the United States. However, as soon as China decided on its wireless strategy, handset cellular network providers around the globe responded immediately to service China's needs. In watching the progress of wireless in more advanced countries, China's governmentally controlled telecom industry was able to sidestep the fallout from mergers and acquisitions and was in a position to judge the technologies and companies that survived the shakeout.

In the Web Space, Reach is Revenue

One of the advantages of interactive advertisement over traditional print and TV advertising is that it is possible to determine how many people are actually exposed to an ad. However, as the banner ads on Web sites demonstrate, most users ignore ads, and the return on investment for Web advertisers has been much lower than initially expected. In other words, the practice of establishing the valuation of a Web site based on the number of visitors to a site has proven to be a poor strategy for financial valuation. On the Web, as in other touch points—print, TV, and radio—what counts is the conversion rate, the number of potential customers who are exposed to an advertisement and then actually form a business relationship with a company.

A Global Touch Point Makes a Company Global

Because of the Internet, a Web site residing on a PC in the dormitory room of the teenager who created it has the same level of access to the global market as does IBM or Microsoft. As such, with enough attention to detail and relevant content, it is impossible for the casual viewer to determine if the company behind the site consists of one or one thousand people. However, the Web has demonstrated that a prerequisite for a company to be successful globally is success locally. That is, a business process must be perfected locally before attempting the much more complex global market.

Companies have to succeed in their local economies and establish a supporting infrastructure before they can establish a global presence, even if they have a global reach by virtue of the Web. Entering and successfully competing in a global market is much more than being accessible, as there are localization issues with user interface design, cultural issues, language, currency conversion, taxes, and other service-fulfillment limitations inherent in dealing with a global business.

Technology is Strategy

Technology can amplify a good or bad customer service strategy, but technology should not be confused with strategy. Good technology, whether it takes the form of a properly implemented Web site or a CRM program, can make a good service strategy great. However, the inappropriate use of technology can make a bad strategy even worse.

In most successful service businesses, technology takes a back seat to the personal element. For example, as described earlier in this book, the human factors associated with technology adoption are much more critical to success than the specific technology involved. Employees involved in customer service typically fear change, do not want to lose the power they have accumulated, and are generally uncomfortable with revolutionary, as opposed to evolutionary, changes that technology can bring about. Without addressing these issues as part of an overall customer service strategy, any technology push is destined for failure.

Growth is Sufficient

The fate of Amazon.com and the other high-profile players in the Web space have demonstrated that a focus on market share at the expense of profitability only works in the short term. Although the strategy of being growth-driven may initially work to gain market share and displace potential competitors, successful long-term companies are profit-driven.

For example, Amazon was growth-driven during its first few years, but then pressure from shareholders for a return on their investment forced it to become profit-driven. The online retailer and bookseller was forced to adopt cost-cutting measures, such as using customer support representatives in India and elsewhere instead of domestic staff. It also established profit-generating business relationships with Circuit City, Toys R Us, and other brick-and-mortar stores that could benefit from—and pay for—Amazon's reach.

COMPANY-DRIVER SCENARIOS

To illustrate the relevance of the Continuum model in everyday business, consider that most companies involved in developing a product and bringing it to market are either new or established companies, and their products are either technology- or market-driven (see Figure 9.1). The first category, the technology-driven startup, involves the entrepreneur-inventor who develops the next new thing and then forms a company to exploit the invention. In the second category, an established company with a marketing and sales division develops a new technology and brings it to market with a mature and experienced management team. In this example, the technology may have come from a merger or acquisition. Microsoft would fall into the third category of a market-driven established company, assuming that the R&D group was driven by data from consumer surveys and not solely from an engineer or programmer enamored of a particular technology. The fourth category of company type is the pure market-driven startup, such as a company started by recent MBA graduates, for example, who are aware of market demand for a product and set out to obtain the resources needed to bring their idea to reality. As described next, the odds of success and the challenges associated with each type of company are very different, and yet the decision makers are faced with many of the same issues.

Figure 9.1   Company-Driver Matrix

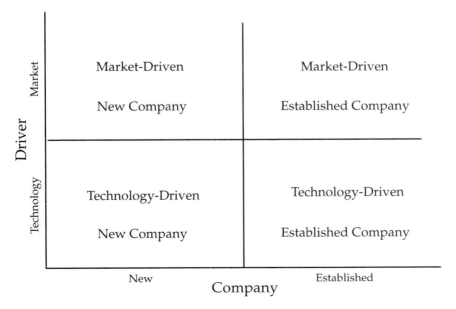

Technology-Driven Startup

Companies that are established primarily to exploit a particular technology have particular challenges along the way to profitability. Most technology-driven companies are small, two- or three-person operations that are characterized by limited resources, which are devoted to developing a viable prototype. The Apple computer and the Visi-Calc electronic spreadsheet are two notable examples of the potential of this type of business venture.

These companies typically start at or near the Technical Gateway of the Continuum, with at least some form of prototype in hand, but with absolutely no knowledge of the potential marketability of the product beyond the developer's typically limited perspective. The challenge facing the decision makers is to take the technically viable concept driving the company and move it along the Continuum to become a successful product. The demographics of the typical user may be undefined, and the viability of the business plan unknown. Also, the soundness of the revenue model and profit potential, based on cost of production, marketing, and distribution, may be undefined, and the availability of resources required for production may not even have been considered. Clearly, the major stakeholders, if any, are the technical experts and their backers. Technology-driven companies that are formed on the basis of nonexistent or potential technology are commonly susceptible to intellectual property and licensing threats from the competition because the company many not have the resources or the energy to devote to protecting its intellectual property. Although there are exceptions, usually the company's decision makers are technocentric, and they usually have difficulty raising capital to address their nontechnologic weaknesses such as hiring employees to adjust the mix for market growth instead of hiring purely for R&D. In addition, if the company is ultimately successful in creating a working product, its success in the marketplace may be usurped by a company that offers a technically inferior product but has better marketing, service support, and customer reach.

Lacking the benefit of a marketing group early on, the product may not be suitable for the potential customers, and there is a greater likelihood that the product will need to be reworked after it is introduced into the marketplace. Products developed by this type of company tend to have the greatest likelihood of consumer recidivism and have a rate of consumer adoption that is slower than market-driven products. Because there is no brand recognition, customer expectations are unknown, and customers may undervalue the product, even if it is technologically superior to similar products on the market.

The major sticking points for the technology-driven new company are the Product Point and, to a much greater degree, the Market Gateway. Many developers never quite manage to create a viable prototype, despite their technical prowess. For example, when Alexander Graham Bell developed his Photophone—a telephone that used light as the communications medium—he was unable to create a demonstration unit that worked in typical weather conditions. Other than carefully controlled demonstrations during Bell's speaking engagements, the Photophone was not widely used.

In addition, the new, technology-driven company typically has major challenges in transforming its corporate culture and developing a marketing vision. There are corporate culture issues of focus, leadership, attracting and retaining quality employees, making payroll, and maintaining employee morale. Because money tends to be in short supply, stock options are commonly used in this type of business to attract and keep good employees—a tactic that works only as long as the potential for success seems significant. In the area of marketing, new companies that are technocentric by design typically face the challenges of assessing the competition, establishing corporate visibility, advertising, and adjusting their products to match shifts in the political economy.

The story of the lone inventor toiling away in her garage or huddled in her computer cubicle creating the next killer application, and bringing it to market is the stuff dreams are made of, but rarely what successful companies are built from. Bill Gates and Larry Ellison, programmers turned multibillion-dollar CEOs because of their entrepreneurial spirit and ability to convert their technical prowess into viable products, have certainly been role models for many other programmers who attempt to follow their footsteps.

However, the authors of this book have worked with companies started by intelligent, well-meaning innovators who poured years of effort into a technology that, although it worked, had mixed long-term viability in the marketplace. A few of these persistent innovators had the knack for marketing or the luck of finding a third party in need of their technology. However, usually the only ones who made money in these arrangements were the original founding team and a host of accountants and business attorneys.

The winners in this type of venture come to realize the value of the concepts embodied in the Continuum model. At some point, typically after they have spent a considerable amount of money developing a prototype or a fully deployed product, they realize that they underestimated the amount or capitol and expertise it takes to establish distribution channels, start a marketing campaign, or use a sales force most effectively. Of course, successful companies come to this realization early on and hire a seasoned CEO, head of marketing, sales, and other specialists needed to attract customers as well as a steady stream of investment capitol. Even these companies pay the price for viewing the development process as a binary one in which a technology focus is suddenly replaced with a marketing focus, instead of the progression defined by the integrated Continuum model.

Many more new, technology-driven companies fail because either they never appreciated the reason that customers did not initially purchase their product or they brought in marketing personnel too late. By the time they have an objective measure of market demand, their fate during initial market introduction has been determined. Although it seems obvious in this extreme case, many established companies act in the same myopic way, thinking that they can handle the customer demand side after a product has been introduced to the marketplace. Unfortunately, many potential inventions die this way, only to be rediscovered later. In this regard, the primary value of the Continuum model in a new, technology-driven company is in proper sales and market planning in conjunction with product development, regardless of whether the founding team has the funds to hire a seasoned CEO or retain a marketing firm.

However, if the organization's leaders work with the understanding of the marketing and customer behavior hurdles ahead, they may be able to direct their work so that, for example, modifications based on changes in customer preferences can be made more readily in the future. A software developer, for example, could make a relatively small investment during the programming stage to use an architecture that supports a variety of end-user interfaces.

If customers do not like the initial interface, the company is in a good position to modify its product quickly. Conversely, coding an application with the mindset that the developers know what is best from a customer perspective could easily result in an application with an interface that is virtually impossible to rewrite affordably and quickly enough to respond to true customer preferences.

Technology-Driven Established Company

Of the technology-driven companies, those with the greatest likelihood of success have already established themselves as capable of surviving in the marketplace. That is, the founders either were aware or became aware of the natural progression of idea to viable product in previous ventures. Often, technologists who have access to talent in other areas as well as technical expertise are called upon to run established companies that use a technology-driven approach to product development. Alternately, the CEO of a technology-driven company can acquire the intellectual property rights to the technology, demonstrate customer demand in the marketplace, and then license the technology to a company interested in growing the market for the product.

Like the new company driven by technology, the established company typically begins with some form of prototype in hand and minimal market analysis. As such, the challenges facing the decision makers are similar to those facing the decision makers in a new company. However, assuming the new technology drive is not completely unlike existing products within the current product pipeline, the decision makers are more cognizant of the likely market demand, and they'll have an easier time of raising capital for the venture because of a successful track record or because the organization is large enough to obtain funding from existing budgets. An established company may already have an internal employee mix that is seasoned for growing a product, including marketing support that can be called upon to help support an initial sales effort.

However, as illustrated by many companies that spun off dotCom entities, success in one type of business does not confer automatic success in ancillary, unrelated ventures. Most of the dotComs established by Fortune 500 companies as potential revenue generators have been relegated to customer support and advertising portals and, in only a few instances, are they providing eCommerce an alternative source of revenue from traditional brick-and-mortar efforts capable of sustaining the online offering. In terms of customer behavior, the rate of adoption, likelihood of customer recidivism, and need to rework the product after introduction are virtually identical to those ascribed to new companies that are technology-driven. However, the customer expectations of an established company's technology product are highly influenced by the previous products released by the company.

Similarly, an established company pursuing the development of a product from a strictly technological perspective is likely to get stuck on the same issues that plague a new company, but to a lesser degree. Among them are marketing-related issues such as establishing an advertising budget, obtaining coverage by the trade press, establishing corporate visibility, and satisfying customer expectations. The issue of expectations should be addressed, at least in part, by the introduction of the company's previous products. However, this advantage is only to the degree that the CEO and other decision makers make use of their knowledge of the market early on in the Continuum.

The primary value of the Continuum model to decision makers is as a streamlined communications medium that keeps marketing, sales, and R&D in sync. Thus, once management decides to expand the effort beyond R&D, product development can move as swiftly as possible through the various phases of the Continuum in collaboration with other departments critical to the successful introduction of the product to the marketplace. For example, if sales and marketing know that the company is still a year away from a fully debugged product (Completion), the organization can plan its budget and resources for initial test marketing and product roll-out activities. Similarly, in communicating with potential investors, the Continuum model can help establish reasonable expectations on time to market, resource requirements, and overall financial risk assessment.

Market-Driven Established Company

Now consider the market-driven established company, whether a Fortune 500 company or small biotech firm. The main difference between this model and the previous two models is that technology is secondary to market considerations. That is, the goal is to satisfy customer wants and needs by providing a product with specific bene-fits, as opposed to a goal of somehow finding a niche for a developed technology. Market-driven product design in these companies begins early on, at Inception, and involves the analysis of customer demographics, likely demand, analysis of the competition, and other long-range projections that relate to the viability of a new product development effort. Because of this focus, many projects never make it to Inception because a viable financial plan cannot be agreed upon, regardless of the technological implications.

Once the project is begun, the major challenge becomes one of creating a technology that will satisfy the needs of the targeted consumers—the converse of the situation in a typical technology-driven company that is headed by developers. As such, there is greater likelihood of reworking the technology and eliminating grand scale features during the development phase of the Product Lifecycle.

One of the greatest advantages that the decision makers in a market-driven company have is that they start with knowledge of the customer's explicit needs and the potential revenue model that a successful product can provide. Then they can establish when to walk away from a technical approach because of unanticipated costs of development or production, and when to keep investing in development. Although a technologist who perseveres despite daunting challenges may occasionally beat the odds and come up with something that is both technically and commercially viable, in most instances it does not pay to follow a pure technology invest-ment with more money until an advanced customer research effort is initiated. An example of an established, market-driven company that is investing heavily in R&D because of the economic potential is Corning. The management at Corning is investing millions in more efficient fiber optics cables, not for the sake of creating a bet-ter fiber, but because of what it considers the vast potential eco-nomic gains for low-loss optical fiber in the next few years based upon projected customer demand.

Of the four models discussed here, a product created by an established, market-driven company has the greatest likelihood of suc-cess. First, it most likely has much deeper pockets than a startup organi-zation. Secondly, assuming the previous products were well received by the public, customer expectations are likely to be enhanced by the company's name and existing brand. Even so, there are many challenges, even for the most established market-driven companies. For example, the major sticking points in the Continuum model are at the Product Point and Completion. That is, compared to a technology-driven company, the sticking points are shifted to later in the Continuum. In addition to the marketing challenges, such as how to allocate advertising dollars to best differentiate the product from the competition's, there are likely to be significant technical hurdles to overcome as well. Dealing with standards, selecting the best technology partners, and evolving platform standards, for example, creates a degree of uncertainty to the company's ability to deliver technically solid products on time and on budget. A disadvantage may be a reliance by senior management on market research data that is either incomplete or unavailable due to the infancy of a new product category with an ill-defined customer base. Examples such as the PC and VCR serve to remind us that initial market research indicating there would be little commercial viability for several of the most commonly used technology products can be misleading.

Finally, compared to the typical startup, the management of an established company is more likely to be familiar with the relative advantages of the various business models, such as limited liability corporations, C-corps, and S-corps in supporting product development, raising capital, and attracting and keeping good talent. For example, a common mistake made by decision makers forming a new corporation is that in defining the initial stock splits they do not put aside sufficient stock for hiring future employees and for providing them with incentives for staying on. Although stock splits can be initiated, doing so has dilution and tax consequences that may be detrimental to existing stockholders.

Market-Driven Startup

The fourth category of product development company, the market-driven startup, has many of the characteristics of an established market-driven company. The main differences are in the areas of customer expectations and business viability. Unless there is a renowned CEO at the helm, customer expectations are unknown because the new company's brand does not have a legacy to build upon. In addition, being a new company, the business plan, revenue model, profit potential, and availability of resources are usually less certain than those of an established company.

A market-driven startup company's common sticking points include market and technology issues and company issues. As in a technology-driven startup, there are issues of how to attract, train, and maintain quality employees; ensure an adequate flow of funding capital; and comply with legal requirements. On the upside, a truly focused market-driven startup may be more flexible in its ability to take advantage of short-term changes in consumer preferences simply because fewer internal divisions and product lines are competing for resources.

The Continuum

In each of the previous four scenarios, the value of the Continuum is in timing, managing risk, predicting resource requirements, assessing the competition, and communicating the state of development to stakeholders inside and outside of the organization. As a concrete example, consider the process involved with bringing a book like this to market with an established market-driven publisher.

Inception: *The publisher first evaluates a proposal for the book in terms of market potential, likely return on investment, likely effect from competing books, and other market-relevant issues.*

Concept Development: *The author reworks the proposal to address the publisher's marketing concerns.*

Technical Gateway: *The author demonstrates his understanding of the task by creating a sample chapter and submitting it to the publisher for review. Assuming the work is in agreement with the publisher's initial feedback, a contract is negotiated between the publisher and the author. The contract specifies deliverables, timetables, and responsibilities.*

Prototype Development: *The author begins to write the book in earnest, working with his team of researchers, readers, and editors, checking in periodically to inform the managing editor of his progress. The developmental editor periodically verifies that the trans-formation of the author's thoughts into the printed word is occurring on schedule and is of adequate quality. As important milestones are reached, such as completion of core manuscript material, marketing and sales personnel are notified. They then start to create promo-tional materials in preparation for sales kickoff in the next publish-ing season.*

Product Point: *The first draft is delivered to the managing editor.*

Clarification: *Working with the managing editor, the author provides refinements in the manuscript to meet the needs of intended readers.*

Market Gateway: *Publication; the book appears on the shelves and is listed in the online bookstores.*

Stabilization: *Rewrites for clarification and omission are made, based on the market response, including reactions from professional review-ers. These edits appear in future editions of the book.*

Completion: *The book's contents are repurposed for magazines, Web sites, symposia, and other markets.*

In other words, the publishing company lives and dies by its abil-ity to forecast exactly when events should and will occur. The publish-ing company orchestrates the work of dozens of professionals—from editors and indexers to publicity agents—in acquiring buy-in from resellers, setting up speaking engagements, and arranging reviews of the book. The printer is told how many copies of the book to print, based on the marketing group's assessment of the marketplace, the economy, the author's reputation, and the timeliness of the topic. In addition, if the publisher learns that a competing firm has signed an author for a similar topic, then the publisher knows when to expect the book on the shelves and whether it will be feasible to speed the book through the publishing process to meet or beat the estimated publication date for the competing work.

In establishing a process that works with a variety of scenarios, the publisher has instituted a form of risk management. For exam-ple, what if the author dies or is otherwise unable to complete the manuscript? What if the market shifts, and there is no demand for the book? What if a competing book appears on the market just before the book is to be released? How will such competition affect the return on investment?

Although this discussion revolves around the type of book you are reading now, it also applies to developing an eBook, software for a computer game, or a movie. Developing each of these media may seem like magic to an outsider, but because the developers and executive managers involved have experience and understand the process of moving from uncertainty to realization, it works. In this regard, a book can be considered a technological development project, where the author's ideas are transformed through a process that results in a marketable product. On a macro process level, most of the magic is gone, but there is still a degree of uncertainty and a need to forecast and maximize the likelihood of success and make provisions for inevitable failures along the way. After all, it is hard to tell if a movie or book will be a success. For example, only about 3% of books are blockbusters; the rest often only break even. However, the 3% that do make the best-seller list make up for all of the loss leaders.

FUTURE SHOCK

CEOs and other decision makers spend much of their time filtering the important data from the noise. There are countless theories and events that may have significant or no effect on their business, and they have to decide which to consider and which to ignore. What is relevant in a booming economy, for example, may be irrelevant when economic conditions are very different.

However, deciding what information is relevant is only part of the challenge facing business leaders today. Knowing what to make of information is often just as difficult. For example, it may be clear that adopting a new approach to developing products is the best thing to do from a business perspective, but acting on that knowledge is typically fraught with challenges. The decision maker may have to decide which functions to automate and how to prioritize implementation in simple, doable steps. Addressing the limited ability of employees and customers to absorb new technologies and process change is generally more challenging than the discrete technological issues involved. In addition, customer expectations regarding product features and benefits will likely continue to rise. In technological arenas, customers expect new products to improve their lives, perform better, and be easier and simpler to use.

As Wall Street searches for the next new thing and investors rethink their investment strategies, the Internet, World Wide Web, and wireless will proceed along the Continuum, just as TV, radio, and AC power did decades earlier. Whether biotech, nanotech, alternative power, or some other area becomes the next "can't lose," sure-fire investment, it will begin as a concept that an entrepreneur or research team brings to the Technical Gateway and then someone with entrepreneurial savvy shepherds to the Market Gateway.

It is up to the CEO and other decision makers to assess and respond to the changes the Web and other technologies made in their industries. For example, banks, which are really information-handling companies, are likely to be affected by even small changes in the effectiveness of data and voice communications technology. Other industries, such as large-ticket consumer electronics, in which the customer often wants to look at, touch, and determine the performance of a device before purchase, may not benefit much from an increased use of online communications.

Taking the global view, as many U.S. companies have been forced to do since the U.S. market stagnation and economic downturn of 2000, entering emerging markets for technology-based goods and services holds enormous potential. For example, in China, where only about 10% of employees have PCs on their desks, the potential for computer sales is significant. However, there is the issue of infrastructure; most provinces do not have any form of wired Internet access. As such, there is a vast potential market for wireless Web access once an open market can be achieved.

In addition, even though the Internet was supposed to be the great leveler, it has not been. To the contrary, those few with access to the technology have excelled in obtaining information more expeditiously, whereas those living in areas not serviced by adequate Internet infrastructures not only do not have access, but they do not have the education required to use and understand how to incorporate the rapidly evolving technology.

Regardless of the state of the economy, businesses operate in a competitive, resource-limited environment, with the reality of finite Product Lifespans, only partially predictable customer behavior, and the need to innovate with an R&D and marketing focus that shifts along with the different stages of product development. The patterns and relationships defined by the Continuum model provide businesses involved in new product development with a tool they can use to successfully lead their companies through the inevitably challenging times ahead.

SUMMARY

The Continuum model is a tool to help steer executives past the potholes that are as common among new technology startups as they are among established blue chip companies. These potholes generally include the inability to understand how to equitably allocate precious financial and human resources to propagate a customer-driven marketing effort while allowing for the right mix of freedom and creativity within the R&D department. It is critical for the CEO to understand how each point along the Continuum demands that the senior management team allocate resources proactively rather than reactively in response to external political and financial change.

The concept of bringing an idea to the marketplace has a romantic quality. Many of us like to imagine the hard-working scientist entrepreneur in his garage working throughout the day and night perfecting the next great invention that will magically change our lives for the better. However, the hard reality is that magic is often the by-product of well-thought-out processes. Just as a magician will not go on stage without thoroughly studying and practicing her craft, a successful entrepreneur must not initiate a new product development or marketplace introduction without a plan for addressing the technical, financial, human-resource, and customer-related issues. In order to keep an organization focused throughout each stage of the product Continuum, the CEO must foster a transparent communication strategy between internal personnel and the external marketplace.

The challenge of removing the traditional friction experienced between technology staff and marketing managers is best accomplished though promoting early interactions between developers and sales staff immediately from the initial concept of a product idea. The average new product development effort traditionally can last anywhere from six months to several years with a development team varying in size between six to over 50 people depending on the complexity of the new technology and availability of investment capitol. Thus a typical work breakdown structure (WBS) or recipe for developing a new product and bringing it to market may comprise well over 450,000 individual tasks over the course of a year. The primary goals and objectives of the management team are to deliver a product offering on time and within budget that can sustain profitability once introduced into the marketplace. In the context of adhering to these goals, if the manager is not capable of establishing continuous communications, and maintaining project team accountability, the likelihood of a successful product development effort that meets the customer's expectations will be low.

Just as with a favorite family recipe that has been handed down generation-to-generation, knowing the ingredients will not ensure a successful cooking experience. Similarly in business, a well-thought-out product development plan, hiring strategy, financial model, and marketing plan are only part of the requirements to guide an organization along the Continuum. The senior management team and founders must provide the vision of knowing when to apply pressure as well as mitigate tensions during the sticking points along the Continuum. For example, it is not enough to tighten the fiscal screws on a sales force struggling to meet volume-driven quotas for a new technology product when the customer base has not been adequately defined. Similarly, it is not particularly productive to reduce the R&D budget when certain product features are discovered not to meet immediate customer needs. As with manufacturing and production systems, the concept of zero-defect management in transforming a new idea into a sellable product is more of a philosophy rather than a realistic or attainable goal. The important concept for the manager is not how to avoid sticking points along the Continuum but how best to negotiate undue delays in bringing a product to market and sustaining a successful revenue stream.

The initial introduction of a new product is often fraught with challenges for both marketing managers as well as the production engineers. A technology product rarely ever works exactly the way the customer wants it to. Establishing a customer relations management (CRM) system that allows for immediate feedback from the customer to the sales manager and on to the product engineer will create the ability to change product specifications that best meet current and future customer needs. A properly working CRM system will also allow for a focused approach in setting realistic short- and intermediate-term development and sales goals.

Just as all politics are local, so are product development efforts. Preliminary sales projections and market forecasts are mere speculation until a technology has obtained customer buy-in beyond the original test market scenarios. The earlier customer expectations and purchasing behavioral patterns are understood for a new product, the greater the likelihood that the development and sales efforts will meet the customer's needs. As discussed in earlier chapters, the demise of the dotCom industry in the 1990s, the Macintosh loss leadership to IBM in the 1980s, and the downturn in domestic car sales to foreign imports in the 1970s are all examples of how once successful organizations lost sight of customer needs and were overtaken by competitors in the marketplace.

A hard lesson learned is that a novel technology or product that is successful at one point along the Continuum does not necessarily get continued acceptance in the marketplace. By continually obtaining and translating end-user feedback into product enhancements, customer support and sales managers can help evolve a new product introduction into one that reaches successful market maturity. Results of this type of due diligence will be to establish brand loyalty and increase total market share.

Crossing the Finish Line: Again, Again, and Again

Imagine after immediately crossing the finish line of the Boston Marathon—one of the most physically grueling challenges the human body can voluntarily seek to endure—the racing committee officials say you must immediately restart the race in order to qualify to compete for next year's race. Yet each time you somehow manage to cross the finish line you are repeatedly told in order to continue to qualify you must repeat the most mentally and physically challenging endurance test that you have ever experienced to date. Aside from the physical pounding and psychological strain of each successive race, the challenge is getting mentally focused and properly motivated to start all over again.

This simple analogy is a reasonable comparison to the continuous, extremely high-level commitment it takes to initially launch a product and sustain profitability and market share growth along the Continuum. Changing customer preferences, emerging competition, turnover in senior management, and an ever-shifting external political landscape all contribute to the need for a CEO to pay unrelenting attention to shifting priorities and resource management across the Continuum.

Bibliography

Aktas, A. *Structured Analysis and Design of Information Systems.* Englewood Cliffs, NJ: Prentice-Hall, 1987.

Bergeron, B. *The Eternal E-Customer: How Emotionally Intelligent Interfaces Can Create Long-Lasting Customer Relationships.* New York: McGraw-Hill, 2001.

Betz, F. *Managing Technological Innovation: Competitive Advantage from Change.* New York: John Wiley, 1998.

Christensen, C. *The Innovator's Dilemma: When New Technologies Cause Great Firms to Fail.* Boston: Harvard Business School Press, 2000.

Foster, R. and S. Kaplan. *Creative Destruction: Why Companies That Are Built to Last Underperform the Market—and How to Successfully Transform Them.* New York: McKinsey & Company, 2001.

Gerber, M. *The E-Myth Revisited: Why Most Small Companies Don't Work and What to Do About It.* New York: HarperBusiness, 1995.

Goff, D. *Fiber Optic Reference Guide.* 2d ed. Boston: Focal Press, 1999.

Hecht, J. *City of Light: The Story of Fiber Optics.* New York: Oxford University Press, 1999.

Heinecke, W. and J. Marsh. *The Entrepreneur: Twenty-One Golden Rules for the Global Business Manager.* Singapore: John Wiley (Asia) Pte Ltd., 2000.

Jennings, J. and L. Haughton. *It's Not the Big That Eat the Small...It's the Fast That Eat the Slow: How to Use Speed as a Competitive Tool in Business.* New York: HarperBusiness, 2000.

Kawasaki, G. and M. Moreno. *Rules for Revolutionaries.* New York: Harper-Business, 1999.

Martineau, B. *First Fruit: The Creation of the Flavr Savr Tomato and the Birth of Biotech Food.* New York: McGraw-Hill, 2001.

Moore, G. *Inside the Tornado.* New York: HarperCollins, 1997.

Moore, G. *Crossing the Chasm: Marketing and Selling High-Tech Products to Mainstream Customers.* rev. ed. New York: HarperBusiness, 1999.

Morrison, I. *The Second Curve: How to Command New Technologies, New Consumers, and New Markets.* New York: Ballantine Books, 1996.

Murphy, D. *The Portable MBA in Marketing.* New York: John Wiley, 1997.

Porter, D. *The Greatest Benefit to Mankind.* New York: W.W. Norton & Co., 1997.

Powell, J. *Eastern Philosophy for Beginners.* New York: Writers and Readers Publishing, 2000.

Ries, A. and L. Ries. *The 22 Immutable Laws of Branding: How to Build a Product or Service into a World-Class Brand.* New York: HarperCollins, 1998.

Silbiger, S. *The Ten Day MBA.* New York: William Morrow and Company, 1993.

Slywotzky, A., D. Morrison, and K. Weber. *How Digital Is Your Business?* New York: Crown Business, 2000.

Index